D1616914

Jonson's Gypsies Unmasked

Jonson's Gypsies Unmasked

Background and Theme of *The Gypsies Metamorphos'd*

Dale B. J. Randall

> Come follow, follow all,
> 'Tis English Iipsies call;
> All you that loue your liues,
> Heres those for profit striues.
> We fare well when thousands lacke,
> None of vs can credits cracke.
> > We fare well, &c.
>
> > *The Brave English Jipsie*

Duke University Press   Durham, N.C.   1975

© 1975, Duke University Press

L.C.C. card number 74–75909
I.S.B.N. 0–8223–0322–1

PRINTED IN THE UNITED STATES OF
AMERICA BY HERITAGE PRINTERS

To Lettie and Kenneth:
like James and George,
you have swum in
the Thames.

Table of Contents

List of Illustrations

Preface

"Truth lyes open to all; it is no mans *severall*," writes Jonson.[1] Hence
it is the more awkward to step forward like little Jack Horner with
the claim that one has plucked forth an interpretive plum that has
lain hidden and plump for three and a half centuries. As we shall
have occasion to see, Jonson himself complains repeatedly about
would-be interpreters. He has Mr. Probee warn in *The Magnetic
Lady* that "It is the solemne vice of interpretation, that deformes the
figure of many a faire *Scene*, by drawing it awry; and indeed is the
civill murder of most good *Playes*..." (HS VI, 545: Chorus before
Act III). Nevertheless he yearns for accurate interpretation, and
it is a simple fact that in many of his works the creative participation
of the audience or reader is essential—in Jonson's time and ours—to
a completion of his design. What this means for us is put very well
by Morton Bloomfield: "True literary scholarship aims at making
literature of the past continuously relevant either by establishing its
original significance or its modern significance."[2]

Establishing the significance of a work by a major writer is a
tempting task when apparently no one has previously tried it, and
especially when the work in question has some particular interest
and appeal. Such is the case here. Jonson's masque called *The Gypsies Metamorphos'd* is the longest, most complex, and most popular
masque by the most prolific and skilled of all English masque writers.
W. Todd Furniss observes that "In the variety of poetic forms, *The
Gypsies Metamorphosed* (1621) is the most ambitious masque Jonson ever undertook..."; and Gerald Eades Bentley informs us that
"the number of extant texts, quotations, and allusions surpasses those
for any other masque except Shirley's *The Triumph of Peace*."[3]

The present study of the gypsy masque's significance began with
a simple impression that the images, action, and diction of the piece
point to a common and intriguing thematic end. Consequently the

1. *Timber*, in *Ben Jonson*, ed. C. H. Herford, Percy and Evelyn Simpson (Oxford, 1947), VIII, 567.
2. "Allegory as Interpretation," *New Literary History*, III (1972), 302.
3. Furniss, "Ben Jonson's Masques," in *Three Studies in the Renaissance* (New
Haven, 1958), p. 141; and Bentley, gen. introd., *A Book of Masques in Honour of
Allardyce Nicoll* (Cambridge, 1967), p. 10.

study is not without its share of "personal Impressionism." Any reader will soon become aware, though, of the large number of supportive footnotes which have been included, partly in a counterbalancing effort to give the study a precise and firm standing. It would be extremely difficult, perhaps impossible, to break down the compound created here of subjectivity and objectivity, of interpretation and fact, and yet the footnotes should help to emphasize the importance of the objective component. In a quite old-fashioned way the author's *auctoritees*, or most of them, are placed in plain sight. One does not attain a view in Darien or anywhere else without the aid of others, and for the present author's purposes it is just as well to acknowledge the fact. Besides, one should note that the footnotes here are used also to provide various sorts of information ancillary to the main task at hand. In other words, they are intended not only as ballast and hence the means to a steadier course in the text, but also as recurrent reminders that our sense of the past should be kept properly complicated.

A special word on Chapter II may be helpful. The seasoned Jonson scholar will hardly expect many major surprises in a chapter entitled "Some Essential Background," and yet the entire reading of the gypsy masque which is proposed in this study depends on a familiarity with certain background material. It is therefore presented here with at least a twofold purpose: first, as a reminder for the old hand (who is likely to find fresh details in some parts, and yet may wish to skim elsewhere), and, second, for the relative neophyte, as a sort of suggestive, ideational scene-setting (which naturally highlights those elements of the Jacobean world that are most germane).

As for mechanical matters, it should be noted that titles of sources have been modernized in capitalization, but their spelling has not been modified beyond regularizing *i*'s and *j*'s, *u*'s and *v*'s. London is the place of publication unless otherwise noted. In all quotations the aim has been to reproduce sources as exactly as possible, complete with any quirks and quiddities. For Jonson himself the main source of quotation is Herford and Simpson's monumental edition, and yet it is necessary to add that the author's constant companions have also been the works of W. W. Greg (for the gypsy masque), Stephen Orgel (for Jonson's masques in general), and William B. Hunter, Jr. (for Jonson's poems).

It is but a step sideways to acknowledge other kinds of indebtedness. Professors John L. Lievsay, Stephen Orgel, and Ernest W. Talbert have been generous enough to look over the manuscript and offer a variety of helpful and much appreciated comments, and Mrs. Phyllis Bowman has helped to brush the cobwebs from a window in a significant corner of Jonson's biography. R. E. Marston (Librarian, County Borough of Derby), Dorothy Stroud (Assistant Curator, Sir John Soane's Museum), and A. G. Veysey (County Archivist, Flintshire) have helped with other specific matters, and His Grace the Duke of Buccleuch has graciously consented to the inclusion here of his Mytens portrait of George Villiers, First Duke of Buckingham. Librarians have been especially kind at the Bodleian, at Worcester College (Oxford), in the North Library of the British Museum (where the author wintered during the power strikes of 1970), at the Folger Shakespeare Library (where *gemütlichkeit* always adds to the pleasures of study), and at Perkins Library, Duke. Thanks are due also to the Duke University Council on Research for its continued aid, and to the John Simon Guggenheim Memorial Foundation, which kindly permitted simultaneous pursuit of two allied subjects in 1970 and 1971.

One last point: it is fatally easy for nearly any student absorbed in a literary subject to lose sight of its true importance. Even if others agree that the hypothesis explored here is correct in its major outlines, this study of Jonson's gypsy masque is scarcely the apple to make the walls of great cities shake. It is much more akin to that bunch of fresh carrots which a decayed gardener once presented to Louis XI—and for which the King is said to have rewarded the old man bountifully. In the present case a bountiful reward would be the knowledge that this study has added even a little to the pleasure of Jonson's readers.

D. R.

Durham, N.C., 1972

A 1974 Postscript: Rather than changing the true date given here, I leave it as a tiny monument to the silence and slow time sometimes required for a manuscript which travels through the vales of Academe.

Jonson's Gypsies Unmasked

James. Ah sir, I knew a time, when two and twen-[ty] yeares was but a merry Christmas, nothing but Ambassadors, Masques, Playes, Entertainements, Hawking, Hunting, Winter and Summer, New-Market and Roiston mourne now, ha! had you seen the Court fox'd upon Gouries night, and the Gunpouder treason began then; oh we had rare sport, and then every body was knighted, they hardly left a Gentleman in those dayes; and afterward they got a tricke of making Lords.

Cavendish, *The Variety* (*ca.* 1641)

Puppy. What might a man doe to be a gentleman of your companie Sir?

* * *

Patrico. Yee aime at a misterie
Worthy a historie.

Gypsies Metamorphos'd (W 981–982, 989–990)

Chapter I. *Introduction*

i. *The Mirror and Its Mystery*

> *King.* Hieronimo, this masque contents mine eye,
>   Although I sound not well the mystery.
>   Kyd, *The Spanish Tragedy*[1]

Ben Jonson's finest achievement as a writer of masques is probably *The Gypsies Metamorphos'd.* This is saying more than first meets the eye, not only because Jonson was the best received and most prolific of English masque writers, but also because in quality of work he was foremost among those writing during the heyday of the genre.[2] Jonson knew better than we, of course, that nearly every time he set himself to compose a masque he was postulating a world which would depend for its realization on "Canvasse, paper, and false lights," a brilliant but ephemeral world fated to be knocked apart in the gray of the following morning.[3] Nevertheless, his mother wit and pride of craftsmanship were such that he produced scripts which are still worth reading. Most notably of all, perhaps, he produced a script for a masque of gypsies. In Stephen Orgel's words, Jonson's "great achievement of the last period is *The Gipsies Metamorphosed*, that vast triumph of vulgarity and wit, crudity and finesse, tastelessness and grace. It was the King's favorite masque, and

---

1. I.iv.138–139 (ed. Philip Edwards [Cambridge, 1959], p. 26). Kyd subtly designed the show in question so that the "meaning" which soon is reached by the Spanish king (with Hieronimo's help) is quite different from that which its English audience is likely to have perceived.

2. He wrote some thirty-three masques and entertainments during the reign of James, and four during that of Charles. As George Gregory Smith says, Jonson's "position as the true creator of the masque and the unchallenged master in the genre was a personal triumph, won in loyalty to ideals and methods of his own making" (*Ben Jonson* [1919], p. 129). At the time of Milton's masterly *Comus* (1634), which comes in the twilight of the genre, Jonson's career was drawing to a close.

3. The quoted phrase is from l. 65 of Jonson's "An Epistle Answering to One That Asked to Be Sealed of the Tribe of Ben," in *Ben Jonson*, ed. C. H. Herford, Percy and Evelyn Simpson (Oxford, 1947), VIII, 220. With the exception of *The Gypsies Metamorphos'd*, all of Jonson's works will be cited from the eleven volumes (1925–52) of this edition.

the court's. It is difficult to believe that it was not Jonson's favorite as well."[4]

Regardless of whether the gypsy masque was Jonson's best or favorite masque, it surely meant something. It was not just an idle show. In the first place, a Renaissance masque depended on the familiarity of its audience with things emblematic. It took for granted an interest in or at least a passing knowledge of symbolic indirection, whether in natural phenomena ("God's hieroglyphics") or in bed-hangings, coats-of-arms, hearses, or inn-signs. In the second place, Jonson believed that all masques, even the slightest of the lot, "eyther haue bene, or ought to be the mirrors of mans life. . . ."[5]

The classic mirror figure to which Jonson turns here had long been a commonplace. His use of it has a relative freshness, nevertheless, because he applies it to a specialized and rapidly evolving form on which he was currently making himself more expert than anyone else in England. What does it suggest? Fundamentally a mirror is a means of reflecting the truth about something, a truth which is always superficial, sometimes profound, and occasionally both. In *Hymenaei* Jonson depicts the figure of Truth with "A christall mirror . . . at her brest,/ By which mens consciences are search'd, and drest. . ." (HS VII, 239: ll. 899–900). The problem is that at a glance a typical masque—even a Jonson masque—may seem to be one of the least truthful of all artistic forms. It usually was presented to its audience by means of elaborately painted scenes and machines, its performers wore fanciful costumes, and its motive was unabashedly "complementall." In what sense could such a work be a mirror?[6]

The question may be brought to a focus thus: when Jonson had Lucy, Countess of Bedford, dance as Aglaia in *The Masque of Blackness*, wherein lay his realism? A full answer would depend on a full

4. "To Make Boards to Speak: Inigo Jones's Stage and the Jonsonian Masque," in *Renaissance Drama*, N.S. I, ed. Samuel Schoenbaum (Evanston, Ill., 1968), 144.

5. From the introduction to Jonson's late masque called *Love's Triumph Through Callipolis* (1631), HS VII, 735: ll. 3–4. Since Jonson's critical views remained more or less consistent over the years, it has seemed reasonable to cite them here whenever they are useful. Probably the reader will wish to bear in mind, however, the chronological problem raised by the considerable length of Jonson's career. See James D. Redwine, Jr., ed., *Ben Jonson's Literary Criticism* (Lincoln, Neb., 1970).

6. Jonson uses the term "complementall" in *The King's Entertainment in Passing to His Coronation* (1604), HS VII, 90: l. 243. The question posed here does not imply that "realism" should be limited to the seamier sides of life. "Realism" might be easier to come by in a scene set at a stall in Bartholomew Fair, but the more relevant point at the moment is that not even court ladies customarily dressed like the ancient queens, goddesses, and graces which in masques they pretended to be.

analysis of that masque, but even to gesture at an answer it is helpful to know that Aglaia—which means "splendor" or "brightness"—is the name of one of the three graces. Frequently regarded as daughters of Zeus and friends of the muses, the graces are personifications of charm and grace in both nature and moral action. In *Cynthia's Revels* Jonson defines Aglaia as *"delectable and pleasant Conuersation*, whose propertie is to moue a kindly delight, and sometimes not without laughter: Her office, to entertaine assemblies, and keepe societies together with faire familiaritie" (HS IV, 166: V.vii.36–40). Furthermore, we have historical reason to think that the charming Lucy was suited to mirror just such qualities. A friend to Jonson's muse, among others, she was indeed a "brightness" at James's court. Punning on Latin *lux* and Lucy, Jonson addressed her in her own person as the "brightnesse of our spheare, . . ./ The *Muses* euening, as their morning-starre."[7]

If we seek more general aid in interpreting such matters we may turn to the distinction which E. M. Waith has drawn between "mirror" and "world of glass."[8] Assuming that it was difficult to write about comedy in the Renaissance without turning back to the old mirror metaphor, and assuming that the comic mirror was used mainly to reflect everyday life and unmask dissimulators, Waith has contrasted this sort of reflector to the world of glass which Spenser speaks of in *The Faerie Queene* (III.ii.19). The world of glass reflects essences. It reflects life in a heightened and more intelligible order than that in which we ordinarily experience it. In the world of glass we find a sort of Platonic "ideality," a realm (to broaden our base a bit) such as we find also in much of Sidney's *Arcadia*. To return to Aglaia, perhaps we may say that Jonson, with the aid of the lightsome Lucy, was setting forth bright and "faire familiaritie" in a heightened and purified form.

Obviously he was attempting no such thing with the rustics in *The Gypsies Metamorphos'd*, and yet the clowns of this later masque are not "real" either. Perhaps one may contrast Jonson's two kinds of achievement here—the creation of Aglaia and, say, Clod—with those highly refined images created by a certain sort of society por-

---

7. "To Lucy, Countesse of Bedford, with Mr. Donnes Satyres," HS VIII, 61: ll. 15–16. Further commentary on the subject is to be found in such places as D. J. Gordon, "The Imagery of Ben Jonson's *The Masque of Blacknesse* and *The Masque of Beautie*," *Journal of the Warburg and Courtauld Institutes*, VI (1943), 122–141.
8. "The Comic Mirror and the World of Glass," *Research Opportunities in Renaissance Drama*, IX (1966), 16–23.

trait painter and the uncensored images of a genre-painter inclined toward caricature. Setting aside gradations between, one might say that to the extent the former is "real" at all, it is realism highly idealized; the latter, though also modified from the "real," might better be called "mock realism."[9] In any case, the world of glass and the comic mirror are concerned with reflecting different kinds of reality and doing it in different ways. Granted this divergence, it is perhaps even more important to bear in mind what they share: the aim of each is not photographic accuracy but symbolic validity. Thus it is that Truth may properly be said to wear either "at her brest."

With the help of hindsight we may see why Jonson used both kinds of reflector in his gypsy masque. Experience had taught him that he could achieve a pleasing and significant variety of effects by playing off the more formal, idealized aspects of a masque against various sorts of (usually comic) disorder. That is, he learned ways to vary his effects by contrasting different amounts of more or less conventional masque elements to assorted kinds of antimasque elements. To push the mirror figure a bit, one might say that he experimented with juxtaposing kinds of reflectors. In the gypsy masque he gives us some brilliant glimpses of an ideal king, but it is perfectly obvious even from a cursory reading that he is interested also in the sort of truth he can catch in his comic mirror.

Any such distinction in terms, it must be admitted, is merely for our own convenience. Whatever the proportional use of different "reflectors" or "realities" in a masque, and however we choose to analyze them, our base for the moment is Jonson's word "mirror." He uses it, in fact, within the gypsy masque itself, and in a context worth a second glance. Though the idea flashes but briefly, one of the gypsies wishes "To the witty all cleare mirrours,/ To the foolish their darke errours. . ." (B 282–283).[10] The passage reaches well beyond masquing and yet embraces it, suggesting that in an art-form such as that in which this gypsy appears, only the most alert and intellectually acute may be expected to see the poet's truth clearly.

9. Jonas A. Barish uses the latter term in a similar context in *Ben Jonson and the Language of Prose Comedy* (Cambridge, Mass., 1960).

10. All quotations from *The Gypsies Metamorphos'd* are from the edition of W. W. Greg, *Jonson's Masque of Gipsies in the Burley, Belvoir, and Windsor Versions: An Attempt at Reconstruction* (1952). Though Greg's own symbols are much more complex, "B" is used here to indicate the postulated Burley version, and "W" to refer to his reconstruction of the version performed at Windsor.

Others in the audience may enjoy or at least be occupied by the surface of the show, but they will perforce remain unenlightened. For the first group a look in the mirror may be epiphanic. The rest will forever see in the glass but darkly.

Jonson's special use of the mirror image may be approached also from a point he makes about masques in a well-known passage in his *Hymenaei* preface: "though their *voyce* be taught to sound to present occasions [i.e., to 'mirror' in some immediate and more or less superficial way], their *sense*, or doth, or should alwayes lay hold on more remou'd *mysteries* [i.e., 'mirror' in some more obscure and profound way]" (HS VII, 209).[11] By definition, in other words, a masque has its "*mysteries*." This passage is as well known as any in the history of masque criticism, and it is quite as important as it is usually thought to be. Equally important for our present purposes, though, and more often forgotten, is the related statement which Jonson makes next:

> howsoeuer some may squemishly crie out, that all endeuour of *learning*, and *sharpnesse* in these transitorie *deuices* especially, where it steps beyond their little, or (let me not wrong 'hem) no braine at all, is superfluous; I am contented, these fastidious *stomachs* should leaue my full tables, and enioy at home, their cleane emptie trenchers, fittest for such ayrie tasts. . . .

From the subject of mysteries, that is, he proceeds at once to insist on his right to set "full tables," complete with "*sharpnesse*," whether or not he drives away those who have come expecting only march-pane castles and honey cakes. Even allowing for a touch of bravado here, it does not sound as though Jonson contemplates limiting himself to a world of glass which is merely "complementall." "*Mirrors*," he writes, "though deckt with diamants, are nought worth,/ If the like formes of things they set not forth. . ." (*Hymenaei*, p. 235: ll. 753–754).

The present study is an attempt to explore some implications which these several views have for Jonson's longest, best received, and best known masque. Despite the many works which have helped us toward a fuller understanding of Jonson's writing generally, none

11. The passage from which this quotation is taken has been analyzed closely by D. J. Gordon, "Poet and Architect: The Intellectual Setting of the Quarrel Between Ben Jonson and Inigo Jones," *Journal of the Warburg and Courtauld Institutes*, XII (1949), 152–178.

thus far has analyzed the rich and varied bill of fare which he provided in *The Gypsies Metamorphos'd*. None has said what "remou'd *mysteries*" his contemporaries might have discerned by looking carefully into this mirror.

ii. *A Summary of the Reading*

> King.   To apt our apprehensions the more
>   To the true understanding of your Maske:
>   You may tell us somewhat of your scope in 't.
> Valdemar.   That is sufficiently inform'd i' the thing
>   It selfe; though lame it be. . . .
>   Burnell, *Landgartha*[12]

Though one may never prove by Euclidean means what Jonson meant to reflect, the present study offers an hypothesis and then supports it with various kinds of evidence. The hypothesis is based on two assumptions: first, that as one of the most metaphorical of literary forms a masque must imply what it cannot state overtly without violating its own nature; and, second, that whatever its complexity, a masque may be regarded in one sense like the simplest of metaphors, since (to borrow Miss Tuve's words) it is "open at one end, allowing interpretations which can be supported by proper evidence but not proven."[13]

As a matter of fact, many students concerned with matters other than Jonson's gypsy masque have raised signposts pointing in the direction of such an hypothesis as is proposed here. Let us start rather distant from the target. Michael Murrin has written of allegory generally as "a figure of speech incomplete in itself, which, for this very reason, makes certain demands on an audience. The hearer by analogy must fill in the proper meaning to complete the figure."[14] This is a simple but significant beginning. Equally significant is the motto for Jonson's impresa: *Deest quod duceret orbem*—That is missing which would complete the circle.[15] A. D. Nuttall takes us a bit farther down the road by observing that the "completion" de-

---

12. (Dublin, 1641), E4r.
13. *Allegorical Imagery: Some Mediaeval Books and Their Posterity* (Princeton, 1966), p. 220.
14. *The Veil of Allegory* (Chicago, 1969), p. 58.
15. Obviously such a motto is a prism which throws various kinds of light. The meaning implied here is one of several.

manded of a reader or an audience, the addition of what is "missing," is made easier because "the fictions of allegory were often seen, not as excursions into the world of fancy, but as a peculiarly intimate way of closing with the real." Although a modern reader may approach a masque "expecting to find pure invention," he is likely to find "instead a curious tendency to 'act out' the real situation in heightened terms."[16] Hence the value of Jonson's mirror figure. This important point is reinforced by Gabriele Jackson, who writes of "the curious coincidence of inner and outer reality upon which Jonson always insists...."[17] Dolora Cunningham helps us yet farther on our way by drawing attention to Jonson's concern for artistic unity. "A masque," she observes, "as Jonson himself conceived it, is a form of dramatic entertainment in which the logical working out of a central idea or device provides the action."[18] If we follow these several signposts—the demand for interpretation which allegory implies, the tendency for allegory in masques to close with reality, and Jonson's penchant for underlying unity, no matter how complicated his surface may seem, and if we add to these (*cum grano salis*, if necessary) the statement by Swinburne that "There is nothing accidental in the work of Ben Jonson," then we should be in a fair way to a reading of *The Gypsies Metamorphos'd*.[19]

For the benefit of fledgling Jonsonians or perhaps even for Jonson veterans who have not read the masque recently, the way may be smoothed if we pause just a moment at this point to remark the basic action of the piece. *The Gypsies Metamorphos'd* begins with the entry of two English gypsies who bring onstage a little pack of gypsy children. The adult gypsies deliver a few lines of merry self-definition, and then the Captain of the gypsies dances in with six more of his band. When the original two gypsies and a third have offered a bit more self-definition, all begin to dance, this time pausing between "strains" or parts of the dance in order to tell the fortunes of the more distinguished persons present, beginning with the King. Creating a sense of place that is conveniently vague, Jonson next has a little clutch of country clowns bumble in. Excited by

16. *Two Concepts of Allegory: A Study of Shakespeare's The Tempest and the Logic of Allegorical Expression* (1967), p. 98.
17. *Vision and Judgment in Ben Jonson's Drama* (New Haven, 1968), p. 103.
18. "The Jonsonian Masque as a Literary Form," *ELH*, XXII (1955), 108.
19. *A Study of Ben Jonson* (1889), p. 9. I am only partly facetious in thus citing Swinburne, for I am working with the assumption that Jonson was the sort of writer and man who virtually always knew what he was doing.

seeing the gypsies, the clowns strike up some music to draw their attention and soon begin dancing themselves, at which point the gypsies move in to display their fortune-telling skills a second time. No sooner have the gypsies finished and gone than the clowns discover that they have been robbed. The Patrico, one of the two gypsies who linger, reassures the country folk that all is not what it seems, the stolen goods are returned (though not necessarily to the persons from whom they were taken), and soon the bumpkins are enthralled again by the gypsies' charms. It is at this point that the gypsies' "songster," the Jackman, sings a ballad of a gypsy captain named Cock-lorrel, whose main claim to fame turns out to be the banquet he once held in Derbyshire for the Devil, at the end of which the Devil broke wind with such memorable force that the place has been known ever since as the Devil's Arse. At last, and ostensibly to impress the clowns still more, the rest of the gypsies are brought back, now changed as if by magic to fine gentlemen. The metamorphosed gypsy-gentlemen dance for their strangely mixed audience (the clowns are somehow at court), and finally the whole piece closes with a series of verses and songs comprised mainly of extravagant praise for the King.

Just what sort of "mirror" do we have here? Most simply this study suggests that the gypsy masque is a brilliant and multi-faceted mirror in which Jonson includes some dangerous truths. As a matter of fact, it may well be that his unifying metaphor and hence the overall *significatio* of the piece have been overlooked so long precisely because they are so audacious, strong, and explicit. Unlikely though it might seem at first, Jonson scarcely could be plainer in implying that the lighthearted Marquess of Buckingham and his numerous relations and friends are, figuratively speaking, a covey of gypsies—gypsies who have flown forth from the Devil's Arse, to put the business as bluntly as Jonson does. "My selfe a Gypsye here doe shine," Jonson has Buckingham declare to King James (W 307), and later the crew of country bumpkins take it for true that *"the King has a noyse* [i.e., a band] *of Gypsies, as well as of Bearewards"* (B 783–784). They may be attractive, "kept" gypsies, but they are gypsies nonetheless.

That Buckingham himself not only starred in the masque but also commissioned it is a significant matter to consider in weighing Jonson's achievement, and a fact to which we must eventually return. The possibility that Buckingham himself even suggested the subject of gypsies is another idea worth considering. Nevertheless, it was Jonson who had the inspiration to use gypsies as animated emblems of a very particular sort. It was Jonson who saw that gypsies would be not merely appropriately colorful but also useful in a variety of double-edged ways. In the hands of Jonson, who long since had shown himself capable of admiration for the cunning and craft of rogues, the image of the gypsies in the masque becomes something like the siren image which Miss Tuve discusses, "delightful-*and-noxious*."[20] For instance, to those who might "squemishly crie out" against his *"sharpnesse,"* Jonson could respond that his main purpose was to avail himself of gypsy talents in the long and largely flattering fortune-telling sequence, which is, after all, intricately interwoven with the long second dance and presumably is, therefore, one of the most important parts of the masque. Gypsies were noted for fortune-telling, and who can resist the lure of looking into the future? In fact, dancing itself is a gypsy specialty. What an ingenious excuse for displaying the performers' terpsichorean skill! To be sure, all gypsies were known to be thieves, but do we not see these gypsies return some of the things they have stolen? Then, too, gypsies were known for "metamorphosing"—and what is a masque without contrast and variety of costume? In the present case the gypsy talent for metamorphosis helps to blur not only the fact that in the world of masques such non-establishment characters as uncouth Irishmen are traditionally transformed by the power of the king, but also the fact that in the present instance it may well *be* the power of a doting monarch which has helped to transform gypsies to courtiers. At the beginning we seem to have courtiers dressed as gypsies, but it may be fully as significant that at the end we seem to have gypsies dressed as courtiers. Or are the gypsies really transformed? At first it would appear that the gypsy garb has been a disguise only on a superficial level. On a more profound level—but how lightly handled!—it may be viewed as an external expression of an inner reality, at once a witty *jeu d'esprit* and a metaphysical demonstration.[21]

Even if one looks at *The Gypsies Metamorphos'd* only casually, one scarcely can miss the fact that Jonson is working here with the illusion-reality theme in a particularly intense and vital way. A typi-

20. *Allegorical Imagery*, p. 20.
21. Angus Fletcher works with this point: "To play what one is a metaphysical game" (*The Transcendental Masque: An Essay on Milton's "Comus"* [Ithaca, N.Y., 1971], p. 13).

cal masque is supposed to conclude by merging the world of the performers with that of the spectators, but here Jonson integrates
worlds very early in the game, firmly binding the King, the principal
spectator of the piece, into its whole scheme and texture. King James
and the rest of Jonson's original audience were not merely passive
spectators but, much more than usual even in a masque, part of the
subject of the show. The people who attended were asked to draw
off their gloves (nearly everyone wore gloves) in order that *their*
palms might be read, and several palms soon were. And all this despite Jonson's use of the masque as a mode of satirical admonishment.
To be sure, there was doubtless an atmosphere of warm and genial
compliment, but it may well be that some of the devil-may-care
excitement of *The Gypsies Metamorphos'd* derives from Jonson's
excited knowledge that this time he was playing with fire.

iii. *A Rationale for the Reading*

> . . . shortly they will play me in what forms they list upon the
> stage.
>
> Essex to Elizabeth[22]

To support such a reading of the gypsy masque and to define it
more completely, one must know something of the temper of the
Jacobean court and the place of Buckingham in it, something of the
attitudes of both James and Jonson towards counsel, criticism, and
allegory, and most important, of course, the specific materials of
the masque. To arrive safely at the thesis just stated, in other words,
we must for a while (in Chapter II) take a route which is rather
circuitous, a route which, it may be hoped, will have some interests
of its own, but the primary purpose of which is to put us in position
to see and understand a quite specific goal. One may arrive at Jonson's removed mysteries only if approaching them by way of his
present occasion.

Upon embarking, moreover, the reader should be assured (or
warned, possibly, depending on his expectations) that this study
will issue in no startling revelation of some particular historical
event which provides parallels for all the gypsy masque's elements.
Much less will it attempt to unveil the gypsies as individuals—with

22. From a letter of 12 May 1600 in Walter Bourchier Devereux, *Lives and Letters of the Devereux, Earls of Essex* (1853), II, 99.

the important exception of Buckingham himself. Jonson simply does not appear to be working in a manner to invite much in the way of specific historical equations.[23] Nevertheless this whole study is grounded on the fact, well documented in recent years, that Elizabethan and Jacobean dramatic writing was commonly used as both a weapon of propaganda and a means of reflecting and commenting on its time. There is evidence aplenty, as David Bevington says, "that allegorical lock-picking was a courtly pastime amounting to a disease"; "the possibilities of allusion were on everybody's mind."[24] Barbara de Luna observes that because it was "an era before freedom of speech was a right guaranteed by either constitution or custom," writers often felt the need to seek "historical and literary parallels as the means of covertly commenting on, and criticizing, the events

23. In this rather tricky business of topical allusion one does well to bear in mind the chastening comment of Josephine Waters Bennett: "Modern attempts to discover and interpret Elizabethan topical allegory have produced such absurdities at the hands of over-zealous devotees, that a scholar who desires a reputation for sanity hardly ventures to touch the subject" ("Oxford and *Endimion*," *PMLA*, LVII [1942], 359).

24. *Tudor Drama and Politics: A Critical Approach to Topical Meaning* (Cambridge, Mass., 1968), pp. 9, 13. A good illustration occurs in Thomas Tomkis, *Lingua* (1607):

> *Memoria*. . . . at my last being at *Athens* (It is now, let me see, about 1800. yeares a goe) I was at a Commedie of *Aristophanes* making, (I shall neuer forget it)[.] The Arch-gouernor of *Athens* tooke me by the hād and placed me, and there I say, I saw *Socrates* abused most grossly, himselfe being then a present spectator: I remember he sate full against me, and did not so much as shew the least countenance of discontent.
>
> *Communis Sensus*. In those dayes it was lawfull, but now the abuse of such liberty is vnsufferable.
>
> *Phantastes*. Thinke what you will of it, I thinke 'tis done. . . .
> (II.iv [D4ᵛ-E1ʳ])

Another useful illustration was published by the dramatist John Ford just the year before the gypsy masque. In *A Line of Life* Ford writes:

> It is an easy vanity, in these days of liberty, to be a conceited interpreter, but a difficult commendation to be a serious author; for whatsoever is at all times honestly intended, oftentimes is too largely construed. General collections meet—not seldom—with particular applications, and those so dangerous, that it is more safe, more wise, to profess a free silence than a necessary industry.

(From *The Works of John Ford*, ed. William Gifford and Alexander Dyce [1869], III, 383.) In the prologue to *The Broken Heart* (*ca.* 1627–31), nonetheless, Ford himself could not forbear hinting that his "fiction" was based on "truth."

Allen Gross, coming at the question through Massinger, protests the view that that dramatist's works are filled with specific references to contemporary politics, and yet he proceeds to argue that Massinger managed to convey his thoughts on such matters as taxation and the intervention of the English in the Thirty Years War: "To express attitudes on these subjects and not to be reprimanded," says Gross, "was a problem that Massinger . . . brilliantly solved" ("Contemporary Politics in Massinger," *SEL*, VI [1966], 279, 280). He concludes that Massinger was "a topical writer partially frustrated in his aims" (p. 290).

of their own times with relative impunity."[25] Thinking in particular
of Shakespeare and Jonson, who "still believed in the power of art to
guide and reform," Bevington writes that "Political dramaturgy was
an inescapable and major portion of their heritage. . ." (p. 4).

When one adds to these facts Jonson's characteristic self-confi-
dence, it is not surprising that he sometimes found himself in conflict with authority. He went to the Marshalsea prison for helping
Tom Nashe with the satirical *Isle of Dogs* (1597). For his barbs in
Poetaster (1601) he was called before the Lord Chief Justice, and
the "apologetical dialogue" which he proceeded to append to that
work was itself officially condemned. Because of *Sejanus* (1603),
the Earl of Northampton had him summoned before the Council
and accused "both of popperie and treason" (HS I, 141). For his
complicity in the satiric comedy *Eastward Ho* he went to prison in
1605. (William Drummond, the gentle laird of Hawthornden, must
have been shocked indeed when Jonson told him later of the report
that he and his collaborators, Chapman and Marston, "should then
[have] had their ears cūtt & noses.")[26] *Epicoene* (1609) drew forth
complaints from the Lady Arabella Stuart, who thought some derogatory passages in that play were aimed at herself. From 1616 we
have a royal order regarding *The Devil Is an Ass*, a courtier having
maintained that his project to raise money by draining land was too
clearly reflected in Jonson's Meercraft. And yet, despite all this, we
find that even toward the end of his career Jonson continued to hurl
barbs. For depicting his sometime collaborator Inigo Jones as Vitruvius Hoop he was ordered to revise *A Tale of a Tub* (1633). He
therefore deleted Vitruvius, but went on to alter the role of In-and-
In Medlay so that one target of the play was *still* Jones. Nothwith-
standing such evidence, however, the real wonder may be that
Jonson's encounters with the law were not more frequent. George
Chapman, who should have known, marvelled at how much Jon-

25. *Jonson's Romish Plot: A Study of "Catiline" and Its Historical Context*
(Oxford, 1967), p. 1. "The fact that we moderns have difficulty seeing 'applications'
where Jonson's contemporaries saw them," she adds, "merely testifies to our relatively slender understanding of the political realities of that age" (p. 5). In *The
Literary Profession in the Elizabethan Age* Phoebe Sheavyn writes of professional
informers who, beginning in the last decade or so of the sixteenth century, "made
it their trade to interpret names as disguises for great personages thereby libelled
. . ." (2nd ed., rev. by J. W. Saunders [New York, 1967], pp. 56–57). Cf. Rhodes
Dunlap, "The Allegorical Interpretation of Renaissance Literature," *PMLA*,
LXXXII (1967), 39–43.
26. *Conversations with William Drummond of Hawthornden*, HS I, 140.

son got away with scot-free: "If all this yett find perdone Fee and grace,/ The happiest outlaw th'art that euer was."[27]

Being a sensible man, Jonson claimed that any attack he made was general, not particular. Any volley he fired was aimed at folly or knavery, not a particular fool or knave. Besides, he said in his dedication of *Volpone*, if ever he *had* become personal in attacking some *"mimick, cheater, bawd, or buffon"* (rather a broad range, in Jonsonian terms), the victim always could have *"wisely dissembled"* that he had been hit (HS V, 18). Proclaiming his own self-righteousness (*"mary,...I beare mine innocence about mee"*), Jonson tried hard to discredit those *"inuading interpreters"* who *"professe to haue a key for the decyphering of euery thing"* (pp. 18–19). But the *"interpreters"* he always had with him. Several years later, in his "induction" to *Bartholomew Fair*, we find him going out of his way to mock any *"State-decipherer"* or "politique *Picklocke"* who might be "so solemnly ridiculous, as to search out, who was meant by the *Gingerbread-woman"* and "what *great Lady* by the *Pigge-woman"* (HS VI, 17). And to give such passages their due, Jonson often must have been innocent.

Even in his masques, nonetheless, he sometimes allowed himself to become pointedly satirical. From the beginning, because of the nature of the form, his masques were allegorical and topical, and being Jonson he could not write thus indefinitely without becoming critical. In *Time Vindicated* (1623), two years after the gypsy masque, he became almost embarrassingly critical, his specific target being the poet Wither ("wretched Impostor,/ Creature of glory, Mountebanke of witte,/ Selfe-loving Braggart..." [HS VII, 658: ll. 96–98]). Apparently the milieu of a courtly masque, as opposed to that of the public stage, was no sufficient reason to Jonson for stifling his impulse to reformation. His whole management of the masquing in *Cynthia's Revels* (1601) is a lesson in the fact that *utile* is as proper to a masque as *dulce*. In this rather early work Jonson explains that since the court is the fountain of manners for the kingdom, every effort should be exerted, even by the writer of masques, to make or keep the court pure. The court is the kingdom's mirror: *"In thee, the whole Kingdome dresseth it selfe, and is ambitious to vse thee as her glasse. Beware, then, thou render mens figures truly, and teach*

27. "An Invective Wrighten by Mr. George Chapman Against Mr. Ben: Johnson," *The Poems of George Chapman*, ed. Phyllis Brooks Bartlett (1941), p. 374.

them no lesse to hate their deformities, then to loue their formes:
For, to grace, there should come reuerence; and no man can call that
louely, which is not also venerable" (HS IV, 33).

If it is true that the kingdom is mirrored in the court, and the
court in the masque, then the masque is capable of being much more
than a pretty show. Nowadays few students would think a good
masque merely a "pretty show," and yet for each courtly entertainment the question still may be posed, Precisely what is it? Though
we shall not be much concerned here with specific equations between Jacobean fact and Jonsonian fiction, the reader is invited to
entertain the idea as we proceed that *The Gypsies Metamorphos'd*
is at least in part a Jonsonian mirror for Jacobean magistrates.

Chapter II. *Some Essential Background*

i. *Aspects of the Jacobean Court*

> 'Twas a busie querulous froward time, . . . much degenerated
> from the purity of the former. . . .
>
> Sir Henry Wotton[1]

At the time Jonson wrote his gypsy masque he had had access to
James's court for a good many years. He had

> . . . eaten with the Beauties, and the wits,
>   And braveries of Court, and felt their fits
> Of love, and hate: and came so nigh to know
>   Whether their faces were their owne, or no. . . .[2]

In his masques, together with Inigo Jones, he himself had contributed to the brightness of those glories "that glister'd in *White-hall.*"[3]
On the other hand, though sufficiently convinced of his own worth
to feel at ease among certain of the nobility (one thinks of his play-
ful lines to Lady Bedford), he often must have felt like a rolling tun
in a china shop amongst those he deemed merely "animated *Porc'lane*
of the Court."[4] He knew well enough that "some" called the court
"*Parasites Place.*"[5] He also knew that while courtly expenses were
continuing to soar, standards of various sorts were continually giving way to expediency. There is no telling what details caught his
eye and ear, but anyone who came occasionally to court could see
and hear in a general way that money was being poured lavishly into
festivities, gems, and grants to favorites. About three months before
the gypsy masque the Venetian Ambassador wrote home that
"everyone spends more than he has, trade has diminished, much gold

1. *Reliquiae Wottonianae* (1651), p. 57.
2. "An Elegie," HS VIII, 200: ll. 33–36.
3. "Clayming a Second Kisse by Desert," from "A Celebration of Charis," HS
VIII, 138: l. 16.
4. "An Epistle Answering to One That Asked to Be Sealed of the Tribe of Ben,"
HS VIII, 219: l. 53.
5. *Timber*, HS VIII, 633.

has been transported and everything is in astonishing disorder."[6]

King James had good intentions but little restraint or even common sense when it came to economic matters. In the spring of 1603, when he first emerged from his rather pinched situation in Scotland, England seemed to lie before him like a new-found-land of milk and honey. Before that first summer was over, however, Queen Anne confided to the Comte de Beaumont, "My husband ruins his affairs by excessive kindness and carelessness."[7] Deluded as to the extent of England's resources, James already had become guilty of what he himself called later the "vastnesse of my expence."[8] Part of the problem was that many of the Scots who followed him into his new realm were poor and importunate, and became no less importunate after learning that there was nothing for which they dared not ask. James could rationalize that his expenses were greater than Elizabeth's because he had more subjects to maintain and royal offspring to rear. The trouble is that from the very beginning he often went to extremes. Both the positive and negative sides of his generosity and pawky Scotch acumen are caught in a statement he made to the Parliament at Whitehall on 21 March 1610: "I hope you will neuer mislike me for my liberalitie, since I can looke very few of you this day in the face, that haue not made suits to mee, at least for some thing, either of honour or profit." Largesse was presumed to be a mark of high birth (*noblesse oblige*), but, beyond that, James's generosity was a mark of his genuinely warm heart. Making fiscal matters worse, he also developed through the years an almost pathetic need to be liked and admired. Though his own personal needs were not unreasonably expensive, he often found it hard to say no to others. In July, 1621, he made a £10,000 " loan" to a foreign am-

6. *Calendar of State Papers and Manuscripts ... Venice ... 1621–1623*, ed. Allen B. Hinds (1911), XVII, 41. These may not be written off as the misimpressions of an outsider. At about the same time a member of the Commons lamented that "we groe every day weaker. Owr Trade is lost, shipping decayed, Tresuer exhausted" (from the notes of Thomas Barrington, in *Commons Debates 1621*, ed. Wallace Notestein, Frances Helen Relf, and Hartley Simpson [New Haven, 1935], III, 351).

Carl Bridenbaugh explores the paradox that James's reign saw both crippling depressions and an overall rise in the living standards for the nobility and most of the "middling people." He notes in particular that the period of 1619–24—beginning well before the gypsy masque and carrying on well after—was one of depression (*Vexed and Troubled Englishmen 1590–1642* [New York, 1968]). See also R. H. Tawney, *Business and Politics under James I* (Cambridge, 1958).

7. Quoted in Frederick Von Raumer, *History of the Sixteenth and Seventeenth Centuries*, trans. from the German (1835), II, 199.

8. This and the following quotation are from *The Workes of the Most High and Mighty Prince, James ...* , "published" by James, Bishop of Winton (1616), pp. 542, 541.

bassador,[9] and yet the very next month, less than a fortnight after the gypsy masque, he was recommending frugality to his candidate for the ambassadorship to Brussels. "I am straungly besett for monie on all sydes," he said, "and must take other and stricter courses then I have."[10] So bad had things become that, shortly before the King was about to begin the progress on which he would see Jonson's gypsy masque, the Venetian Ambassador had the distinct impression that there was scarcely money enough for the journey.[11] Whatever details helped Jonson to formulate his own impression, he knew—and had the Third Gypsy mention in the masque—that men's pensions were not being paid on time (W 422). With still greater audacity Jonson assigned the same gypsy the quite extraordinary task of informing the Lord Treasurer of England, "Your fortune is good and will be to sett/ The office vpright and the Kinge out of debt. . ." (W 420–421)!

Perhaps the plainest symptom of the general malaise at court was the devaluation of titles. During his first four months as king, James dubbed over nine hundred knights. Elizabeth died in March, 1603, and by December of 1604 England's supply of knights had nearly trebled.[12] In *Eastward Ho*, as we have seen, Jonson, Chapman, and Marston dared to point satirically at this sudden flowering, and Jonson, even after a stay in prison, returned to the topic in *Volpone* (1606; HS V, 95: IV.ii.29–30) and *The Alchemist* (1610; HS V, 320: II.ii.86–87). After a relative lull, then, in the knighting process—and the King was rather proud of it—the creation of new knights began to climb again, reaching an average of 120 per year for the period of 1615 to 1619. The reason that matters began to

9. John Finett, *Finetti Philoxenis. . .* (1656), p. 90 (i.e., 80), writes that "The Polonian Ambassador . . . departed, having obtained of his Majesty (by the cunning assistance of the Count *de Gondemar* [the Spanish Ambassador], the loane (I may say) the gift (as never to be restored) of ten thousand pound sterling."

10. Diary of Sir George Chaworth, in *The Loseley Manuscripts*, ed. Alfred John Kempe (1835), p. 421. Just a few weeks after the gypsy masque, on 11 September 1621, the Privy Council was "by his Majestie's order and commandement resolved to take into . . . serious consideration the true causes of the decay of trade and scarcitie of coyne within this kingdome and to advise of some fitt course for the remooving of soe great inconveniences. . ." (*Acts of the Privy Council of England 1621–1623*, ed. J. V. Lyle [1932], p. 40).

11. *Calendar of State Papers . . . Venice . . . 1621–1623*, XVII, 92.

12. Lawrence Stone, *The Crisis of the Aristocracy 1558–1641* (Oxford, 1965), p. 74. Elizabeth had been niggardly in the matter, but now James tipped the scales the opposite way. He himself said, "I haue enlarged my fauour in all the three degrees, towards as many and more than euer King of *England* did in so short a space . . ." (*Workes*, p. 495). The other figures on knighting in this paragraph are also from Stone, pp. 80, 103.

grow worse in 1615 was the inauguration of a new policy involving the direct cash sale of titles and also, as a reward for courtiers, the granting of nominations. Within this period a particularly high peak was attained in 1617; in that year, when James made his expensive pilgrimage back up to Scotland—drawn, he said, by a salmonlike instinct—he made 199 knights. Even later on, however, in the period from 1620 to 1625, there were about seventy creations a year.

Naturally men were moved to comment. "Come all to *Court*, & be made *Knights*," one Jacobean versifier jeered; "*Honour* is sould . . . *Dog-cheeap* now."[13] Archie Armstrong, the King's fool, was credited with telling how one time,

> KIng *Iames* being a hunting and very earnest in his sport, a Countrey fellow crost it, in so much that the dogs were at a losse: At which the King being extreamely angry, drew his Skeine [a kind of sword], and rides after the man, with all the speed he possibly can. Who perceiuing the King to pursue him in his anger, cryed out aloud, I beseech your Maiesty to pardon me, for I haue no desire to be knighted yet: and this hee spoke so often, that hee turned the Kings rage into laughter, who bid him to ride fast enough, and farre enough and bee hang'd, for he better deserued a halter, then to be knighted.[14]

In short, when it comes to knighthood in James's reign, the real blends into the absurd: knighthood is said to have come to Montgomery's barber, the Queen's laundress's husband, an earless ex-convict, and—*domine, dirige nos!*—a Lancashire loin of beef, in honor of which men still call that part "sir-loin."

Another sure sign of the times toward the close of James's reign was the decline in the price of baronetcies, a rank he himself had introduced. Baronetcies sank from £700 in 1619 to a shocking low of £220 in 1622. By offering more than a hundred in a single five-year period, the King had flooded the market, and, as the price declined, so did the quality of buyers.[15] In the spring preceding the gypsy masque Sir Henry Withrington rose in the Commons to voice a widely held view: "this byeing of honor is base; and for Barronetts, that every skipp Jack shall precede both me and my posteryty, I confess it greives me."[16] In the following year, nonethe-

---

13. From British Museum Add. MS 5832, fol. 206. In 1621 a knighthood sold for £44-16-0 (Finett, p. 78).
14. *A Banquet of Jeasts* (1630), pp. 184–185.   15. Stone, p. 93.
16. From the notes of Thomas Barrington, *Commons Debates 1621*, III, 104.

less, there was talk of setting up a new title of "vidams," to help fill the gap between knights and baronets.

Naturally one price for such a state of affairs was a diminution in the respect which Englishmen accorded to titles. Smouldering antagonisms between titled old families and rising new ones in James's reign blazed rather spectacularly in the House of Lords in the May preceding the gypsy masque, when Arundel taunted Spencer for his ancestry.[17] By all odds the most sobering aspect of the problem, however, and the one which ultimately affected Jonson's gypsy masque most profoundly, time-honored concepts of order, degree, and vocation were being undermined by the very man who should have been their chief defender.

Jonson, it is clear, was by no means unique in realizing that "Who e're is rais'd/ For worth he has not, He is tax'd, not prais'd." There may even have been some Englishmen of the time who would have agreed that " 'Tis Vertue alone, is true Nobilitie."[18]

ii. *George Villiers*

> ...the whole Kingdome hath cast their eye upon you, as the new rising Star....
>
> Bacon to Villiers[19]

The example *par excellence* of what was happening to English titles was George Villiers, the young man (he was approaching twenty-

---

17. Looking back on events in 1621, Arthur Wilson recalled (in his *History of Great Britain* [1653], pp. 186–187) that the

> Lords began to consider how cheap they were made by the multitude of *Irish*, and *Scotch* Earls and Viscounts, the King had accumulated, not the Natives of those *Kingdoms*, but private *English* Gentlemen, who had procured, and assumed those Titles, to perch above the *English* Baronry, to their great regret and dishonor. And after some debate, and canvassing in it, they resolved, That though they could not debar the King from making such swarms of *Nobles* with *Outlandish Titles*, yet they would let him know what prejudice it was to them, and if it produced no other good effect, the King might at least see they took offence, and were not well pleased with it....

The resultant petition bore the names of thirty-three peers. See Robert Ashton, ed. and introd., *James I by His Contemporaries* (1969), and L. C. Knights, *Drama & Society in the Age of Jonson* (1937).

18. "To My Muse," HS VIII, 48: ll. 15–16; and "To Kenelme, John, George" (from "Eupheme"), HS VIII, 282: l. 21. In fairness it should be recalled that Jonson decried ills even at the court of Gloriana. Probably *Cynthia's Revels* constitutes the fullest evidence on the subject, but especially relevant here is Macilente's outburst in *Every Man Out* against "these mushrompe gentlemen,/ That shoot vp in a night to place, and worship" (HS III, 449: I.ii.162–163).

19. *A letter of Advice Written by S*ʳ*. Francis Bacon to the Duke of Buckingham*

nine) for whom Jonson wrote his gypsy masque. Probably never an embodiment of Jonson's ideas of "Vertue," Villiers, at least to begin with, was liked by nearly everyone. When first he swam into the ken of the court his pride was not outsized and his basically good nature shone to good advantage. He was lighthearted, lightfooted, affable, generous, charming, and, perhaps most important of all, he was strikingly handsome. "A man to draw an Angel by," said James Shirley.[20] According to Goodman, "He was the handsomest bodied man of England; his limbs so well compacted, and his conversation so pleasing, and of so sweet a disposition."[21] Jonson himself comments on Buckingham's good looks within the gypsy masque. According to the Third Gypsy, he is "as handsome a man as ever was Adam" (B 359). In fact, using the Nurse's praise of Romeo's rival, he says Buckingham is "A man out of wax" (B 360). The King, who had a weakness for good-looking young males, became completely infatuated. Goodman wrote that "it was impossible for one man to dote more upon another."[22] Sir John Oglander went a step farther, declaring that he had never seen "any fond husband make so much or so great dalliance over his beautiful spouse. . . ."[23] And James himself eventually spoke of Villiers as his "cheiffest Man."[24]

One result of being thus "prais'd" by the King was that Villiers came to be "tax'd" by most of the English people. To Clarendon later in the century it seemed that Villiers throughout "his Life of favour, stood the mark shot at by the most petulent and malicious

---

. . . *Never before Printed* (1661), p. 4. Among helpful studies of Villiers are Katharine Thomson, *The Life and Times of George Villiers, Duke of Buckingham*, 3 vols. (1860); M. A. Gibb, *Buckingham 1592–1628* (1935); Charles Richard Cammell, *The Great Duke of Buckingham* (1939); Philippe Erlanger, *George Villiers Duke of Buckingham*, trans. Lionel Smith-Gordon (1953); and Hugh Ross Williamson, *George Villiers First Duke of Buckingham* (1940).

20. "Epitaph on the Duke of Buckingham," *The Poems of James Shirley*, ed. R. L. Armstrong (New York, 1941), p. 15.

21. *The Court of King James the First*, ed. John S. Brewer (1839), I, 225–226.

22. Goodman, I, 393.

23. *A Royalist's Notebook: The Commonplace Book of Sir John Oglander Kt. of Nunwell*, ed. Francis Bamford (1936), p. 196. The fact is, however, that Buckingham turned out to be something of a ladies' man. There is no reason to doubt James's homosexual tendency, nor any good evidence for saying to what extent it was gratified by his favorites.

24. From a poem by James, "Off Jacke, and, Tom," reprinted in *The Poems of James VI. of Scotland*, ed. James Craigie (Edinburgh, 1958), II, 192. "Christ had his John," James told the Privy Council, "and I have my George" (quoted by Samuel R. Gardiner, *History of England from the Accession of James I. to the Outbreak of the Civil War* [1901], III, 98; this invaluable work appeared in an earlier form in the years 1863–82).

Spirits this Climate ever nourished."[25] In the first place, and certainly relevant here, Villiers was regarded by many as an upstart,
"a novice in Nobility."[26] He was descended from respectable gentry, but gentry were the mere bottom "Round in the Scale of
Honor."[27] Some gossips went so far as to say that George Villiers
was meanly descended, despite the fact that his family had been
seated at Brokesby, in Leicestershire, since the time of Henry III.
As a matter of fact, his father, Sir George Villiers, had for a while
been sheriff of the county. And still it is fairly said that Sir George
remained relatively "obscure amongst Gentlemen."[28]

Sir George's wife Mary was also from Leicestershire and presumably, to begin with, still more obscure. She was the daughter of
Anthony Beaumont, Esquire, third son of William Beaumont of
Cole-Orton Hall. Her detractors would have it that she had been a
poor relation serving in the household of one of Sir George's relatives, but one may put a better face on the matter by saying that she
had served as a young waiting gentlewoman in the household of
Henry Beaumont. Malicious gossips even twisted the facts so that
Mary appeared to have been a kitchen-maid in Sir George's own
household. They claimed he gave her £20 to buy a new dress, and
that then, in response to her metamorphosis, his "affections became
so fired that, to allay them, he married her."[29] Fortunately one may
chronicle the lady's rise without resorting to such means. Though
she was, indeed, an "obscure" country gentlewoman, she rose to be
Countess of Buckingham because she had young George as her son
and because she herself was a determined and ambitious woman.
After the death of Sir George in 1606 she married first Sir William
Rayner and then Sir Thomas Compton. The latter, who was stepfather to the favorite at the time of the gypsy masque, was said to
have "the remark of a slow-spirited man when he was young, and
truly his Wife made him retain it to the last."[30] According to Gar-

25. Edward Hyde, Earl of Clarendon, *The Characters of Robert Earl of Essex,
. . . and George D. of Buckingham, . . . with a Comparison* (1706), p. 2.
26. E.g., George Eglisham, one of James's physicians, *Fore-runner of Revenge*
(1642), p. 12—a violently anti-Buckingham source who says that the favorite's
career proves the proverb "*Nothing more proud then basest blood, when it doth
rise aloft*" (p. 11).
27. Francis Markham, *The Booke of Honour* (1625), p. 58.
28. Eglisham, p. 12.
29. Quoted by Hugh Ross Williamson, p. 30.
30. Wilson, p. 147. An anonymous poem written close to the time of the gypsy
masque includes these lines:

diner, "all the world knew" that Lady Mary "hated and despised" Sir Thomas and "had only been attracted by the prospect of sharing his wealth" (III, 87). Such a judgment sounds harsh, but the simple truth is that the poor man proved to be little more than a rung to assist his wife in her climb.

A younger son of Sir George Villiers's second marriage, and one born to a family of no great means, scarcely could have hoped for a sizeable patrimony. Still, George was reared comfortably enough. Since he demonstrated no bent toward academic learning, his mother saw to it that he was instructed instead in all the more vital areas of courtly learning—dancing, riding, fencing, and French. The latter in particular, after several years of schooling in Leicestershire, he learned in France itself. France was the best of courtly finishing schools, and apparently it was his mother's wish that somehow George might eventually land on his feet at court. That he really would do so was by no means clear for a while. Gossip had it later that when he returned "from his *French* Travels, and sought his Preferment in Marriage with any body [!]," he "mist of a Match for want of an hundred Marks. . . ."[31] More convincing and still striking enough is the antagonistic Wilson's observation that he returned to England "in no greater a *condition* than fifty pounds a year is able to maintain."[32] Writing of the period immediately before the young man caught the King's eye, Sir Simonds D'Ewes claimed in his memoirs that "Mr. Villiers" had been seen

at a horse-race in Cambridgeshire in an old black suit, broken out in divers places; and at night much of the company lying at Linton, near which town the race had been, he could not get a

---

A countesse doth her husband rebuke
& bids him goe & com at her call
but when her Sonne is created a Duke
the day will com shall pay for all[.]

(MS Ashmole 38, 229ᵛ, Bodleian)

31. Cited but denied by William Sanderson, *A Compleat History. . .* (1656), p. 455.

32. *History of Great Britain*, p. 79. Sixty pounds per year, it was claimed in *A Cat May Look upon a King* (1652), p. 76. Thirty pounds, said Edward Peyton, *The Divine Catastrophe of the Kingly Family of the House of Stuarts* (1652), p. 37. Although it is difficult to translate such figures into practical terms, Carl Bridenbaugh is helpful: "Possession of a sufficient landed estate to enable the owner to live off its income identified the country gentleman. . . . 'Northward and farr off' this indicated £300 to £400 a year. . ." (p. 57).

room in the inn to lodge in, and was therefore glad to lie in a trundle-bed in a gentleman's chamber, of a mean quality also at that time. . . .[33]

It is pointless to argue the validity of D'Ewes's story. Whether or not it was true, it was true to what many men thought.

Whether or not it was true, furthermore, the new favorite was knighted and sworn a Gentleman of the King's Bedchamber in less than a year, and from thence he proceeded to accumulate more titles and to climb even higher than Lady Mary might have hoped. Once within range of the royal eyebeams—it seems that the two men met on 3 August 1614, when George was approaching twenty-two—he so enchanted James that by the next Christmas season Ben Jonson was engaged to write a Twelfth Night masque (*The Golden Age Restored*) which would serve to launch the new minion and display to advantage his talent and looks.[34] After this, to quote Wilson,

> To speak of his Advancement by *Degrees*, were to lessen the Kings Love; for *Titles* were heaped upon him, they came rather like *showers* than *drops.* . . . Knighthood [1615], and Gentleman of the Bed-Chamber [1615], were the first sprinklings. . . . And Sir *George Villers* (Baron of *Whaddon* [1616], Viscount *Villers* [1616], and Earl of *Buckingham* [1617], also of the Privy Council) is made Master of the Horse [1616]. In this glory he visits *Scotland* with the King, and is made a Privy Counsellor there [1617].[35]

Then in the following year, 1618, he was made Marquess of Buckingham and Lord High Admiral of England. As Wilson puts it, casting a sidelong glance at Buckingham's dancing ability, "he jumpt *higher* than ever *Englishman* did in so short a time. . ." (p. 105). Within ten years (1614–23) he was metamorphosed from a mere gentleman to a dazzlingly wealthy and powerful duke.[36] *The Mir-*

---

33. *The Autobiography and Correspondence of Sir Simonds D'Ewes, Bart.,* ed. James Orchard Halliwell[-Phillipps] (1845), I, 86.

34. Judging from a letter which John Donne wrote to Sir Henry Goodyer, preparations for the masque were under way at least as early as 20 December 1614 (*John Donne: Selected Prose,* chosen by Evelyn Simpson, ed. Helen Gardner and Timothy Healy [Oxford, 1967], p. 145).

35. *History of Great Britain,* pp. 104–105.

36. The dukedom came after the gypsy masque, but Buckingham's upward trajectory was already unmistakable. Nineteen lines are required to list his titles in Dudley Digges's *A Speech Delivered in Parliament . . . Concerning the Evill Con-*

rour of Majestie, an emblem book of 1618, depicts him as the single "glorious *Starre* attending on the *Sunne*," a star so bright as to burn the fingers of Envy, a *"Heliotropium"* which moves serenely "Aboue the danger of *Detractions* curbe."[37]

As it turned out, Villiers ascended into power and glory trailing clouds of relatives. A court wit prophesied,

> Above in the skies shall Gemini rise,
> And Twins the court shall pester,
> George shall call up his brother Jack
> And Jack his brother Kester.[38]

Obviously it was necessary for the King to play a major role in effecting this multiple ascent, and fortunately for the Villierses he did so eagerly. What he did for them he did for George—or "Steenie," as he called him, because of a fancied resemblance between the favorite and a picture the King knew of St. Stephen. At the time when Christopher Villiers ("Kit," the "Kester" of the verses) became an earl, James wrote to assure Steenie that "thus was thou born in a happy hour for all thy kin."[39] In fact it appeared to Sir Henry Wotton that Buckingham's "noble care of his Family, confirm'd him in the estimation of his Master, who knew that all fountains ought to bestow themselves upon their Neighbour brooks. . . ."[40] In the summer of 1618, at Buckingham's new estate at Wanstead in Essex (once the home of Elizabeth's favorite, Leicester), the King drank a toast to the house of Villiers, which he said he hoped "to advance above all others."[41] With plenty of encouragement from Buckingham and his mother, the royal wish inevitably proved capable of fulfillment. Of George's older half-brothers by his father's first marriage, the first, William, was made a baronet, and the second, Edward, was variously Master of the Mint, Ambassador to Bohemia, and President of the Province of Munster in Ireland. George's elder full

---

sequences, That Doe Attend This State, by Committing Places of Trust, into the Hands of Court-Favourites (1643), p. 4.

37. By "H.G." (Sir Henry Goodyer?), p. 21 (reproduced here as plate No. 1). Bacon, Wotton (*Reliquiae Wottonianae*, p. 55), Clarendon (p. 19), and Digges (p. 6) are among others who speak of Buckingham as a star.

38. Quoted by D. Harris Willson, *King James VI and I* (1956), p. 387.

39. *Letters of the Kings of England*, ed. James Orchard Halliwell-Phillipps (1848), II, 195.

40. *Reliquiae Wottonianae*, p. 61.

41. John Nichols, *The Progresses, Processions, and Magnificent Festivities, of King James the First* (1828), III, 484.

brother, John, was created Baron of Stoke and Viscount Purbeck. His only younger brother, Christopher, was made Baron Villiers of Daventry and Earl of Anglesey. His brother-in-law, William Feilding, became Baron Feilding and First Earl of Denbigh. And his mother was created Countess of Buckingham. It is therefore all the more striking that his rather dull stepfather remained earthbound. In fact, being excluded from his wife's preferments, Sir Thomas posed something of a problem for the heralds.

Meanwhile no one bothered about pretending that marriages in the family were made in any sphere more celestial than the court. The Villierses carried the conventional marriage of convenience to extremes. George himself married sixteen-year-old Katherine Manners, who loved him dearly, it turned out, but also happened to be the only heir to the Rutland fortune, one of the greatest in England. George's good-natured but mentally unstable brother John, after much ado (it was reported that the lady had to be tied to her bed and beaten),[42] was married to Frances Coke, the beautiful daughter of Sir Edward Coke and Lady Hatton. To bring off this match, Coke had to scrape together a tremendous dowry, the money and the girl presumably being the sum required to buy his way back to favor at court. Numerous other if lesser transformations were wrought by hitching wagons of various country cousins to various courtly stars. According to one source, Buckingham summoned

> up all his Countrey kindred, the old Countesse providing a place for them to learne to carry themselves in a Court-like garbe, but because they could not learne the French Dances so soone as to be in gay Clothes, Countrey Dances must be the garbe of the Court, and none else must be used.
>
> Then must these women-kindred be married to Earles, Earles eldest sonnes, Barons, or chiefe Gentlemen of greatest estates, insomuch that the very female kindred were so numerous, as sufficient to have peopled any Plantation; nay, very Kitchin-wenches were married to Knights eldest sonnes.[43]

42. Thomas Longueville, *The Curious Case of Lady Purbeck* (1909), p. 54.
43. *The Court and Character of King James*, a notorious work ascribed to Sir Anthony Weldon (1650), pp. 134–135. John Chamberlain wrote that Buckingham's mother "is to be commended for having such care to preferre her poore kinred and frends, and a speciall worke of charitie yt is to provide so younge maides, whereof there be six or seven more (they say) come lately to towne for the same purpose" (*The Letters of John Chamberlain*, ed. Norman Egbert McClure [Philadelphia, 1939], II, 338).

Overplump Anne Brett, a niece of Buckingham's mother, was the price of political advancement for Lionel Cranfield, later Earl of Middlesex—who would have much preferred to marry someone else.[44] Susan Hill was forced onto the heir of Henry Montagu, Earl of Manchester. Audrey, Mary, and Jane Boteler were the means to promotions for, respectively, Francis Lord Leigh, Edward Lord Howard of Escrick, and James Earl of Marlborough. "But above all, the miracles of those times, old Sir *Anthony Ashley*, who never loved any but boyes, yet hee was snatcht up for a kinsewoman. . . ."[45] All too soon it was possible to say, *"These* are *they,* beare the *Sway,* in *Courte* & *Citty:* / And yet *fewe* love them, thoe *greater's* the *Pitty."* [46]

Perhaps the basic point of family advancement—of metamorphosis —is adequately conveyed by these facts relating to titles and marriages. One may reinforce it, however, as well as pursue the broader subject of Jacobean malaise, by considering the official side of Buckingham's position as James's "cheiffest Man." An observer from France, the Comte de Tillières, provides a convenient summary: on 19 July 1622 he reported that "the government of the whole State appears to have no other end than the elevation of Buckingham, his friends and relations."[47] It was no secret how this had come about. In some verses designed merely to flatter (and published in the same year as the gypsy masque), William Slatyer noted blandly that since Buckingham "is among his Peeres possessest of chiefest place," so "T'is he can giue thee free accesse vnto thy Kings good Grace. . . ."[48] More explicit is this gall-steeped passage from another topical versifier of just about the same time:

When Yelverton shalbe released[49]
& buckingham begine to fall
then will the comons be well pleased
& that hath Long bine wishet of all

44. Chamberlain reported that Cranfield "had noe greate fancy" to the lady (II, 281).
45. *Court and Character of King James,* p. 136.
46. British Museum Add. MS 5832, 206ᵛ.
47. Quoted by Von Raumer, II, 272.
48. *The History of Great Britanie . . . to This Present Raigne* (1621), Cc4ᵛ.
49. Sir Henry Yelverton was released from the Tower on 18 July 1621. He "had ostensibly been committed for malfeasance [as Attorney General], but the real reason was widely guessed: his stubborn opposition to Buckingham" (Robert Zaller, *The Parliament of 1621* [Berkeley, Calif., 1971], p. 30).

They Say Seianus Doth bestowe
what euer offices Doe fall
but tis well knowne it is not so
for he is Soundly payed for all [.] [50]

To give him his due, one must admit that Buckingham achieved some reforms in public affairs—in the Royal Household, the Treasury, the Wardrobe, and the Admiralty. James spoke proudly of his young favorite's success in reducing various expenses. Eventually it was to seem, however, that all the evils toward the end of James's reign and the beginning of Charles's converged "in one Center, met in one great man, the cause of all, . . . *Buckingham*." These are the words of Sir Dudley Digges, speaking in the Parliament of February, 1626, shortly before Parliament was dissolved to prevent Buckingham's impeachment.[51] Even in 1621, however, at the time of the gypsy masque, the French Ambassador saw Buckingham's less attractive qualities quite clearly. Tillières reported that

> The Marquis, with his vanity, takes every thing under his charge, affairs internal and foreign, although, in fact, he knows nothing of either, and they are objects of interest to him, not in regard to the good of his country, nor the honour of his master, but simply with respect to his own advantage. Every thing thence is in confusion. . . . Thus in the end he exhibits nothing estimable, and he is hated to the uttermost. . . .[52]

The parliamentary spokesman had an ax to grind, and the French Ambassador might be expected to cast a particularly critical eye on the pro-Spanish favorite. On the other hand, their statements are supported by a good many other sources. Arthur Wilson, for one, writing specifically of 1621, realized that Buckingham had not yet reached his zenith, nor James his nadir: "*Buckingham*, though he

50. MS Ashmole 38, 229ᵛ (Bodleian). Sir John Eliot was later put in the Tower for comparing Buckingham with Sejanus (1626). Though he owed to Buckingham his appointment as Vice Admiral of Devon (1619), Eliot pulled back from the favorite when convinced he was incapable of managing England's foreign policy. Jonson's play about Sejanus came too early (1603) to be applicable in any specific way to Buckingham, but it appears to have been a topical warning about some problems which continued to plague England throughout James's reign.
51. Digges, *A Speech Delivered in Parliament* (1643), A2ʳ. Bad as he became, Buckingham was not the monster he seemed to some. See Samuel Rawson Gardiner, ed., *Documents Illustrating the Impeachment of the Duke of Buckingham in 1626* (1889).
52. Quoted by Von Raumer (II, 262) from a report dated 25 November.

were well grown, had not yet *sap* enough to make himself swell into *exuberancy*, as he did afterwards, nor was the peoples *malice* now against him so fertile, as to make every little weed, a dangerous and poysonous plant . . ." (p. 158ʳ). Wilson added, however, that even then *"Buckingham* ruled as a Lord *Paramount"* (158ᵛ).⁵³

Even then, moreover, Buckingham's involvement in the abuses relating to patents had become public knowledge. Patents were grants to individuals which afforded them certain privileges, powers, and exemptions. Most patents entailed control over some trade or industrial process and were known as patents of monopolies. And most laid open a fertile field for the "weeds" of corruption. In 1621 the most notorious abuses were those of Sir Giles Mompesson, a distant in-law and close associate of Buckingham (he was married to the sister of Edward Villiers's wife). Mompesson's doings touched practically all Englishmen because he held the patent for inns. Late in 1620 Bacon warned Buckingham that Mompesson's patent and the one for alehouse recognizances held by Buckingham's brother Christopher were "more rumoured, both by the vulgar and by the gentlemen, yea, and by the Judges themselves, than any other patents at this day."⁵⁴ Bacon was Lord Chancellor of England and yet even he could do little more than suggest politely that in the matter of patents Buckingham might initiate such action as would let him "rather take the thanks for ceasing them, than the note for maintaining them." Buckingham was not interested in such advice, however.

53. John H. Barcroft, after investigating the subject of "Carleton and Buckingham: The Quest for Office," decided that, though Buckingham did his part to corrupt the English system of patronage, corruption during his administration was a lesser evil than inefficiency (from an essay in *Early Studies,* ed. Howard S. Reinmuth, Jr. [Minneapolis, 1970], pp. 122–136). A more typical conclusion is that of Trevor-Roper, who describes Buckingham as "the universal manager and profiteer of all those marketable offices, benefices, sinecures, monopolies, patents, perquisites and titles which together constituted the nourishment of the Court" (*Religion the Reformation and Social Change* [1967], p. 85). Lawrence Stone writes that "Royal administration entered its most squalid phase during the rule of the Duke of Buckingham who elevated corruption to the status of a system. . ." (*Crisis of the Aristocracy,* p. 493).

As a gracenote to this theme, it is interesting to find that in 1618 the Venetian Secretary in England, Pier Antonio Marioni, reported that James himself said, "if he punished his subjects like your Serenity [the Doge] for appropriating money to themselves, he would have none left" (*Calendar of State Papers . . . Venice . . . 1617–1619,* ed. Allen B. Hinds [1909], XV, 585). James found "trifling" the accusation by Venice that their ambassador in England, young Antonio Donato, had been found guilty of large-scale embezzling (p. 595). In the same year as the gypsy masque, it should be recalled also, the Lord Chancellor of England, Bacon, was found guilty of taking bribes.

54. Reprinted by James Spedding, *The Letters and the Life of Francis Bacon* (1874), VII, 148–149.

At that very time he was promoting still another patent for Christopher. The bad situation grew gradually worse, therefore, until February of 1621, when the House of Commons opened an investigation of patent abuses. By 26 March the King, though unwilling as always to do anything to hurt George, realized that he must act. He appeared in the House of Lords to announce that he had cancelled the patents for inns and alehouses, as well as the one for gold and silver thread (which had been promoted by Edward Villiers). "My Purpose is," he said, "to strike them all dead...."⁵⁵ On 10 July twenty more patents were struck down by royal proclamation. Meanwhile, Buckingham had conceived a means to remove himself from the path of the sickle. On 13 March he announced that if any of his brothers were found to have done something wrong, he would not defend them. In fact, said he, "the womb that bare them hath also borne one that will seek to have them punished."⁵⁶ It was a tricky caper and it worked. Nevertheless, a good many Englishmen would have been willing in August, 1621, to cry amen to the statement made then by Tillières: "Buckingham ruins England...."⁵⁷

The present reading of *The Gypsies Metamorphos'd* rests in part on Jonson's knowledge and disapproval of all these various matters —the extravagant but dangerously thin façade of courtly glister, the ease of obtaining titles, the specific and meteoric rise of young George Villiers and his family, and the dangers of profiteering and chicanery, together with the easy morality which was at once their cause and corollary. Jonson was neither ignorant nor unconcerned about such things.⁵⁸

In particular we should note that Jonson was aware of James's weakness in matters involving Buckingham. In 1618, when John Selden's *The Historie of Tythes* created a storm among churchmen, James summoned Selden to Theobalds, and Selden went accompanied by two learned friends, Edward Heyward and Ben Jon-

55. *Journals of the House of Lords, Beginning Anno Decimo Octavo Jacobi Regis, 1620* (1771?), III, 69. A significant postscript is to be found in the *Calendar of State Papers, Domestic*, for 23 September 1622: "Grant to Sir Edw. Villiers of a lease of the customs and subsidies on gold and silver thread, &c; similar to a grant heretofore made..." (X, 448).
56. From *The Anonymous Journal* in *Commons Debates 1621*, ed. Wallace Notestein, Frances Helen Relf, and Hartley Simpson (New Haven, 1935), II, 212.
57. Quoted by Von Raumer, II, 261.
58. Jonson's advice to kings in *Timber* is crystal clear: "Choose neither Magistrates *civill*, or *Ecclesiastick*, by *favour*, or *Price*: but with long disquisition, and report of their worth, by all Suffrages. Sell no honours, nor give them hastily; but bestow them with counsell, and for reward..." (HS VIII, 602).

son. Before appearing in the presence of the angry King, however, Jonson took the precaution of enlisting Buckingham's aid. It would seem that for the sake of a good friend Jonson was willing to make use of the fact that any case presented by Buckingham was likely to prosper. (The story is related in *Joannis Seldeni Vindiciæ Secundùm integritatem Existimationis suæ* [1653], quoted in HS XI, 384–385.)

It is obviously significant that Jonson felt he could approach Buckingham in this matter, but lest we read too much warmth into their relationship we should recall also that a few years later Jonson was suspected by his contemporaries of committing some strongly anti-Buckingham views to writing. When Buckingham was assassinated by John Felton in 1628, verses sympathetic to Felton appeared in profusion, including some thought to be by Jonson. Jonson was called in and examined by Sir Robert Heath, the King's Attorney General, on 26 October. Though Jonson admitted having seen the verses in question while visiting the Westminster home of his friend Sir Robert Cotton, he firmly denied writing them and denied holding the sentiments they expressed, adding that he had heard they were the work of Zouch Townely, a friend of his who by then was safely out of England.

Herford and Simpson exclude the poem from the Jonson canon, probably correctly, and add the suggestion that Jonson was unlikely to write laudatory verses on an assassin whose victim was one of his own patrons. One might demur that it is a bit misleading to refer to Buckingham as a "patron" of Jonson. More certain, in any case, is Herford and Simpson's statement "that Cotton's circle mistook the eulogy on Felton for a poem of Jonson's" (I, 243). This is an especially thought-provoking observation, since Jonson's private views may have been better known to Cotton's circle than to us. No matter what Jonson's private views may have been, though, he was cleared of writing the poem and soon was enjoying the favor of Charles.

Whoever wrote it, furthermore, the poem is a noteworthy expression of one loyal Englishman's feelings toward the man who killed Buckingham. In part it reads,

Farewell: undaunted stand, and ioy to bee
Of publique sorrow the epitomie.
Let the dukes name solace and crowne thy thrall:
All wee by him did suffer, thou for all.[59]

59. From Frederick W. Fairholt, ed., *Poems and Songs Relating to George*

iii. *Jonson and the Theme of* Cupiditas

> O! but to strike blind the people with our wealth, and pompe,
> is the thing! what a wretchednesse is this, to thrust all our riches
> outward, and be beggars within. . . ?
>
> Jonson, *Timber* (HS VIII, 605)

Granted the times in which he lived, it is no surprise that Jonson
was interested in moral aspects of economic questions. The *cupiditas*
theme became one of his most frequent means of exploring the dual-
edged subject of how men flout genuine values and exalt false ones.
Krishnamurthi observes "that in his most successful as well as in his
doubtful achievements Jonson is concerned with the same theme
. . . . He explores . . . manifestations of . . . the acquisitive attitude."[60]
Helena Baum makes a similar point: "Jonson's dramatic use of avarice
began in 1598 and ended in 1632, and he utilized it in almost every
possible fashion."[61]

Though Jonson's range of interest should never be underestimated,
the fact is that Avarice to him was the "Grandame vice." As Jonson
viewed her, the old harridan's offspring include Fraud, Slander, and
(how well he puts it!) "Corruption with the golden hands."[62] To
cite but a few specific instances of his attitude, we have from fairly
early in his career Volpone's hymn to gold and a veritable covey of
avaricious scavengers (1606). Toward the middle of his career, in
The Devil Is an Ass (1616), we have his bitter observations on the
opportunism of Jacobean patentees and projectors—some five years
before the House of Commons began its investigation. And late in
his career, in *The Staple of News* (1626), we encounter the Lady
Pecunia (i.e., "wealth" or "property"), whom he significantly has a
character term "The *Venus* of the time, and state" (HS VI, 319:
II.v.34). In other words, during a career which began in Elizabeth's
reign and stretched on into that of Charles, Jonson showed a con-

Villiers, Duke of Buckingham (1850), p. 75. One need not place much weight on
"A Grace by Ben: Johnson. Extempore. Before King James," which asks God's
blessing on "Buckingham the fortunate." This is an occasional piece which asks
God's blessing on "every living thing./ That . . . loves the King." Given its shape
and nature, it was bound to include the King's favorite (HS VIII, 418–419).

60. "The Ethical Basis of Ben Jonson's Plays," *Journal of the Maharaja Sayajirao
University of Baroda*, XI (1962), 154.

61. *The Satiric & the Didactic in Ben Jonson's Comedy* (Chapel Hill, N.C.,
1947), p. 84.

62. *The Golden Age Restored*, HS VII, 422: ll. 36, 39.

tinuing concern for the ascendancy of false over genuine values. Even in his late plays he was still holding a mirror to the venality of the world in which he lived.

A picture in a mirror which Jonson created for the public stage is usually amusing, to be sure, but it is also likely to be somewhat troubling, especially when one ponders its "more remou'd *mysteries.*" It is likely to be disturbing because one of Jonson's several aims was to alert men to their need for reform. His abiding dream, if not, perhaps, his belief, was that poetry in general and dramatic entertainment in particular could be the means to reform. He appears to have been quite serious when he declared in his dedicatory epistle of *Volpone* that "*doctrine . . . is the principall end of* poesie . . ." (HS V, 20). And some of his contemporaries must have agreed. Whatever laughter Jonson's drama provoked, and whatever Jonson's own delight in the Moscas and Subtles he created, Falkland remembered "th' *Ethicke Lectures* of his *Comedies,*" and Richard West wrote soberly that "*Thy Scænes* are *precepts,* every *verse* doth give/ Councell, and teach us not to *laugh,* but *live.*"[63]

No matter how often a theme appears in a dramatist's work, it is possible—perhaps even salutary—to argue that in any given character, scene, or play he may not be speaking for himself. Be this as it may, the criticism of acquisitiveness which is so pervasive in Jonson's drama is carried over into his non-dramatic prose. "Wee serve our avarice," he complains in *Timber,* though "*Money* never made any man rich, but his mind" (HS VIII, 605). In a situation where no stage character obtrudes between us and the light of Jonson's mind, he here denounces man's covetousness: "What need hath nature of silver dishes, multitudes of Waiters, delicate Pages, perfum'd Napkins? She requires meat only, and hunger is not ambitious. . ." (VIII, 606). Of course it may be argued that even in *Timber,* a work constructed in part from other men's sentences, we are still at some remove from Jonson's own innermost thoughts. Nevertheless, all things considered, such a passage as the following is persuasive evidence of Jonson's concern about the acquisitive scramble which he saw in the world around him:

> this is that, wherewith the world is taken, and runs mad to gaze on: Clothes and Titles, the Birdlime of *Fools.*

63. Both in *Jonsonus Virbius* (1638), reprinted in HS XI, 432 and 468.

What petty things they are, wee wonder at? like children, that esteeme every trifle; and preferre a *Fairing* before their Fathers: what difference is betweene us, and them? but that we are dearer Fooles, Cockscombes, at a higher rate? They are pleas'd with Cockleshels, Whistles, Hobby-horses, and such like: wee with Statues, marble Pillars, Pictures, guilded Roofes, where under-neath is Lath, and Lyme; perhaps Lome. . . . Nor is it onely in our wals, and seelings; but all that wee call happinesse, is meere painting, and guilt: and all for money: what a thinne Membrane of honour that is? and how hath all true reputation falne, since money began to have any? Yet the great heard, the multitude; that in all other things are divided; in this alone conspire, and agree: To love money.

(VIII, 607–608)

Jonson was too honest to depict *cupiditas* as peculiar to those with titles. He has Subtle, Face, and Doll set up their fleecing alchemical corporation in his own neighborhood of Blackfriars. But *cupiditas* is nonetheless characteristic of people of "honour."

What bearing on *The Gypsies Metamorphos'd* have such comments and quotations on genuine and false values, on acquisitiveness and avarice? They converge in the point that we had better not suspend our knowledge, while reading this masque, of what Jonson continued to say about such matters throughout the rest of his work —most strikingly in *Volpone* and *The Alchemist*, but in many other places as well. We should use such knowledge, instead, to enrich our understanding of Jonson's gypsies, light-fingered frauds who come to dance before the King, then "change" and settle down to live at his court.

It would be wrong to heap on the shoulders of a single courtier the blame for everything which Jonson deplored at James's court, but the fact remains that James's "cheiffest man" is also Jonson's chief gypsy. In both the actual court and the masque which mirrors it, Buckingham is a major figure and must bear a major responsibility. Though certain things about the historical Buckingham are puzzling (his epitaph in Westminster Abbey calls him the enigma of the world), we have seen that he was most emphatically an acquisitive man. Probably at the beginning of his career as royal favorite he merely provided the strong, broad shoulders on which the doting

King might heap honors as he pleased. Moreover, young Villiers, like his royal master, did have a generous strain. Flecknoe observed, more truly than he knew, that Villiers scattered gifts "With such Liberality, he scant/ Thought's gold his owne, whilst other men did want."[64] If he could be lavishly generous, however, he also learned quickly enough how to look after himself, and his own acquisitive skills, coupled with the King's generosity, inevitably resulted in riches. After the King gave him land worth some £80,000 Buckingham was said to be second in wealth only to the Earl of Montgomery.[65] However attractive such a man may have appeared to those on whom he beamed his "Liberality," there were many who might cry "aye" to such accusations as the Earls of Clare and Devonshire were finally moved to make. The former decried Villiers's "Subtilties, which he used to wind himself into the Possession of the King's Money, and to get that by Cunning Steps and Degrees, which per-adventure he could not have obtained at once."[66] And Devonshire brought into public view the role that Villiers was playing in the manufacture of titles, explaining how the favorite "not only sets Titles of Honour to Sale, come buy that will, and awards to his Agent a *Venditioni exponas* for them; but hath compelled others, that were modest, and could have been contented to have remained in their own Rank, to take them at a Price set by himself."[67] To the keen-eyed French Ambassador Villiers's rapacity was, quite literal-ly, something to write home about.[68]

All in all, then, it is well to remember that Jonson writes of Lady Pecunia as "The *Venus* of the time, and state," the embodiment of modern love. Of course he is writing generically, but he is also writ-ing of an English situation in which George Villiers and his clan were deeply implicated. Five years after the gypsy masque Jonson still could write that Pecunia

64. "On the Late Duke of Buckingham," in *Miscellania. Or, Poems of All Sorts, with Divers Other Pieces* (1653), p. 43.

65. Godfrey Davies, *The Early Stuarts 1603–1660* (Oxford, 1967 printing of 2nd ed., 1959; 1st ed., 1937), p. 269.

66. *Journals of the House of Lords*, III, 615. Sir John Holles became Earl of Clare in 1624. The price of his earldom was set originally at £6,000, but later was reduced to £4,000. Holles agreed "to give £5,000 to whomever Buckingham as-signed, with the hope that the favorite would remit the other thousand" (Charles R. Mayes, "The Sale of Peerages in Early Stuart England," *Journal of Modern His-tory*, XXIX [1957], 24).

67. *Journals of the House of Lords*, III, 611. Mayes points out that the sale of peerages stopped abruptly after Buckingham's assassination (p. 33).

68. Tillières, quoted by Von Raumer (II, 273), from a report of 19 July 1622.

> *... holds a Faire of* Knights, *and* Lords,
> *A Mercat* [market] *of all Offices,*
> *And Shops of honour, more or lesse. ...*
> (HS VI, 351: IV.ii.110–112)[69]

iv. *Jonson and the Need for Flattery*

Lysippus. What think'st thou of a maske, will it be well?
Strato. As well as masks can be.
Lysippus.   As masks can be?
Strato. Yes, they must commend their King, and speake in praise
Of the assembly, blesse the Bride and Bridegroome,
In person of some god, there tied to rules
Of flatterie.

> Beaumont and Fletcher[70]

Granted the important, interlocking circles of his moral and ethical concerns (which do not, of course, either alone or together encompass so large a poet), the demand for flattery in masques constituted a continuing problem for Jonson. Whatever the theme of a masque, its "present occasion" always called for some encomiastic rhetoric. Though masquing had undergone considerable evolution during the course of its history, it had been regarded as a medium for complimenting monarchs ever since the fourteenth century, and after so long a time as that, the affinity between masquing and praise was not likely to fade from the court of a monarch so conceited as James. The vanity of James is beyond question. Des Marets wrote in 1616 that "Always and in every thing does King James insist upon flattery."[71] Besides, one perforce speaks with a circumspection akin to flattery when addressing a monarch who holds that "God and Kings doe pace together."[72] No matter how James drooled or slurred

69. It should be noted that Pecunia takes an honorable place in the play as soon as her real nature is understood. Jonson scorned the abuse of money, not money itself.

70. *The Maid's Tragedy*, I.i.6–11 (ed. Robert K. Turner, in *The Dramatic Works in the Beaumont and Fletcher Canon*, gen. ed. Fredson Bowers [Cambridge, 1970], II, 29).

71. Quoted by Von Raumer, II, 233, from reports of February, 1616. At the opening of his reign James said of himself and Henri IV "that not for a long time, not for a century, had two kings of their quality been to be found" (Von Raumer, II, 199). Earlier still James had gone so far as to insert some flattery of himself in a wedding masque he composed. See p. 43.

72. "The Wiper of the Peoples Teares," from *Poems*, II, 182.

words, no matter how loud his belches nor how indecorous his grab-bling at his codpiece, he presented himself to his subjects as God's own lieutenant, and at least for public purposes he rested assured in thinking of "the blessings which God hath in my Person bestowed vpon you all."[73]

It is clear that the requirements of masques in general and James in particular presented Jonson, the chief writer of masques, with a dilemma which was not merely ethical and moral, but political as well. What could he do? Like any man, Jonson sometimes fell short of his goals, but he apparently held that "To flatter my good Lord" is "To lose the formes, and dignities of men...."[74] When writing for the public stage, there was little temptation for him or any play-wright to flatter, but what could he do—what could the leading satiric dramatist of the day do—when the job at hand was a masque? In *Pleasure Reconciled to Virtue* Jonson hailed James in the reful-gent form of Hesperus. In *Oberon* he wrote of James as "the matter of vertue," "a god, o're kings" (HS VII, 353: ll. 341, 344). And in *The Masque of Blackness* he declared that the royal rays "shine day, and night, and are of force/ To blanch an Æthiope, and reuiue a Cor's" (HS VII, 177: ll. 254–255). Little wonder, then, that in *The Gypsies Metamorphos'd*, though James in places is addressed in a much more personal and realistic way (as a "lucky bird" who loves "a horse, and a hound, but no part of a swine" [B 250, 255])—little wonder that even here there is praise:

Could any doubt, that saw this hand,
Or who you are, or what command
    You have upon the fate of things,
Or would not say you were let downe
From Heave'n on earth to be the crowne,
    And top of all your neighbour kings?
                    (B 288–293)

One might ask how these can be the words of a man who "of all stiles ... loved most to be named honest, and hath of that ane hundreth letters so naming him" (HS I, 150).

73. *Workes*, p. 486. He clarified his stand on the divine right of kings in his *Trew Law of Free Monarchies* (1598) and elsewhere. Godfrey Davies notes that James's persistence in stating and defining his concept of kingship probably stimu-lated other formulations and hence hastened trouble (p. 33).
74. "An Epistle to a Friend, to Perswade Him to the Warres," HS VIII, 166–167: ll. 146–147.

A major explanation, beyond the levels of literary convention and social constraint, is that Jonson esteemed the kingship highly. He held that all men belong in their proper places, that they are absurd when they try to be something they are not, and that the place of a king, whoever he may be, is at the top. A king is therefore to be honored. Like Marlowe and Shakespeare before him, Jonson saw plainly the disparity between a king's place and his person, and, ironically, it may have been this very fact which made it possible for him to hold that patriotic "honoring" is not personal "flattery." In *Timber* we find that

> *After God*, nothing is to be lov'd of man like the Prince: He violates nature, that doth it not with his whole heart. For when hee hath put on the care of the publike good, and common safety; I am a wretch, and put of [f] man, if I doe not reverence, and honour him: in whose charge all things *divine* and *humane* are plac'd.
>
> (HS VIII, 594)

It follows that another justification for expressing praise in masques is simply that the king really does have powers which can alter men's lives. His favors really can transform their fortunes. His "beames" really can, when he is so inclined, "salue" at least some of "the rude defects" of those on whom he smiles.[75]

Nor are these the only important reasons for the presence of flattery in a masque. There are at least two more, and both are the stronger for being expressed by Jonson. First, he makes the obvious but important observation in *Timber* that "*Flattery* is a fine Picklock of tender eares. . ." (HS VIII, 596). Flattery is a practical means of securing interested attention. The second he gives in his verse epistle to John Selden:

> . . . I confesse (as every Muse hath err'd,
> And mine not least) I have too oft preferr'd
> Men past their termes, and prais'd some names
>   too much,
> But 'twas with purpose to have made them such.
>
> (HS VIII, 159: ll.19-22)

75. *Masque of Blackness*, HS VII, 177: ll. 254-257. See John C. Meagher, *Method and Meaning in Jonson's Masques* (Notre Dame, Ind., 1966), esp. pp. 110-112.

Jonson admits that in the past he has erred sometimes in administering proper doses of the stuff, but his intent has been to use praise at least in part as a gentle persuasion towards improvement. A counsellor, he says in *Timber*, ought to behave as if "the *Prince* were already furnished with the parts hee should have, especially in affaires of *State*" (VIII, 566). Ernest Talbert and Allan Gilbert long ago pointed out that Jonson held "praise can be counsel, not flattery, and is fitting for an address to great persons."[76] Much the same view (as Talbert notes) was held by Jonson's friend Bacon: "Some praises come of good wishes and respects, which is a forme due in ciuilitie to Kings and great persons, *Laudando praecipere*, when by telling men what they are, they represent to them what they should be."[77] Furthermore, it is worth adding that both the great instaurator and the great neoclassicist had classical precedent for their stand. Plato himself had spoken of the didactic value of praise.[78] One may shy away from an either-or reading (*viz.*, that the praise is either flattery *or* counsel) in favor of one which sees Plato's interrelation, but ever since the articles of Talbert and Gilbert it has been impossible to ignore the advisory aspect of Jonson's *laudatio*.

There is yet another aspect to the question of praise which relates to *The Gypsies Metamorphos'd*. Provided one dared at all to offer council to King James, its disguise as praise was more than ever politic in 1621. James at this time was especially sensitive to the criticism of his policies. Ever since the outbreak of the Thirty Years War in 1618, and especially since it had become clear that James was holding to his pro-Spanish policies, the average Englishman's political interest had been growing more intense, finding expression in sermons, pasquils, pamphlets, and songs, and in conversations everywhere. In 1620 James finally became so annoyed by self-appointed critics and advisers that on 24 December he issued a proclamation (Bacon wrote it) *Against Excess of Lavish and Licen-*

76. Ernest W. Talbert, "The Interpretation of Jonson's Courtly Spectacles," *PMLA*, LXI (1946), 458. See also Allan H. Gilbert, "The Function of the Masques in *Cynthia's Revels*," *PQ*, XXII (1943), 211–230, and, more recently, Meagher, who nevertheless admits, after discussing the matter, that "It can hardly be doubted that he often sinned against sincerity, in the modern sense of the word" (p. 160).

77. "Of Praise," *Essaies* (1624), H6ᵛ.

78. See O. B. Hardison, Jr., *The Enduring Monument: A Study of the Idea of Praise in Renaissance Literary Theory and Practice* (Chapel Hill, N.C., 1962), pp. 26–27. Hardison notes also that "Pliny defended his servile flattery of Trajan with the argument that in it 'good princes might recognize what they have done; bad, what they ought to have done'" (p. 31). Hardison's whole chapter on "Rhetoric, Poetics, and Theory" is helpful.

tious Speeche of Matters of State. The document even took a certain sort of flattery into account: "Neither let any man mistake us so much," it concluded, "as to think that by giving fair and specious attributes to our person they can cover the scandals which they otherwise lay upon our government, but conceive that we make no other construction of them but as fine and artificial glosses the better to give passage to the rest of their imputations and scandals."[79] Then on 26 July 1621, just a few days before the first performance of the gypsy masque, another proclamation was issued reinforcing the first. Since Jonson had surely composed the masque by then, except, perhaps, for any last-minute revisions, one might wonder if he grew apprehensive. The Venetian Ambassador later reported the general situation to the Doge and Senate, and noted, immediately after describing the King's visit with Villiers, that everyone had been forbidden "to speak about affairs of state even in the court, upon pain of death. . . ." Little wonder that "the progress . . . continued in profound silence. . . ."[80]

It was towards the end of this same year, 1621, after the Commons had passed its famous Protestation, that James angrily called for its Journal, tore out the offending passage with his own hands, and adjourned the Parliament. Somewhat later but during the same general period he went so far as to record his thoughts on unsought advice in the following extraordinary lines:

Come Counsell me when I shall call
Before bewarr what may befall
Kings will hardly take aduice
Of Counsell they are wondrous nice
Loue and wisdome leads them still
Their Counsell tables vpp to fill
They need noe helpers in their choice
Their best aduice is their owne voyce. . . .[81]

He even included a couplet which points defensively at Buckingham: "Content your selfe with such as I/ Shall take neere, and place on highe" (II, 184).

Jonson's *laudando praecipere*, therefore, and still more his depiction of Buckingham as a saucy gypsy rogue begin to seem all the

79. Quoted by Spedding, *The Letters and the Life of Francis Bacon*, VII, 157.
80. *Calendar of State Papers . . . Venice . . . 1621–1623*, XVII, 117.
81. "The Wiper of the Peoples Teares," II, 190.

more bold. Sure enough, he had bragged to Drummond some three years earlier that if he "might have favour to make one Sermon to the King, he careth not what y^r after sould befall him, for he would not flatter though he saw Death" (HS I, 141). As he said in *Timber*, "Soveraignty needs counsell: Learning affords it" (HS VIII, 565). Nevertheless, it is perfectly clear that not even Jonson could afford to write a masque without a good deal of praise. It was fortunate indeed, therefore, that learning could express itself properly in a masque by means of praise.

Still more fortunate in the case of the gypsy masque the *mise en scène* allowed Jonson to place all the praise on the lips either of gypsies or of courtiers who have just metamorphosed from gypsies. What could be more appropriate? Gypsies are supposed to be charming deceivers. The machinations of gypsies are supposed to be oiled by wily flattery. In denouncing the astrologer William Lilly, who later became notorious for predicting the death of Charles I, an anonymous broadside writer could say nothing worse than, "Hence, *Baser Gypsees*! here is one that can/ Out do *ye all*, in flattering any man...."[82] Gypsies aside, Jonson was sufficiently clear-eyed and hardheaded when it came to writing a masque to accept the necessity of sweetening his preaching with praise, but it turns out that part of his special achievement in *The Gypsies Metamorphos'd* is that here he has made a special and appropriate virtue of that necessity.

v. *James, Jonson, and Allegory*

> Are not the choisest *fables* of the *Poets*,
> That were the fountaines, and first springs of
>   wisdome,
> Wrapt in perplexed *allegories*?
>
> Jonson, *The Alchemist*[83]

When it came to indirection in literary genres, James himself was not uninformed. In 1596, for example, he had been aroused by Spenser's allegorical depiction of his mother in *The Faerie Queene*. No matter what personal sentiments he may have had about Mary of Scotland, his official feelings prompted a protest to London regarding her transparent disguise as the False Duessa.[84] In fact, James

---

82. *Lilly Lash't with His Own Rod* (1660).
83. HS V, 327–328; II.iii.205–207.
84. He requested that Spenser "be duly tried and punished" (Frederic Ives Car-

himself when a teen-ager had composed a long poem called *Ane Metaphoricall Invention of a Tragedie Called Phoenix* (1584), which is an allegory concerning his early favorite Esmé Stuart, the dashing Duke of Lennox. (The phoenix reborn was Esmé's son Ludovick, one of those whose fortunes were told by Jonson's gypsies at Windsor.) In 1588, on the occasion of the marriage of Esmé's daughter Henrietta to George Gordon, Earl of Huntly, James had even put his royal hand to the writing of a masque. Furthermore, and much closer in time to *The Gypsies Metamorphos'd*, he had become so intrigued by the *roman-à-clef Argenis* (1621), John Barclay's monumental attempt in Latin to merge courtly prose fiction with contemporary European politics, that he asked none other than his "welbeloved Servaunt" Ben Jonson to turn it into English.[85]

James knew perfectly well, then, that the purpose of the allegorist is to write so that all may hear or read, but only the wiser understand. In his early days he even acknowledged in his own writings that the figurative approach is particularly suitable for a writer who wishes to handle a subject so delicate as politics. Here is King James on the subject of indirection:

> Ze man . . . be war of wryting any thing of materis of co*m*moun weill, or vther sic graue sene subiectis (except Metaphorically, of manifest treuth opinly knawin, zit nochtwithstanding vsing it very seindil [i.e., seldom]) because nocht onely ze essay nocht zour awin *Inuentioun*, . . . bot lykewayis they are to graue materis for a Poet to mell in.[86]

This canny bit of self-preserving literary criticism sounds very much like James. Tiresias, he might have added, was struck blind for having looked on Pallas naked.

It is of interest and importance to know that during the period with which we are mainly concerned—the years closest to the gypsy masque—some men proceeded as if they had read James's advice and accepted at least some of it. Convenient illustrations of metaphorical "melling" may be found in certain sermons of the time. For

---

penter, *A Reference Guide to Edmund Spenser* [Chicago, 1923], p. 41). Jonson, by the way, mentioned the Mary-Duessa parallel to Drummond (HS I, 137).

85. The patent for Jonson's pension of 1616 is reprinted in HS I, 231–232. His version of *Argenis* was registered with the Stationers' Company in 1623, in which year a fire at his home presumably destroyed the manuscript.

86. *Ane Schort Treatise, Conteining Some Reulis and Cautelis to Be Observit and Eschewit in Scottis Poesie*, in Craigie (Edinburgh, 1955), I, 79.

instance, on that day in 1616 when George Villiers became Viscount Buckingham, none other than William Laud preached on the story of how Miriam had been stricken with leprosy for speaking against Moses.[87] Often, however, the men of the cloth spoke otherwise than James would have wished. In December, 1620, one of the preachers at Paul's Cross spoke "very freely" on Prince Charles's proposed marriage to the Spanish (and naturally Roman Catholic) *infanta*, using the text "thou shalt not plow with an ox and an ass."[88] The Spanish Match, to which Jonson alludes with approval in the gypsy masque, was a subject of intense interest and also some danger at this time. Another preacher, after speaking on the damnable condition of those who forsake their faith (the worry was all for the Prince, not the *infanta*), finished by saying that his congregation might now expect him to proceed to a current application, "but he was not ambitious of lying in prison, and so ended."[89] Arthur Wilson is doubtless remembering correctly, therefore, when he generalizes that in sermons of that day "there were no plain downright blows to be given, but if they cunningly, and subtily, could glance at the misdemeanors of the Times, and smooth it over *metaphorically*, it would pass current, though before the King himself" (p. 151). Such a practice and cast of mind are worth recalling when we think of Jonson, who himself had given thought to what it would be like to deliver a sermon to James.

It was very much in character for Ben Jonson to preach even without a pulpit, and also to "mell" metaphorically. "Phant'sie," he wrote four years before the gypsy masque, "has dreams that have wings,/ And dreams that have honey, and dreams that have stings ...."[90] Not only was Jonson willing to preach in his poetry by means of praise, in other words; he was willing to point that preaching with satirical barbs. Traditionally masques were supposed to praise by allegorical means, and Jonson, who was fond of allegory anyway, was far too much a traditionalist to neglect this function; but the indirection proper to allegorical writing in general and masques in particular was proper also to satire. If it is true that Jonson was "the only thoroughly serious satiric author in this period,"

87. D. Harris Willson, p. 383.
88. Chamberlain, II, 331.
89. Noted by Godfrey Davies, "English Political Sermons, 1603–1640," *HLQ*, III (1939), 12–13.
90. From *The Vision of Delight*, HS VII, 465: ll. 61–62.

and much "concerned with the moral and sanative purpose of satire, not just with exciting theater,"[91] the more shocking discovery would be that somehow he managed to write so many masques for the Jacobean court *without* letting loose some "stings."[92] Of course in a masque the stings, the "sharpness" we have touched on earlier, might or might not be felt, depending on the varying sensibilities of those in the audience and depending on which points the poet chose to bate and how he decided to deploy them. Precisely here lay Jonson's great gamble—and perhaps his salvation—in the gypsy masque. As was his custom, at any rate, he proceeded on the assumption that "a *Writer* should alwayes trust somewhat to the capacity of the *Spectator*, especially at these *Spectacles*; Where Men, beside inquiring eyes, are vnderstood to bring quick eares...."[93] Since a writer could not "say" all he "meant," he had to "trust somewhat."

Sharp eyes and quick ears could have discerned that at least since *Mercury Vindicated* (1615), where he had concerned himself with alchemists, the greatest satirist of the English theater *had* been tossing satiric darts in his masques.[94] It should therefore come as no

91. Alvin Kernan, *The Cankered Muse: Satire of the English Renaissance* (New Haven, 1959), p. 156.

92. Ellen D. Leyburn has taken note of the affinity between allegory and satire in *Satiric Allegory: Mirror of Man* (New Haven, 1956). See also John MacQueen, *Allegory* (1970), esp. pp. 68–69.

93. From *The Masque of Queens*, HS VII, 287: ll. 105–108.

94. *For the Honor of Wales* (1618) was designed to honor the Prince of Wales, and yet it opened with a satiro-comic conversation between contentious, chauvinistic Welshmen. The newly emerging fourth estate was the target of the prose induction to *News from the New World* (1620); here Jonson played with the fantastic idea that a man might bring back news from the moon. In *Neptune's Triumph for the Return of Albion* (1624), an allegory mirroring the return of Charles and Buckingham from Spain, Jonson indulged himself in fashioning some barbs for the Spaniards, and the King ordered some of the sharper passages cut. In *Time Vindicated*, two years after the gypsy masque, Jonson let loose the savage personal satire mentioned here earlier—satire against Wither—which from the beginning was recognized as such. And scarcely less plain was the satire in *Love's Welcome at Bolsover* (1634), a royal entertainment in which Jonson mocked his sometime collaborator Inigo Jones under the thin guise of Coronell Iniquo Vitruvius.

About the same time William Cartwright made it perfectly clear in *The Lady-Errant* that masques had come to be one means of administering a public needling. A lady who is determined to pester certain courtiers proposes in that play that

We will vex 'em through
All sorts of Torment, meet 'em at each Corner,
Write Satyrs, and make Libels of 'em, put 'em
In Shows, & Mock-Shows, Masques,
     & Plaies, present 'em
In all Dramatique Poetry....

(I.ii.199–203, from *The Plays and Poems of William Cartwright*, ed. G. Blakemore Evans [Madison, Wis., 1951], p. 99.)

surprise that he availed himself of his satirical armory in writing *The Gypsies Metamorphos'd*. Bagged for the Devil's feast in the masque, and served on the surface for all to see, are promoters and panders and painted ladies. A more important point, however—and one to be developed here presently—is that Jonson's more massive and deadly satire in this masque is implicit in the figurative material relating to his fundamental courtier-gypsy conceit.

Before exploring some implications of this conceit it may be useful to remind ourselves of the related fact that in matters allegorical Jonson specifically advocated clarity and underlying unity. Though sometimes his mirror proved hazy (sometimes because he had stirred too deep in the Pierian spring, sometimes for other reasons), he wrote in *Timber* that allegory should not be overextended "lest either wee make our selves obscure, or fall into affectation, which is childish" (HS VIII, 625).[95] As for unity, he wrote in his *Part of the King's Entertainment in Passing to His Coronation* that one's chances for comprehension were enhanced precisely because the poet held to the principle that the "nature and propertie" of an allegorical device were "to present alwaies some one entire bodie, or figure, consisting of distinct members, and each of those expressing it selfe, in the [i.e., its] owne actiue spheare," with all contributing to a "generall harmonie" (HS VII, 90–91). However complex the multeity, it was to be informed by some sort of unity, and grasping the unifying principle was all-important. Late in his career, in his "induction" to *The Magnetic Lady* (1632), Jonson hit on a particularly happy simile to suggest not only something of the nature of the unity proper to allegory, but also something of the pleasure to be derived from grasping it aright. "A good *Play*," he writes,

> is like a skeene of silke: which, if you take by the right end, you may wind off, at pleasure, on the bottome, or card of your discourse, in a tale, or so; how you will: But if you light on the

95. He had held much the same view for a long time. In 1604, in the commentary for his "device" celebrating the King's coronation the preceding year, he wrote that

> Neither was it becomming, or could it stand with the dignitie of these shewes (after the most miserable and desperate shift of the Puppits) to require a Truch-man, or (with the ignorant Painter) one to write, *This is a Dog*; or, *This is a Hare*: but so to be presented, as vpon the view, they might, without cloud, or obscuritie, declare themselues to the sharpe and learned. . . .

(HS VII, 91)

wrong end, you will pull all into a knot, or elfe-lock; which nothing but the sheers, or a candle will undoe, or separate.

(HS VI, 512: ll. 136–141)

In this passage, of course, he is writing of drama proper, not a civic show or masque, but, rather than turning us aside, this fact should impress us with the pervasiveness of his views on unity.

Since the idea of underlying unity was important to Jonson throughout his career, it surely is worth some emphasis by those who write about him. We have glimpsed it here earlier in the words of Dolora Cunningham,[96] and now having amplified it a bit, we are in a better position to appreciate the value of an insight offered by Ray Heffner. Noting that "the essential unity of Jonson's comedy is thematic," Heffner has gone on to point out that "the central expression of the unifying idea is usually not in a fully developed plot but in a fantastic comic conceit, an extravagant exaggeration of human folly...."[97] Thus are we brought back to Jonson's gypsies. Whether one chooses finally to call them allegorical or symbolic, Jonson's courtier-gypsies constitute precisely the sort of conceit that Heffner describes: "an extravagant exaggeration of human folly." It is a unifying device which beautifully fulfills the requirements of clarity, and, however the verse-writing King may have responded to it, it enabled his chiefest poet to "mell" in "graue materis" with admirable ease.

vi. *Gypsies in Tudor and Stuart England*

> ...the counterfoote theiveis and lymmairis [i.e., rogues or scoundrels] callit Egipsianis...committ infinite thifte, insolenceis, and oppressionis upoun his Majesteis goode subjectis in all pairtis quhair they hant and frequent....
>
> Register of the Privy Council of Scotland, 1619[98]

In considering various aspects of the basic image in the gypsy masque one might well bring to bear on it the light of Michael

96. See p. 9. Eliot was getting at the same fundamental phenomenon when he observed that in Jonson's work, "The plot does not hold the play together; what holds the play together is a unity of inspiration that radiates into plot and personages alike" (*Elizabethan Essays* [1934], p. 77).

97. "Unifying Symbols in the Comedy of Ben Jonson," from *English Stage Comedy*, ed. W. K. Wimsatt, Jr. (New York, 1955), p. 75.

98. David Masson, ed. (Edinburgh, 1895), XII, 152.

Murrin's observation that "Every trope represents a value judgment made by comparison. No one can juxtapose a man and a toad or a man and an angel without making a moral judgment of some kind . . . ."[99] The creator of a man-toad trope or a man-angel trope assumes that his audience has some more or less fixed notions about toads and angels, and that he can use these notions to say something about man. Given our present topic it behooves us to consider what thoughts, feelings, facts, and impressions the Jacobeans had about gypsies. Granted that Jonson could do what he chose with them—anything from contradicting them completely to capitalizing on them as he found them—it is essential that we understand the conventional role played by gypsies during the Tudor and Stuart periods.

No one is sure when gypsies first appeared in England. They were ordered out of France in the summer of 1504, however, and soon afterwards made an appearance and a good impression in Scotland. One wispy tradition would have it that they turned up in Scotland in 1460, but our first certain knowledge is that in April, 1505, the sum of ten French crowns was granted to certain gypsies by the great-grandfather of Jonson's King. Having introduced themselves to the Scots as "Egyptians" (from which word the aphetic "gypsy" derives), they prevailed on James IV to write them a letter of introduction to the King of Denmark. After "a few months," said James, "Anthony Gawin, Earl of Little Egypt," and his retinue appeared to be wretched but honorable wanderers.[100]

The earliest known gypsy reference in England comes from 1514. In *A Dyalog of Syr Thomas More Knyghte*, written at the time of the inquiry into Richard Hunne's hanging in the Lollards' Tower, we find a talkative witness wishing he could consult a woman, now "gone ouer see," who could as well have told "who kyld Hunne as who stale an horse," merely by lokyng in onys hande. Therwyth the lordys laughed and asked what is she. Forsoth my lord quod he an egypcyan . . ." (xci[r]).[101]

Andrew Borde, writing about thirty years later, takes us closer to

99. *The Veil of Allegory* (Chicago, 1969), p. 65.

100. A translation of the letter is given in Henry T. Crofton, *The English Gipsies under the Tudors* (Manchester, 1880), pp. 4–5. With regard to Gawin's claim to be "Earl of Little Egypt" Crofton observes that "Before they were unmasked these people used to affect all kinds of titles from distant countries. . ." (p. 3).

101. A nearly contemporaneous allusion to "Egyptians" occurs in the descrip-

what was to become the prevailing image of "Egyptians." In his chapter on Egypt in *The Fyrst Boke of the Introduction of Knowledge* (1542), Borde says that "The people of the coũtry be swarte and doth go disgisyd in theyr apparel contrary to other nacyons they be lyght fyngerd and vse pyking [i.e., stealing] they haue litle maner and euyl loggyng & yet they be pleasunt daunsers. Therbe few or none of the Egipciõs y^t doth dwel in egipt for Egipt is repleted now w^t infydele alyons" (Nii^r). Confusion lies near the surface here, however, for it is a rare nation in which the native costume is a disguise.

Putting together a number of scrappy sources such as these, we may gather that from a very early time the gypsies were associated with roaming, fortune-telling, strange costumes, and dancing. Furthermore, we may infer that their initial good impression became tarnished when people found that "they be lyght fyngerd and vse pyking."

Fortunately for our purposes here, early notions about gypsies are as useful as hard facts about them, but we need to be aware that the two do not always square. If Borde were really writing about Egyptians, for instance, he would help us not at all with gypsies, who, we now know, came originally not from Egypt but from north and northwest India.[102] Borde is correct, however, in his im-

---

tion of a disguising of 1520. Edward Hall's *Union of the Two Noble and Illustrate Famelies of Lancastre & Yorke* records that after a comedy of Plautus had been played in the "greate chambre at Grenewiche," there entered "eight ladies in blacke veluet bordred about with gold . . . , and tired like to the Egipcians very richely . . . ," and that after a while the ladies were joined by eight men, similarly dressed (lxvii^v–lxviii^r). To James McPeek it has seemed that Henry's entertainment "may have been suggestive to Jonson for his *Metamorphosed Gypsies*" (*The Black Book of Knaves and Unthrifts* [Storrs, Conn., 1969], p. 257). This is unlikely on several counts, however, not least because the metamorphosis in Jonson's masque is a rags-to-riches transformation, and the performers at Henry's court are from the beginning "very richely" attired.

102. According to Chaman Lal, the Romany language is derived from Sanskrit and is closest to Punjabi (*Gipsies: Forgotten Children of India* [Delhi, 1962], pp. xi and 11). The same author notes that Romany "has thousands of words from Hindi, Punjabi, Gujarati and the dialects of Rajputana and Malwa" (p. xi).

On their move westward the gypsies also must have spent a long time in Greek- and Slavic-speaking lands, since they picked up many words from the Greek world. The earliest known reference to gypsies in the Byzantine Empire comes from about 1068 and describes the gypsies as *Adsincani* (cf. Fr. *Tsiganes*, Ital. *Zingari*, etc.), a people famed as sorcerers and magicians. It is noteworthy that early Byzantine popular literature yields illustrations of the term for gypsy being used already as a pejorative epithet, e.g., "a liar, a thief, and a Gypsy" (George C. Soulis, "The Gypsies in the Byzantine Empire and the Balkans in the Late Middle Ages," *Dum-*

plication that gypsies already had come to be regarded as accomplished thieves. By the year 1530 the gypsies in England had committed so many felonies and robberies that the first of several official measures was taken to bring them under control (22 Henry VIII, cap. 10). The new act forbade any more gypsies to enter the realm, and, equally significant, changed the conditions under which gypsies already within the realm could be tried. Until 1530 a gypsy accused of robbing or murdering an Englishman could demand a jury made up half of gypsies, but no more was this true. During the pre-1530 period an ordinary, run-of-the-ditch English rogue was, legally speaking, disadvantaged, in effect encouraged to become a counterfeit gypsy or even, if real gypsies would allow it, to join their bands.

The latter fact introduces an important and complex subject. In those days as always an irresponsible way of life appealed to many non-gypsies, and the "gypsy" tradition became immensely complicated by the "conversion" of some Britons to gypsyism. William Harrison in his *Description of Britaine* (1577) deplored how the tribes of English rogues, including English "gypsies," had increased:

> . . . they are nowe supposed of one sexe and another, to amount vnto about .10000. persons, as I haue harde reported. Moreouer, in counterfaiting the Egyptian roges, they haue deuised a lāguage among themselues, which they name Canting, but other[s] pedlars Frenche. A speache compact 30. yeares since of English, & a great number of odde words of their owne diuising without all order or reason: and yet such is it as none but themselues are able to vnderstand. The first deuiser thereof was hanged by the necke, a iust reward no doubt for his desartes, and a common ende to all of that profession.[103]

---

barton *Oaks Papers*, XV [1961], 143–165). In very early times in Byzantium, furthermore, the legend of the Egyptian origin of gypsies was known. John Hoyland in the last century made an acute observation on such self-advertisement by the wanderers: "The fame of Egypt in astrology, magic, and soothsaying, was universal; and they could not have devised a more artful expedient, than the profession of this knowledge, to procure for them a welcome reception by the great mass of the people" (*A Historical Survey of the Customs, Habits, & Present State of the Gypsies* [1816], p. 80).

103. From *The Firste Volume of the Chronicles of England, Scotlande, and Irelande . . . by Raphaell Holinshed*, p. 107[r]. Frank Aydelotte observes sensibly that Harrison's figures and others like them are useful even if not accurate because they indicate "that in the eyes of contemporaries the vagrants were a large and important class" (*Elizabethan Rogues and Vagabonds* [Oxford, 1913], pp. 4–5).

One cannot imagine that there really was much intermingling be-tween genuine gypsies and English rogues. Most gypsies are endogamous and have always felt quite removed from *Gorgios*. Nevertheless, as Harrison suggests, some English rogues at a fairly early period did become "counterfeit Egyptians." When later we come to ponder what sort of gypsies Jonson created for his gypsy masque, therefore, we will do well to recall that the terminology of the subject is more than a little confused. Strictly speaking, genuine gypsies were counterfeit Egyptians, too, and making matters still murkier after laws against gypsies began to be passed, the gypsies themselves were tempted sometimes to pass themselves off as Eng-lish rogues.

Specifically addressed to such ambiguities was the 1562 "Act for the punyshement of Vagaboundes, callyng them selues Egiptians" (5 Elizabeth, cap. 20). This was created because

> there is a scruple and doubt rysen, whether such persons as beyng borne within this Realme of England, or other the Quenes highnes dominions, and are or shall become of the felowshyp or company of the sayde vagaboundes, by trans-formyng or disguysyng them selues in theyr apparell, or in a certayne counterfait speache or behauour, are punyshable . . . in lyke maner as others of that sort are being straungers borne, and transported into this Realme of Englande.[104]

The Act resolved the doubt with a resounding Yes. English vaga-bonds condemned themselves either by allowing themselves to be found in the "felowship" of gypsies or by "counterfaityng, trans-formyng, or disguising them selues by theyr apparell, speache, or other behauour, lyke vnto suche vagaboundes cōmonly called or callyng them selues Egiptians..." (55ʳ). Living with gypsies as long as a month made one subject to the same penalties as gypsies; in the eye of the law one became a felon and was subject to death. Such severity was called forth partly by notions about gypsy sor-cery and witchcraft, and by the supposed concealment by gypsies of Catholic priests and spies, but it was also and more generally based on the notion that all gypsies and counterfeit gypsies were conscienceless tricksters and thieves. Never, however, one should note, was the banishment of a race intended. The goal was to urge

104. *Anno Quinto Reginae Elizabethe. At the Parliament Holden at West-mynster the .xii. of January . . . Were Enacted as Foloweth* (1562), 55ʳ.

gypsies and counterfeit gypsies alike "to leaue theyr . . . naughtie, ydle, and vngodly lyfe and company, and to place them selues in some honest seruice or . . . worke" (55ᵛ).[105]

That the gypsy problem was not readily solved by such laws we have seen already in the passage by Harrison written in the next decade. Gypsies may even have begun to operate a bit more freely again toward the end of Elizabeth's reign, for on 5 September 1596 Sir Edward Hext of Netherham, Somersetshire, informed the Lord Treasurer that "that wicked sect of rogues the Egyptians" was again becoming troublesome. "And they laugh in themselves," he said, "at the lenity of the law, and the timorousness of the executioners of it. . . ."[106] That same year an important new Act affirmed the labels of rogue and vagabond for all persons "wandering and pretending them selues to be Egyptians, or wandering in the habite, forme, or attire of counterfeit Egyptians" (39 Elizabeth, cap. 4); but possibly the more significant fact may be that the Act did not so readily equate gypsies with felons.[107]

Such was the state of affairs in England when Elizabeth was succeeded by James. Since in his gypsy masque Jonson is quite alert to some of James's notions (the masque being very much a custom-made form), the poet who seldom overlooked anything may well have turned his thoughts to James's view of gypsies. For one thing, to begin positively, the scholar-poet probably knew that the scholar-King was aware of a tradition that "the ancient nation of the Scots" was "descended of the victorious Greeks and learned Ægyptians."[108] On the other hand, in the very first year of his English reign James had issued a proclamation "for the due and

---

105. For a while it must have appeared that this 1562 Act had achieved its ends. In 1567, in his *Caveat for Commen Cursetors*, Thomas Harman wished that certain other rogues might have

> as short and as spedy a redresse . . . as hath bene of late yeres for yᵉ wretched, wily wandering vagabonds calling and naming them selues Egiptians, depely dissembling and long hyding & couering their depe decetfull practises, feding the rude common people wholy addicted and geuen to nouelties, toyes, and new inuentions, delyting them with the strangenes of the attyre of their heades, and practising paulmistrie to such as would know their fortunes. And to be short all theues and hores. . . .

The Epistle, Aiiiᵛ. This description by Harman merits particular attention because, unlike most early commentators on rogues, who tended to quote one another and Harman, he took pains to garner firsthand knowledge of his subject.

106. Crofton, *English Gipsies*, pp. 23–24.

107. *Anno xxxix. Reginae Elizabethae. At the Parliament. . .* (1597), B6ᵛ.

108. The typography here has been regularized from that in *Ta ton mouson eisodia*, ed. John Adamson (Edinburgh, 1618), p. 137.

speedy execution" of the old 1596 Act concerning rogues and vagabonds. From that law, in previous years, "great good ensued to the
whole Common weale of this Realme, but now of late by the remisse-
nesse, negligence, and conniuencie of some Justices of the Peace,
and other Officers in diuers parts of the Realme, they haue swarmed
and abounded euery where more frequently then in times past
...."[109] Certain additions were made, therefore, to stiffen the old
Act. Since banished rogues had no distinguishing mark and might
return or retire somewhere within the realm and so escape punishment, it was ordained that thenceforth such rogues as were deemed
still dangerous were to "be branded in the left shoulder with an hot
burning Iron of the breadth of an English shilling with a great
Romane R. ...." If anyone bearing such a brand offended again,
"begging or wandering . . . , then in euery such case, the party so
offending shall be judged a Felon...." Nor did the matter rest there.
In 1609 there appeared a book called *Foure Statutes, Specially Selected and Commanded by His Majestie to Be Carefully Put in
Execution by All Justices and Other Officers of the Peace Throughout the Realm*; and one of the four statutes singled out was, significantly, the old 1596 Act, supplemented now by its Jacobean
"branches."[110] Clearly the King was mindful of the problem posed
by rogues, including those "wandering and pretending themselues
to bee Egyptians, or wandering in the habite, forme, or attire of
counterfeit Egyptians. . ." (p. 33).

Following the legal trail still further, we may approach to within
two or three months of the first performance of Jonson's gypsy
masque. On 26 May 1621 a bill was introduced in the Commons for
the continuance of a number of old statutes, including 39 Elizabeth,
cap. 4 (amended in 1 James, cap. 25) and 7 James, cap. 4, on rogues
and vagabonds. A couple of days later, however, Sir Samuel Sandys
arose to express the view which was to prevail: "Tis not fitt for the
labor of this time to perfect bills, but to applye our selves to greivances which are to be redressed. . . . There are greivances of Patents,
Monopolies, etc., and many such greivances...."[111] It was a matter
of priorities. Monopolies and patents raised problems of much
greater magnitude than did gypsies or, indeed, all kinds of rogues

---

109. *A Booke of Proclamations, Published Since the Beginning of His Majesties
Most Happy Reigne . . .* (1609), pp. 44–45.
110. The two preceding quotations are from pp. 47–48 of this work.
111. From Thomas Barrington, *Commons Debates 1621*, III, 309–310, 327.

and vagabonds put together. The problems, moreover, had nothing to do with one another. A poet in 1621 might work very well by thinking of one in terms of the other, but a Parliament had to keep them separate.

Up in Scotland, meanwhile, gypsies had for a long while fared better than their brothers in England. As a matter of fact, despite some alternations of leniency and severity, James's Scottish predecessors, at least since the time of James IV, generally had treated gypsies rather kindly. It is thus the more significant that after James VI took over the reins of Scotland's government, the laws against gypsies became markedly more severe. In 1579 a law was passed *"For punischment of strang and Idill Beggars,"* and it was aimed at nothing less than their "vtter suppressing."[112] Among its features is a description of gypsies. "And that it may be knawen," the law specifies,

> quhat maner of persones ar meaned to bee idle and strang beggares, and vagabounds, . . . IT IS declared, that [they are] all idle persones, ganging about in ony Countrie of this Realme, vsing subtill, craftie, and vnlauchfull playes, as Iuglarie, Fast-and-lous, and sik vthers. [Included are] The idle peopill calling themselues *Ægyptians* or any vther, that feinzies [feigns] them to haue knawledge or [of] Charming, Prophecie, or vthers abused sciēces, quhairby they perswade the peopill that they can tell their weirdes [fates], deathes and fortunes, and sik vther phantasticall imaginations. . . .
>
> (33ʳ)

The punishment prescribed was hard. It was decreed that offenders should

> be put in the Kingis Waird or irones, sa lang as they haue ony gudes of their awin to liue on. And fra they haue not quhairvpon to liue of their awin, that their eares bee nayled to the Trone, or to an vther tree, & their eares cutted off, & [themselues] banished the countrie, and gif there-after they be found againe, that they be hanged.
>
> (32ʳ)

112. From 32ᵛ in section on Parliaments of James VI in *The Lawes and Actes of Parliament, Maid Be King James the First and His Successours Kings of Scotlãd* . . . (Edinburgh, 1597). It is probably worthwhile to add that James bragged as a young king that he never signed anything important until first he had mastered it (Godfrey Davies, "The Character of James VI and I," *HLQ*, V [1941], 38).

In 1592 the matter was considered important enough for the old statute to be ratified and confirmed. And some seventeen years later, in 1609, after James had occupied the English throne for six years, the Parliament of Scotland felt the need for a statute pertaining exclusively to gypsies. When passed, the 1609 Act provided for nothing less than perpetual banishment of all those "vagaboundis sorneris [i.e., spongers, idlers, sturdy beggars] and cōmoun theiffis comounlie callit Egiptianis. . . ."[113] Thenceforward any gypsies who remained in the country and any who returned were to be executed. So sure were some Scots that to be a gypsy was to be a thief, in fact, that the rovers might be put to death merely upon proof that they were "knawin repute and haldin Egiptianis. . . ."

Apparently in Scotland as in England the main goal was to end "Egyptian" idleness, vagrancy, and thieving, not to end the gypsies as a race. James *did* exercise clemency in some cases involving gypsies. "Nevertheless," writes MacRitchie,

> the last quarter of the sixteenth, and the first quarter of the seventeenth century is a period more adverse to the Gypsies, by reason of its stern and continuous anti-Gypsy legislation, than any period before or since. And this seems in a great measure due to the personal influence of James VI. of Scotland . . . ; a monarch who, in spite of his pedantry and other faults, thoroughly realised his duty of bringing the whole United Kingdom into a state of order and civilisation.[114]

As James was fond of saying, "Order is the daughter of Heaven."[115]

We have at least one specific glimpse of the royal attitude at a time fairly close to Jonson's gypsy masque. The Register of the Privy Council of Scotland for 21 December 1619 records a petition

113. Cited from *The Acts of the Parliaments of Scotland*, ed. Cosmo Nelson Innes (Edinburgh, 1826), IV, 440. According to Walter Simson, the first gypsies to be tried under the statute were four persons named Faa, who on 31 July 1611 were sentenced to be hanged (*A History of the Gipsies*, ed. James Simson [New York, 1866], p. 118). Cf. n. 120.

114. *Scottish Gypsies under the Stewarts* (Edinburgh, 1894), pp. 77–78. The situation is to some degree clarified if we know "that Gypsies were then regarded as 'witches'" (p. 79). James, however, was also set strongly against rogues *qua* rogues. In a speech delivered in the Star Chamber in 1616 he said, "For Rogues, you haue many good Acts of Parliament: *Edward* the sixt, though hee were a child, yet for this, he in his time gaue better order then many Kings did in their aage [*sic*]: You must take order for these Beggars and Rogues; for they so swarme in euery place, that a man cannot goe in the streetes, nor in the high wayes, nor any where for them" (*Workes*, pp. 566–567).

115. Noted by Bacon in 1620 (*Letters and the Life of Francis Bacon*, VII, 89).

which had been made to the King on behalf of three men, one of
them Alexander Forbes, a "servitour" to the Duke of Lennox,
Ludovick Stuart (he whom we have met earlier as the "phoenix"
reborn). Perhaps Forbes's connection with Lennox is irrelevant.
At any rate, Forbes apparently requested permission to serve as
something of a secular "pardoner" for those who harbored gypsies.
He was to be permitted—probably after buying a sort of hunting
license—to ferret out and fine as many wealthy victims as he found
guilty of the crime of assisting gypsies. Obviously a sufficient number of the gentry sheltered gypsies to make the post attractive to a
certain sort of man, though the position was itself illegal according
to the Act of 1609. James turned the case over to the Privy Council
with a recommendation for favorable action, provided that the
pardoners divulged the names of the guilty. Furthermore, everyone
was reminded at this time that gypsies "committ infinite thifte, insolenceis, and oppressionis upoun his Majesteis goode subjectis in all
pairtis quhair they hant and frequent."[116]

Granted that Jonson had a generally accurate impression of
where gypsies stood in the eyes of the law and, possibly, the eyes
of the King, and setting aside the interesting possibility that he may
have encountered English or Scottish gypsies personally during his
four-hundred-mile walking tour to Scotland in 1618 and 1619
(when he certainly met country and village folk something like
those he put in the gypsy masque), what other factors should be
weighed at this point? What other evidence do we have concerning
gypsies in the Jacobean milieu? This is not the place to run down
all the sources available to Jonson, nor even his specific borrowings,
but a few representative passages from some relevant works should
be helpful. Let us start with two of Jonson's sources, Dekker and
Rid, then proceed to note briefly a small handful of other works.

116. Masson, p. 152. See Eric Otto Winstedt, "Early British Gypsies," *JGLS*, N.S.
VII (1913–1914), 5–37; and David MacRitchie, "The Crime of Harbouring Gypsies," *ibid.*, pp. 243–247.

A rigorous search might turn up relevant legal data yet closer in time to the
performance of the gypsy masque. Such a search would involve, for instance,
weighing the information that on 15 September 1621 (five or six weeks after the
first performance of the masque, and within days of its third performance) the
Privy Council of England was considering that, "through the neglect and slacknes
of inferior officers in execution of the lawes against rogues and vagabondes, that
kind of people is of late become verie frequent in all places and (it may well be
feared) will daily increase to the scandall of this government and dommage of the
subjectes if speedy prevention be not used. . ." (*Acts of the Privy Council*, p. 43).
Further data, however, probably would not alter the basic outlines of the picture
sketched here.

To Thomas Dekker (though Jonson thought Dekker a rogue, he did not hesitate to borrow from him), gypsies are "the onely base Runnagates vpon earth. . . . They are a people more scattered than Jewes, and more hated: beggerly in apparell, barbarous in condition, beastly in behauiour, and bloody if they meete aduantage."[117] Since gypsies constantly seek new victims, they constantly travel, and their transportation as described by Dekker is much like that in Jonson's masque. The gypsies "forrage vp and downe countries, 4, 5. or 6. in a company," says Dekker; they travel with their harlots and

> a number of little children following at their heeles: which young brood of beggers, are sometimes carried (like so many gréene geese aliue to a market) in paires of paniers, or in dossers like fresh-fish from Rye that comes on horsebacke, (if they be but infants. But if they can straddle once, then as well she-roges as the he-roges are horst, seuen or eight vpon one iade, strongly pineond, and strangely tied together.
>
> (F2ʳ)

One suspects that in this matter of travel, necessity was the mother of invention, yet some of the gypsies' odd ways may really have been lures for people to come and "wonder at their fooleries, or rather ranke knaueries" (F2ʳ–F2ᵛ). Young people, writes Dekker, are particularly susceptible to gypsy wiles, but sometimes the old, too, are taken in, "olde doting fooles, that should be beaten to this world of villanies, and forwarne others" (F3ʳ). A typical reward for succumbing is that "within halfe an houre after [your palm has been read] you shal haue your pocket pick'd, or your purse cut" (F3ʳ). One cannot trust gypsies even to look the same when one sees them next. They are so skilled in assuming different shapes that sometimes they are called moon-men. Especially versatile among the metamorphosers, one supposes, and therefore all the more treacherous, are the "counterfeit Egyptians," those base Englishmen who have made themselves look like "Tawny Moore bas-

117. *Villanies Discovered by Lanthorne and Candle-light* (1620), F1ᵛ. Obviously this little work enjoyed more than usual attention, having appeared in several previous incarnations (1608, 1609, 1612, and 1616), as well as in some later ones. Its earliest version was called *The Belman of London*. The version of 1620 has the advantage for us of being enlarged by the author as well as bringing us closest in time to the gypsy masque, which was written the following year. It would be hard to say whether Jonson was more familiar with the pamphlet in its original form or as buttered over and re-served.

tards," though "not borne so, neither hath the Sunne burnt them so, but they are painted so. . ." (F1ᵛ). In short, according to Dekker, the gypsies and counterfeit gypsies—whose traditions for our present purposes may remain intermingled—are guilty alike of all "black and deadly-damned Impieties" (F3ʳ).

Samuel Rid is a valuable supplement to Dekker. He begins *Martin Mark-all* (1610) by noting the great popularity of Dekker's work ("These volumes and papers . . . [are] now spread euerie where" [A2ʳ]), but he does so only to undercut his rival by saying that most of Dekker's material was set forth forty years earlier by Thomas Harman. On the other hand, he himself has no scruples about plagiarizing from Harman, who, after all, was a very good source. He also offers the new information that the "fellowship" of counterfeit English gypsies was "invented" in 1528 by one Giles Hather, who was the "Captaine" (Jonson also uses the word) of the band.[118] As Rid tells the story, a group

> of Vagabonds (at the diuels-arse-a-peake in Darbishire) began a new regiment, calling themselues by the name of Egiptians: These were a sort of rogues, that liued and do yet liue by cousening and deceit, practising the arte called legerdemaine, or fast and loose, whereby they got to themselues no small credite among the Countrey people by their déepe dissembling and deceitfull practises, féeding the common people wholly addicted and giuen to nouelties, toyes and new fangles, delighting them with the strangenesse of the attire of their heads, and practising palmistry to such as would know their fortunes.
>
> (G4ʳ)

It is worth noting that even in this passage some phrases are filched from Harman. Again, however, Rid furnishes new information: Giles Hather had a whore, Kyt Calot (Kate Harlot), and she "was termed the Quéene of Egypties" (G4ʳ).

Just prior to launching into his passage on gypsies, Rid has been discussing a series of rogue leaders, which comes to a climax and concludes with Cock-lorrel. Since Jonson makes important use of

118. According to John Awdeley, "Gyle Hather" is no gypsy, but one of the "Orders of Knaues." More exactly, he is one "that wyll stand by his Maister when he is at dinner, and byd him beware that he eate no raw meate, because he would eate it himselfe. This is a pickthanke knaue, that would make his Maister beleue that the Cowe is woode" (*The Fraternitye of Vacabondes*, 1575, Bivʳ&ᵛ; 1st ed., 1565).

Cock-lorrel in the gypsy masque, it is of interest that Rid describes him as the "most notorious knaue that euer liued" (G3ᵛ).[119] Rid did not invent him, of course. The earliest known reference to Cock-lorrel occurs in Wynkyn de Worde's *Cocke Lorelles Bote* (*ca.* 1510), where he is depicted as a merry captain, specifically a "knyght," engaged in taking various kinds of rogues aboard his ship. His attitude and that of his crew accord well with the more raucous elements of Jonson's gypsy masque:

> They banysshed prayer peas and sadnes
> And toke with them myrthe sporte & gladnes
> They wolde not haue vertu ne yet deuocyon
> But ryotte and reuell with Ioly rebellyon
> They songe and daunsed full merely
> With swerynge and starynge heuen hye. . . .
> (Ciiʳ–Ciiᵛ)

Rid's information is tonally somewhat similar to this, but factually quite different. According to Rid, Cock-lorrel headed a gang of thieves in the days of Henry VIII, beginning about 1511 (i.e., some seventeen years before Hather presumably organized the English gypsies). By trade he was a tinker, and consequently often carried "a panne and a hammer for a shew: but when he came to a good booty, he would cast his profession in a ditch, and play the padder . . ." (G3ᵛ–G4ʳ). Despite the bond of tinkering which Cock-lorrel therefore shared with gypsies, however (tinkering was as respectable work as the average gypsy ever did), he does not seem to have been a gypsy leader until Jonson made him one in his famous ballad in the gypsy masque (B 820–884). Strangely enough, it may be that the reason for Jonson's placement of the honor is nonetheless traceable to Rid. After Rid has explained that Cock-lorrel's special achievement as a leader of English rogues is that he "reduced and brought in forme the Catalogue of Vagabonds or quarterne of knaues . . ." (G4ʳ), he begins in the very next paragraph to tell of Giles Hather's gypsies in the North. Having damned the latter by definition, he proceeds to explain how Hather *and* Cock-lorrel, *both* "vp-start Lossels," met together at the Devil's Arse concerning the establishment of "their new found gouernment." It was there and then, says Rid, that they assigned labels to various levels of operators in their company and also devised a new language so that "their

119. See also pp. 79–82.

cousenings, knaueries and villanies might not be so easily perceiued and knowne. . ." (G4ᵛ). Then Rid returns to the specific subject of Cock-lorrel, and then once again to Giles Hather. In other words, a hasty reading of Rid could have led Jonson to think that Cock-lorrel was a gypsy. On the other hand, Jonson simply could have decided that, for his own purposes in the gypsy masque, Cock-lorrel's qualifications were the better ones. Given the choice, one may more readily imagine an inventive Jonson than a muddled one.

In broadening our range of reference just a bit further, it may be well to glance at the role of gypsies in the drama.[120] Probably Middleton's *More Dissemblers Besides Women* (*ca.* 1615) takes us closer to the temper of Jonson's masque than does any other contemporary play. Though its lines lack the keenness they would have in an occasional piece like a masque, Middleton's gypsies are likewise both merry and reprehensible. They enter with *"Booties"* of hens and ducks, then sing a song which epitomizes their carefree gaiety. The final chorus is, *"We laugh, we quaff, we roar, we scuffle./ We cheat, we drab, we filtch, we shuffle."*[121] Most Jonsonian of all (Jonsonian in that it resembles the gypsy masque) is the speech of the gypsy captain when he explains to Dondolo what it means to be a gypsy:

> Get me Gipseys brave and tauny;
> With Cheek full plump, and Hip full brauny.
> Look you prove industrious dealers
> To serve the Commonwealth with stealers,
> That th'unhous'd race of Fortune-tellers
> May never fail to cheat Town-dwellers;

120. Other gypsy references of interest occur in John Melton's *Astrologaster* (1620) and John Cowell's famous *Interpreter* (1607). Cowell, Professor of Civil Law at Cambridge, notes that gypsies claim curative powers, that the Welsh are guilty along with native Englishmen, and, most important, that all gypsies are by definition counterfeits (Bb1ʳ).

Quite unusual for its sympathetic handling is the famous passage on gypsies in Joseph Glanvill's *The Vanity of Dogmatizing* (1661), the source of Arnold's scholar gypsy. It tells of an Oxford student whose "need" forced him to join a gypsy band, the result being that he learned how one man's imagination may be heightened and used to control another's (pp. 196–198). Glanvill cut the incident, however, when he reworked his book as *Scepsis Scientifica* (1665).

Cf. also the rather romantic ballad called *The Gypsy Laddie*, which tells of gypsies casting a "glamer" over a fair lady, who then runs off with Johnny Faa, the gypsy chief. Faa is said to have been a real figure who was executed in 1624 along with seven others for refusing to leave Scotland (Francis James Child, ed., *The English and Scottish Popular Ballads* [Boston, *ca.* 1898], IV, 61–74); but "Faa" is a common gypsy name.

121. From *Two New Playes* (1657), p. 50.

Or to our universal grief,
Leave Country Fairs without a Theif.
This is all you have to do,
Save ev'ry hour a filch or two,
Be it money, cloth or pullen,
When the ev'nings browe looks sullen.
Loose no time, for then 'tis pretious,
Let your sleights be fine, facetious;
Which hoping you'll observe, to try thee
With rusty Bacon, thus I Gipsifie thee.

(p. 53)

In view of the relative dating of both works, however, it may make more sense to call Jonson's gypsies Middletonian. *More Dissemblers*, after all, antedates *The Gypsies Metamorphos'd* by several years.

In 1623 Middleton joined with Rowley to write *The Spanish Gipsie*, a pleasant if shallow work in which all the gypsies are really courtiers. Offhand it might be supposed that these high-born counterfeits would resemble Jonson's courtier-gypsies more than do those in Middleton's own *More Dissemblers*. The Middleton-Rowley gypsies have none of the zing of Jonson's rogues, however. If anything, they suggest how much farther Jonson could have gone had he really wished to wash his gypsies clean. As a matter of fact, the collaborating dramatists go out of their way to contrast their Spanish gypsies to English ones, and thus they give us yet another glimpse of English gypsydom. The Spanish courtiers, we find, will be "Gipsies, but no tann'd ones, no red-oker rascalls umberd with soot and bacon as the English gipsies are, that sally out upon pullen, lie in ambuscado for a rope of onions, as if they were Welsh free-booters; no, our stile has higher steps to climbe over, Spanish gipsies, noble gipsies."[122] The Spanish captain, Alvarez, admonishes his companions in the same scene, "Be not English gipsies, in whose company a man's not sure of the eares of his head they so pilfer; no such angling; what you pull to land catch fair..." (p. 24).[123]

---

122. *The Spanish Gipsie*, ed. Edgar C. Morris (Boston, 1908), p. 22.
123. I have wondered whether one response to *The Spanish Gipsie* may have been a broadside called *The Brave English Jipsie*. This was supposed to be sung to the tune of "the *Spanish Iipsie*," and it concludes, "So Spanish Iipsies all adue,/ For English equall are to you."
It is also possible that the ballad represents an effort to capitalize on the stir caused by Jonson's masque. Unfortunately we cannot date it certainly. Issued by

If one wishes to track gypsies still farther in the field of drama, Shakespeare's plays yield a few scattered allusions. Rather noncommittal is the mention in *As You Like It* of two pages who are to sing "both in a tune, like two gypsies on a horse" (V.iii.14–15). More memorable is the fact that the charms of Romeo's Rosaline will presumably make Cleopatra seem a mere gypsy, one to be contemptuously categorized with dowdies, hildings, and harlots (II. iv.43–45). In *Antony and Cleopatra* the same great queen is said to have a gypsy's lust (I.i.10). And it should be recalled that one source of Othello's anguish is a handkerchief given to his mother by a gypsy (III.iv.56). In each of these cases, however, Shakespeare is appealing to established notions, not pausing as he might to modify or qualify them. Since he is not directly interested in the subject of gypsies, he tends to use them, significantly, rather like negative counters.

If we note any other dramatist, it should be Jonson himself. Aside from the work which is our main concern, the masque in which he sets forth Buckingham and his friends, does Jonson anywhere else tip his hand concerning his attitude toward gypsies? Granted that a man may use an image (Yeats a swan) in different ways at different times, its recurrence in a writer may sometimes help us understand a bit better both writer and image.

In the 1616 Folio version of *Every Man in His Humour* we find that the plain-speaking squire Downright uses the term "gypsy" as a derogatory epithet for the loudmouthed fraud, Captain Boba-

---

John Trundle (a bookseller mentioned by Jonson in *Every Man in His Humor*, HS III, 312: I.iii.63), the ballad cannot have appeared later than 1626 (Claude M. Simpson, *The British Broadside Ballad and Its Music* [New Brunswick, N. J., 1966], p. 676). It is included in *The Roxburghe Ballads*, ed. William Chappell (Hertford, 1875), vol. III, pt. 1, pp. 328–333.

Whatever its inspiration, the ballad expresses one of the most sympathetic attitudes toward gypsies—specifically counterfeit gypsies—that may be found in the period. For example, "We beare this honest mind,/ To loue all friends are kind," and "Wheresoere we come, we find/ For one that hates, an hundred kind. . . ." The ballad itself repeatedly qualifies its own air of jollity, however. The kindness which the gypsies find as they roam through the countryside is the simple effect of a specified cause: "He that freely giues, shall find/ The English Iipsies alwaies kind." Even in this sunshiny version of English gypsying, the gypsy spokesman admits,

Our foes we can requite,
with hatred and despight:
For we can plague our mortall foe,
Yet he the actors neuer know.

A crude cut which illustrates the ballad is reproduced here as Plate No. 5.

dill, one of whose oaths is "By Pharoah's foot." "Come, draw," says Downright, "to your tooles: draw, gipsie, or Ile thresh you" (HS III, 378: IV.vii.120–121). In the Folio version of *Cynthia's Revels*, on the other hand, there is a lively song beginning, "*Come follow me, my wagges, and say as I say./ There's no riches but in ragges; hey day, hey day*" (HS IV, 80: II.v.1–4); and if we turn to the longer quarto version of 1601 we find that the song goes on to include gypsies among the various types of ragged "*wagges.*" Here is the alliterative context in which they appear:

> *Pedlers, and Puppit-players.*
> *Sow-gelders, and Sooth-saiers.*
> *Gipsies and Iaylers,*
> *Rat-catchers, and Raylers. . . .*
> (HS IV, 80)

In other words Jonson has rather cheerfully placed gypsies amongst other kinds of riffraff. Similar in its "placing" technique but more venomous by far is the use of the word "*Gipseys*" in *Volpone* (1606), when Mosca answers Corvino's question as to whether the "dying" magnifico has children. The purpose of neither Jonson nor the parasite is in doubt when Mosca replies that Volpone has "Bastards,/ Some dozen, or more, that he begot on beggers,/ *Gipseys*, and *Iewes*, and black-*moores*, when he was drunke" (HS V, 42: I.v.43–45).

At the other end of Jonson's career, and not far from the time of the gypsy masque, he mentions gypsies in *The Staple of News* (1626), alluding to their jargon as a language such as "*Pedlers* trade in" and "no honest *Christian*/ Can vnderstand. . ." (HS VI, 347: IV.i.53–54). In *The New Inn* (1629) he includes an Englishman, Lord Frampull, who, along with his servant Fly, has gone to live for a while with gypsies. Frampull regards gypsies as "Reduced vessels of ciuility" (HS VI, 488: V.v.129), but he does not denigrate them. In *The Magnetic Lady* (1632), on the other hand, when Jonson has Polish reach for the most potent epithets she can find to hurl at Keepe, she comes up with

> . . . catife witch!
> Baud, Begger, Gipsey: Any thing indeed,
> But honest woman.
> (HS VI, 568: IV.iv.1–3)

Even in what is probably Jonson's last play we find him returning yet again to the subject of gypsies. In *The Sad Shepherd* (1637) the wicked witch Maudlin has a magic girdle which, like Desdemona's handkerchief, was made by a gypsy.

If we look into Jonson's non-dramatic works we find in his *Epigrams* ("*the ripest of my studies*," published in 1616) that No. 41 is a quatrain entitled "On Gypsee":

> GYPSEE, new baud, is turn'd physitian,
> 　And get[s] more gold, then all the colledge can:
> Such her quaint practise is, so it allures,
> 　For what shee gaue, a whore; a baud, shee cures.[124]

Bold bawdry and acquisitiveness: it is not a pretty picture. As a man of great intellect and tremendous vitality, Jonson apparently found something attractive in such ingenious and free spirits as gypsies, just as, to a still greater degree, he apparently delighted in those shameless parasites Mosca and Face; but it is clear beyond reasonable doubt that he also shared the broadly and basically condemnatory attitude of his age toward gypsies. Considering that gypsies were disruptors of order, we should be surprised to learn otherwise.

Can we find any other evidence of Jonson's views in the writing of other men about him? Not much, but there may be a scrap in Dekker's *Satiromastix* (1601). When Dekker wished to sting Jonson as sharply as he could in this play, he did not stop short of attacking Jonson's physical appearance, and since he took pains to fashion barbs that would smart, it is of interest to learn that this man who knew Jonson better than we ever can called him (i.e., had "Tucca" call "Horace") a "poore saffron-cheeke Sun-burnt Gipsie."[125]

If we stand back and ponder the sampling here of facts and opinions, it is clear that for Elizabethans and Jacobeans alike, gypsies were a baleful influence in the land. It cannot be denied that their taking ways exerted a certain fascination. Gypsies sometimes danced and plied their tricks even "where great men dwell,"[126] even, at an early date, at Holyrood itself. Still the fact remains that

124. HS VIII, 39. Here Jonson makes use of the gypsy talent for cures, mentioned by Cowell and others. The "colledge" he refers to is the Royal College of Physicians, and the phrase "quaint practise" is a pun.

125. I.ii.367–368, from *The Dramatic Works of Thomas Dekker*, ed. Fredson T. Bowers (Cambridge, 1953), I, 326. Though the point is not crucial here, perhaps it should be noted that Marston also had something to do with the creation of *Satiromastix*.

126. *The Brave English Jipsie*.

gypsies had a very bad name. Foreign or domestic, they were deemed a blight, a plague, a swarm of caterpillars upon the land.

Two final facts may stand as summarizing evidence. The first is as suggestively ambiguous as Jonson's gypsies themselves, and the second flashes a harsh, historical ray of light on the negative aspect of Jonson's "dark conceit."

The first concerns a weed, the bright and cheery blue field scabious, the name of which reflects the fact that it is "the herb for scabies, the scab, the mange, the itch. . . ."[127] It is commonly known by such other names as cornflower and bachelor's-buttons, and, in Scotland, blue bonnet. Some time during the period with which we are concerned, it began to be known also as the gypsy flower. Pretty it may be, but the flower is a weed, and Gervase Markham, the master of all such matters, lumped it with certain other plant pests: "by all meanes you shall pull these weeds vp by the roots whilst they are tender" or else "in their stronger growth, sith their sufferance breedeth great losse and distruction. . . ."[128] Probably no one would dare to say now whether the gypsy flower came to be associated with gypsies because it was in some way gypsy-like or presumed to be liked by gypsies, or even because it was related to certain skin diseases. In any case, it was an undesirable invader popping up everywhere in the midst of England's cultivated corn, and the nature of gypsies was known widely enough for their name to be given to it.

For a final bit of evidence on the place of gypsies in Tudor and Stuart England we may turn to the deathbed of the Earl of Sussex in the summer of 1583. Sir Thomas Radcliffe, the third Earl, warned those who were gathered about him to beware of Queen Elizabeth's long-time favorite, Leicester. Like Buckingham in the next reign, Leicester was a man of good looks and high spirits, both set off by courtly skills. Like Buckingham he had received the Mastership of the Horse, which placed him in close attendance on his sovereign. And like Buckingham he had come to be bitterly resented by many of the old nobility. Therefore the terms as well as the target of Sussex's warning invite reflection: *"I am now passing into another world,"* he said, *"and I must leave you to your fortunes, and the Queenes grace and goodnesse, but beware of the Gipsey, meaning* Liecester, *for he will be too hard for you all, you know not the beast*

---

127. Geoffrey Grigson, *The Englishman's Flora* (1955), p. 361.
128. *Markhams Farwell to Husbandry* (1620), p. 61.

so well as I do.[129] The presence of a "gypsy" at Elizabeth's court in the form of a lord—a dangerous royal favorite—was to the dying Sussex a matter of deep concern.

Weighing these miscellaneous facts and attitudes about Tudor and Stuart gypsies, and considering them in connection with James's court and Jonson's aims, we are in a better position to apply to the gypsy masque the observation of Murrin that "Every trope represents a value judgment made by comparison. No one can juxtapose a man and a toad or a man and an angel without making a moral judgment of some kind. . . ." When Jonson chose to compare and contrast gypsies and lords in his masque for Buckingham, he could assume that his audience had some more or less fixed notions about both. He could present his lively and attractive gypsy-lords so as to imply and invite a moral judgment. However delightful and distracting their performance might be, and however skillfully their show might be sweetened by praise and salted by wit, he could use the figure of gypsies to imply—and invite his audience to infer—that something was rotten in the Jacobean state.

129. Robert Naunton, *Fragmenta Regalia* (1641), p. 7 (i.e., 17).

Chapter III. *Some Significant Aspects of the Masque*

i. *The Original Setting*

> Sir, you haue euer shin'd vpon me bright,
> But now, you strike and dazle me with light:
> You England's radiant sunne, vouchsafe to grace
> My house, a spheare too little and too base. . . .[1]
>
> Sir John Beaumont

In defining an approach to Jonson's gypsy masque we have been advancing thus far along a winding way, touching a variety of social, literary, and historical matters ranging from the Jacobean court to Jacobean gypsies. Now it is possible to move in closer to the masque to consider its immediate ambience and some of its themes and characteristics.

Part of the proof of the masque's success is that, quite extraordinarily, it was performed on three occasions, first on 3 August 1621, at Buckingham's home, Burley-on-the-Hill; next on 5 August at Belvoir, the estate of Buckingham's father-in-law, Francis, Sixth Earl of Rutland; and finally some time in September at the court at Windsor. That the masque was performed three times is of considerable importance. It is a significant clue both to the King's taste and to Jonson's knack for satisfying it.

The multiple performances of the masque also help to account for the textual complexity of the versions which have come down to us. We are fortunate, indeed, that W. W. Greg has given his attention to this problem.[2] Not only does it appear unlikely that

---

1. From a poem written for Buckingham on the occasion of the King's visit. Reprinted in *The Poems of Sir John Beaumont, Bart.*, ed. Alexander B. Grosart (n.p., priv. circ., 1869), p. 157.
2. *Jonson's Masque of Gipsies in the Burley, Belvoir, and Windsor Versions: An Attempt at Reconstruction* (1952). As noted previously "B" is used here to cite passages from the probable Burley version, and "W" those from the Windsor. Another major edition is that of George Watson Cole, *The Gypsies Metamorphosed . . . Edited from Original and Unexpurgated Sources . . . A Variorum Edition* (New York, 1931).

textual work more accurate than Greg's is to be done on the masque, unless fresh sources are discovered, but Greg has also, in particular, given us a brilliantly and painstakingly reconstructed version of the script as it was probably first performed at Burley. This is of importance here because it is the Burley version which requires our closest attention. No matter how valuable the insights afforded by Jonson's later modifications of the masque, a search for its essence should be concentrated on its first performance. The reason is simple: a masque was by definition conceived and designed for a particular audience in a particular place on a particular occasion. Chapman, whom Jonson thought capable of making a good masque, analyzed the matter thus:

> *as there is no Poem nor Oration so generall; but hath his one perticular proposition; Nor no riuer so extrauagantly ample, but hath his neuer-so-narrow fountaine, worthy to be namd; so all these courtly, and honoring inuentions (hauing Poesie, and Oration in them, and a fountaine, to be exprest, from whence their Riuers flow) should expressiuely-arise out of the places, and persons for and by whome they are presented; without which limits, they are luxurious, and vaine.*[3]

Whatever life the text of a masque may have when detached from its proper habitation should be remarked and appreciated, but it is also, in a sense, almost extraneous. This is true even of the gypsy masque, which is unusual in that it was modified so as to enable its performers to repeat their roles elsewhere. In trying to recapture something of the atmosphere of the original gypsy masque we must bear in mind that it was designed to be performed first on the occasion of a visit by the King of England to the home of his favorite.[4]

3. From Chapman's comments on his masque for the marriage of Princess Elizabeth, ed. G. Blakemore Evans, in *The Plays of George Chapman: The Comedies*, gen. ed. Allan Holaday (Urbana, Ill., 1970), p. 569.

4. One may not discount the information that Richard Harris (a gentleman usher) and seven assistants were paid for two days' work in July to make ready for "a maske" at Belvoir (*Dramatic Records in the Declared Accounts of the Treasurer of the Chamber 1558–1642*, ed. David Cook, assisted by F. P. Wilson, Malone Society Collections [Oxford, 1962], VI, 120). Nor may one discount Greg's statement that "The double performance at Burley and Belvoir must clearly have been provided for when planning the progress, and the necessary alternatives were presumably written at the time of the original composition" (p. 29). On the other hand, no one knew in July that the masque would be a success. A second performance could have been planned but not assured. What if James had been offended rather than pleased? Besides, even if Greg were completely correct, adapting the masque for presentation at the home of Buckingham's father-in-law a few miles

And it will do no harm to postulate that somebody in that Burley audience may have recalled that Friday, 3 August 1621, the day of the performance, was a special day in the relationship of James and Buckingham: it appears to have been the seventh anniversary of their first meeting.[5]

Far from being threadbare any longer (the term may stand if taken metaphorically), George was now master of an estate described by John Evelyn as "among the noblest seates in England."[6] If Jonson did not know in advance what sort of place he would be visiting, he could have learned from Camden that Burley was "most daintily seated, and overlooking the vale."[7] In the county of Rutland, about three miles to the northeast of the town of Oakham, which itself was some ninety-six miles from London, the house stood high "on a hill, a princely Park and Woods adjoyning, overlooking the little, but rich, Vale of Catmus, and several fair Lordships belonging to the same Owner."[8] Along with the shrievalty of Rutland, the lordship of Oakham had been granted by Edward II to his minion, Piers Gaveston, in 1309, and by Richard II to *his* favorite, Robert de Vere, Earl of Oxford, in 1385. That some Englishmen were alert to this sort of historical precedent and parallel scarcely needs demonstration here.[9] Buckingham, however, was too full of his own splendid vitality to worry about ghosts. Burley was beautifully situated, and, besides, it had the advantage of being near

from Burley would not have diluted beyond recognition the essentially Buckinghamian flavor of the work. Moreover, the most important point is that the main base, the psychic and symbolic home of the masque, was the place of its initial presentation, the home of its sponsor and star.

5. There is some confusion as to the date of their introduction, but 3 August seems probable (Charles Richard Cammell, *The Great Duke of Buckingham* [1939], pp. 114-115, and Hugh Ross Williamson, *George Villiers First Duke of Buckingham* [1940], p. 91). James's visit to George in 1621 lasted from Sunday, 29 July, to Saturday, 4 August.

6. *The Diary of John Evelyn*, ed. E. S. de Beer (Oxford, 1955), III, 124. A study of the estate has been made by Pearl Finch, *History of Burley-on-the-Hill Rutland* (1901).

7. *Britain*, trans. Philemon Holland (1610), p. 526. There is no harm in assuming with Herford and Simpson that Jonson was present (HS XI, 70).

8. James Wright, *The History and Antiquities of the County of Rutland* (1684), p. 30.

9. It happens, nevertheless, that we have some specific evidence in the present case. In the Upper House on 30 April 1621, three months before the gypsy masque, Sir Henry Yelverton bared some of Buckingham's wrongdoing and compared him with Hugh Spencer, another of the notorious minions of Edward II. The Prince arose, pale, and demanded that Yelverton be silenced. He would not allow his father's reign to be "paralelled and scandalised." Buckingham, who was also present, coolly requested that Yelverton be allowed to proceed (Robert Zaller, *The Parliament of 1621* [Berkeley, Calif., 1971], p. 120).

to Brokesby, his early home in Leicestershire, and also to his wife's home, Belvoir.

Buckingham had purchased Burley in 1620 from Lucy, Countess of Bedford, daughter of Sir John Harington of Exton—the same excellent lady, be it noted, who had brightened Jonson's masques of *Blackness* and *Beauty*, as well as *Hymenaei* and *The Masque of Queens*. In Elizabeth's time her father had lived there in a house which Camden found "stately and sumptuous" (p. 526). The modern reinventor of the flush toilet, that more famous "cosin" of Sir John who was also named Sir John Harington, thought especially well of the place. Were his invention to be installed there, he said, it might be inventoried at £1,000. "Not that . . . wit and art can be rated at any price, but that I wold accept it as a gratuitie fit for such houses and their owners."[10] With or without plumbing, however, the master of Burley welcomed Elizabeth's successor to his home during the Easter season of 1603, when James was delightedly making his first journey down into England.[11] That event, like the present one eighteen years later, was the occasion for royal flattery; James heard a long panegyric by the well-languaged Samuel Daniel. In July of the same year Sir John was made Baron Harington of Exton, and in October he was honored—and correspondingly burdened—with the guardianship of the Princess Elizabeth, whom he took to Combe Abbey near Coventry. Eventually he fell into debt because his allowance to keep the Princess was too small. Then in 1613, the year of her marriage, he died. His only son died a short time later, his title became extinct, and after a few more years Burley was put up for sale.

However grand it had been during Harington's heyday, George Villiers proceeded to tear down all or most of the old house in order to build one better suited to his eminence. Employing the verses of his maternal kinsman Sir John Beaumont (a brother of the famous playwright and a friend of Jonson), Villiers welcomed his King as "England's radiant sunne" to a Burley which was a "spheare too little and too base." The worthy Tom Fuller, however, records that Burley was "so beautified with buildings by the Duke of *Buckingham*, that it was inferiour to few for the House, superior to all for the Stable; where horses (if their *pabulum* so plenty as their *stabulum*

10. *Sir John Harington's A New Discourse of a Stale Subject, Called the Metamorphosis of Ajax*, ed. Elizabeth Story Donno (New York, 1962), p. 178.

11. He returned in 1614, 1616, 1617, 1619 (probably), 1621, and 1624 (William Page, ed., *The Victoria History of the County of Rutland* [1908], I, 184).

stately) were the best accommodated in *England*."[12] Fuller's reference to horses should come as no surprise. Since 1616 young Villiers had been Master of the Horse, a very significant post considering the significance of hunting to the King. Though Buckingham also had other and still grander titles now, it was fitting that at Burley he build a mansion for his horses. Some bore such names as "Bay Burley with the Saddle Spots," "White Gray Burley," and "Burley with the Cloud."[13] And one bit of historical flotsam informs us—we may infer the pride and pleasure of Buckingham and his sovereign—that on 1 August 1621, two days before the gypsy masque, "there passed through Exon six horses and mares which the marquis of Buckingham sent for into Barbary."[14]

No picture of the mansion itself has survived. Among the drawings of John Thorpe, however, there are three alternative floor plans which suggest the terms in which one architect conceived of the place. The particular Thorpe sketch which a later hand has labelled as Buckingham's "Burghley" depicts a large inner-courtyard house that is seemingly derived from plans for the Palais du Luxembourg, which was built in Paris for Marie de Médicis.[15] Presumably a palace for Marie de Médicis would be suitable for the young English favorite. Also of interest, though much more crude and not a part of the Thorpe group, is a sketch depicting the Burley stables as we know them to have been built, as well as a ground-plan of the ruins of Buckingham's house and the place where it stood. This second drawing is as full of puzzles as facts, however, and scarcely capable of suggesting the grandeur of the place.[16]

Whatever facts about Burley have dropped from sight, we may construct our mental image of it with the certain knowledge that nothing was too good for Buckingham. In the year of the gypsy masque he sent Balthazar Gerbier into Italy on the first of several art-buying missions, and, aided by Sir Henry Wotton in Venice, Gerbier eventually acquired a staggering array of treasures. These included one Titian masterpiece, the *Ecce Homo*, for which the Earl of Arundel offered Buckingham the then fantastic sum of

12. *The History of the Worthies of England* (1662), p. 346. Wright, p. 32, provides us a picture of these stables, reproduced here as Plate No. 6.

13. Cammell, p. 115.

14. *Diary of Walter Yonge, Esq.*, ed. George Roberts (1848), p. 42.

15. See John Summerson, ed., *The Book of Architecture of John Thorpe in Sir John Soane's Museum*, Walpole Society Volume XL (1966), esp. pp. 30–31 and Plate 49.

16. It is reproduced in Finch (plate preceding p. 7).

£7,000.[17] In 1625 Gerbier boasted to his master, not without cause, that among all collectors, including princes and kings, "there is not one who has collected in forty years as many pictures as your Excellency has collected in five."[18] Of special interest here are two works which crop up in a 1635 inventory of Buckingham's paintings. One is by the Fleming Abraham Blyenberch, "A Picture of Ben: Johnson," and the other by Bartolomeo Manfredi, "An Egiptian telling Fortunes."[19]

In the summer of 1621, when Jonson penned a poem to express the Villierses welcome of James to Burley, it is significant that he expressed in it also Buckingham's warm thanks for this "house your bounty'hath built, and still doth reare" (B 13). The passage refers in part, of course, to the classical idea of "rearing" a family, but it also points to the King's munificence as it was reflected specifically and physically at Burley-on-the-Hill. Though Jonson would not have known any details of the financial picture as it finally was revealed, he knew, as everyone else did, that Burley was itself a sort of monument to the King's weakness. It later came out that because of some shrewd bargaining on the part of Lionel Cranfield regarding duties on coal, the King had been able to help Buckingham pay for Burley. The "farmers" of the coal duties paid £16,000 for a new imposition, and Secretary of State George Calvert informed Cranfield that "His Majesty told me that £8,000 must be for my Lord Admiral."[20] On 12 August 1620, therefore, £8,000 was paid to Sir Robert Pye for Buckingham's purchase of Burley. Naturally this did not end the matter. On 21 January 1622 the King himself wrote to Cranfield concerning Buckingham:

> I find he must pay twenty thousand pounds for his lands at Burghly, . . . besides three thousand for his new house, and all this he must borrow. I need say no more; if he once run in arrear, he will ever go backward. Do quickly, therefore, what

17. See L-R. Betcherman, "Balthazar Gerbier in Seventeenth-Century Italy," *History Today*, XI (1961), 325–331. Arundel's great interest in the arts is recognized by Jonson within the gypsy masque. The Third Gypsy speaks of him as both a "father . . . and a nurse of the artes" (W 440).

18. Quoted in translation by Godfrey Goodman, *The Court of King James the First*, ed. John S. Brewer (1839), II, 370.

19. MS Rawlinson A.341.(30), 31ʳ–31ᵛ and 32ᵛ (Bodleian). See Randall Davies, "An Inventory of the Duke of Buckingham's Pictures, etc., at York House in 1635," *The Burlington Magazine*, vol. X, no. xlviii (1907), pp. 376–382. Most of Buckingham's treasures went eventually to York House.

20. Quoted by Menna Prestwich, *Cranfield: Politics and Profits under the Early Stuarts* (Oxford, 1966), p. 271.

you are to do for him, and remember a thing done in time is twice done: comfort me with some present good news on this point; for, till then, I protest I can have no joy in the going well of my own business. . . .[21]

In other words, though Burley looked very grand in August, 1621, the King was concerned that still more money was needed to pay for it. Whether James had a hand in any particular transaction does not so much matter after a certain point, however, since Buckingham's own hand was in so much of the King's business.

It has been suggested that James's 1621 visit to Burley may have been timed to celebrate an "august house-warming."[22] Whether this is accurate punning or not, the King found Burley a "goodly house,"[23] and his entire visit seems to have gone very well. The weather for some time had been rainy (crops were poor that season), but now it cleared and the hunting was good. Probably everyone had misgivings for a while about the "indisposition" which recently had troubled Buckingham, but that cleared, too, and Jonson's masque was apparently performed with verve. Thus it is no surprise to learn (the Venetian Ambassador is our source) that his Majesty

> showed the favourite as much honour at Burli as he received from his Excellency, as at a state banquet which took place on the morning of his departure [4 August], his Majesty rose from the table where he was sitting apart with the prince, and went to the head of another at which were the leading lords and ladies, and drank standing and uncovered to the health of the Lord High Admiral, . . . and finally read some verses which he had composed in honour of this splendid host and ordered that they should be written on the walls and carved in the marble of the doors, for a perpetual memorial.[24]

The marble doors (door *frames*, surely), carved or not, failed to survive the ravages of sluttish time. (One recalls Jonson's observation

21. *Letters of the Kings of England*, ed. James Orchard Halliwell-Phillipps (1848), II, 158.

22. *The Victoria History of the County of Rutland*, ed. William Page (1935), II, 113.

23. "Verses Made by the Kinge, When Hee Was Entertaynd at Burly in Rutlandshire, by My L. Marquesse of Buckingham," in *The Poems of James VI. of Scotland*, ed. James Craigie (Edinburgh, 1958), II, 177.

24. Girolamo Lando, 27 August 1621, in *Calendar of State Papers . . . Venice . . . 1621–1623*, ed. Allen B. Hinds (1911), XVII, 117.

that "marble Pillars, Pictures, guilded Roofes" are the toys of "Fooles" and "Cockscombes.") The Parliamentary forces in Rutland captured Burley when the civil war broke out, and for a couple of years they made it their headquarters. Then in 1645, apparently thinking themselves too weak to retain it, they set the place ablaze. The land and such of the buildings as survived were granted to Thomas, Lord Fairfax, commander in chief of the Parliamentary army. Then Fairfax and Parliament fell out, and in 1650, the year Fairfax resigned because of his unwillingness to invade Scotland, Burley was sold by the trustees for forfeited estates. This time the buyer was Oliver Cromwell. The world was now a very different place from that one thirty years earlier when Great Britain's King, in one of the happiest times of his life, basked at Burley in the company of Buckingham and his wife, "Beholdinge of this blessed couple deere,/ Whose vertues pure no pen can duly blaze."[25]

ii. *The Devil's Arse, the Devil, and Buckingham*

> And now we're come (I blushing must rehearse)
> As most does stile it to the *Devils Arse*;
> *Peaks Arse* the Natives.
> A noble Cave between two Rocks appears,
> Unto the Sun unknown, but to the Stars
> Fearing to be immerg'd, and both the Bears
> Turn'd, it its mouth with horrour does present:
> Just like a furnace, or as Hell they paint,
> Swallowing with open Jawes the Damned croud....
> Hobbes, *De Mirabilibus Pecci*[26]

Even if Jonson had never laid a brick in his life, a whole range of other experiences allowed him to see that Burley was no Penshurst. The "ancient pile" of the Sidneys, together with the honorable activities pursued there, embodied for him what Parfitt has described as "that ideal of the virtuous and satisfying life for which he is, in a sense, searching throughout his work, the ideal which underlies all his satire."[27] Buckingham's Burley was doubtless a

25. "Votum," Craigie, II, 177.
26. Latin version by Hobbes (1636), English "by a Person of Quality" (published 1678), p. 30.
27. "Ethical Thought and Ben Jonson's Poetry," *SEL*, IX (1969), 125. See also J. C. A. Rathmell, "Jonson, Lord Lisle, and Penshurst," *English Literary Renaissance*, I (1971), 250–260.

more dazzling place. Though no picture of it survives, there is every reason to suppose that it was very much the sort of thing that Jonson had in mind when earlier he wrote of the "proud, ambitious heaps" which men have "built to enuious show."[28] Evidence in the matter must remain circumstantial, but the temper of its master would seem to be reflected in the fact that Jonson constructed his masque there so as to make Burley, Buckingham-the-courtier's palace on a hill, a sort of counterpart to Buckingham-the-gypsy's "famous Palace" within a hill (B 218). In passing it might be noted that the idea of having a palace inside a hill is not likely to have strained the powers of perception of a court which previously had seen Jonson's *Oberon* (for ocular proof we have Inigo Jones's drawings of Oberon's palace inside a huge hill). At any rate Jonson lost no time in the masque in establishing the location of the gypsy Captain's base.[29] In the first song after the Captain enters, the Jackman, on behalf of the gypies, tells of

> ... the famous Peak of Darby
> And the Devills-Arse there hard by,
> Where we yearely keep our musters. . . .
>   (B 96–98)

The fact that Buckingham is "Captain" at both Burley and the Devil's Arse sets up some inescapable vibrations between the two, both contrasts and correspondences, superficial and underlying, all together quite enough to illustrate the truism that Jonson, like a good many other writers (Shakespeare, for one), knew that setting may function as symbol. Jonson's settings are always appropriate, but more than that he sometimes manages to show by means of them how "appearance and reality are in the end the same."[30]

The most famous of Derbyshire's limestone caverns, the Devil's Arse was created on an even grander scale than Burley.[31] It extended

---

28. "To Penshurst," HS VIII, 93 and 96: ll. 1, 101.

29. Naturally gypsies are wanderers, but the word "base" may be justified by Jonson's designation of the Devil's Arse as a "palace."

30. Gabriele Bernhard Jackson, *Vision and Judgment in Ben Jonson's Drama* (New Haven, 1968), p. 78.

31. It has been known also by such names as the Devil's Arse A-peake (and o'Peak), Devil's Cave, Devil's Hole, Péac's Arse, Peak's Arse, Peak's Hole, and Peak Cavern. Camden says the region "throughout riseth high and peaketh up with hils & mountaines, whence in old time it was called in the old English tongue Peac-lond" (*Britain*, p. 556). More persuasive is the suggestion that the Old English name of the cave, "Péaces ærs," reflected an early association of the place with a demon called "Péac," whose name was cognate with O.E. "Púca" or Puck.

half a mile into a hillside, had a broad, arched entry forty-two feet high (Defoe found it "*Gothick*"[32]), a great hall some two hundred feet long, and passages leading "to chamber after chamber, galleries and halls."[33] A subterranean supply of water flowed through the cave, adding weird sounds to the place, and sometimes after a heavy rain it even came boiling up with appropriate hellishness from among the stones near the entrance.

Jonson could have read about this underground "palace" in such places as Camden's *Britannia* (1586) or in John Speed's *Theatre of the Empire of Great Britaine* (1611), or even in Gervase of Tilbury, to whom Camden and Speed both refer. As a matter of fact, one of Jonson's sources on gypsies said on its very first page that the place was well suited for a convocation of rogues, "it being hollow, and made spacious vnder ground, at first by estimation halfe a mile in compasse, but it hath such turnings and roundings in it, that a man may easily be lost, if hee enter not with a guide."[34] For illustrative purposes here, the most helpful early sources are a drawing made by Elias Ashmole in 1662 and a rather uninhibited passage in the *Journal of a Tour* made that same year by Edward and Thomas Browne, sons of the famed physician.[35] The *Journal* narrative runs thus:

> And so wee led our horses downe a steep mountain to Castleton, so called from the castle situated upon the left buttock of the peak hill.[36] As soon as wee were got to the town, wee prepar'd our selves to see this place so much talk'd of, called (save your presence) the devill's arse. ... At the bottome of the backside of a high rocky mountain, bipartite at the top and perpendicularly steep from thence to the leavell of the ground, wee beheld

32. *A Tour Thro' the Whole Island of Great Britain Divided into Circuits or Journies*, Letter No. 1 (1727), III, 64.

33. Arthur Mee, *Derbyshire*, rev. ed. F. R. Banks (1969), p. 55.

34. Samuel Rid, *Martin Mark-all* (1610), A2^r.

35. Ashmole's sketch is in the Bodleian Library, MS Ashmole 854, p. 41. It is reproduced here as Plate No. 7. See also Plate No. 8, the interior of the cave as pictured on *A New & Correct Map of Great Britain and Ireland*, an eighteenth-century work by Charles Rice, published by John Bowles (British Museum, uncatalogued). The passage from *Journal of a Tour* is cited from Simon Wilkin's edition of *Sir Thomas Browne's Works* (1836), I, 32–33. Other seventeenth-century descriptions include those of Michael Drayton, *The Second Part, or A Continuance of Poly-olbion* (1622); Charles Cotton, *The Wonders of the Peake* (I have seen only the second edition, 1683); and Celia Fiennes, *The Journeys* (which records her visit of 1697), ed. Christopher Morris (1947).

36. A reference to so-called "Peverel" castle, familiar by name through Sir Walter Scott's *Peveril of the Peak*, though built after the Peverels lost the property.

a vast hole or den which was presently understood by us to bee the anus, into which by the helpe of light and guides wee did not onely enter, but travailed some space up the *intestinum rectum*, and had made further discovery of the intralls had the way been good, and the passage void of excrement; but the monster having drunke hard the day before, did vent as fast now, and wee, thinking it not good sayling up Styx against the tide; after some inspection, with no small admiration of these infernall territories, wee returned again to the upper world, at our entrance wee found the countrey inhabited, but scarce gesse by their habit what kind of creatures they were, whither they were onely Ascarides, which did wrigle up and downe and live in the devil's postern, answerably to wormes in men, or whither they were shades dwelling in these Tartarean cavernes, to us at first was doubtfull. They looked indeed like furies, but for manners sake wee ask'd whether they were Gipsies. By the answer wee gathered indeed those wandering tribes did some-times visit them, but these famous Πρωτοπωλιται [proto-citizens] did make good their mansions in this cave and reserved to them-selves a more fixed habitation, skorning to change theirs for any mortal mansion having greater accommodations in this their commonwealth, then in other that are beholden to the sun or annoyed by the weather, both which they seem to contemne, and having got so strong a shell upon their backs, they fear'd no externall weapons, and if their Nile overflows not its bankes too high they can suffer no inconvenience at all; for you must understand, this retromingent divell, whose podex they inhabit, is alwaies dribling more or lesse whereby these doe sometimes suffer inundations.

From very early times the residents of the cave were regarded as the Devil's children, "and their excursions from the mouth of their gloomy abode, like a foul excrement, gave its earliest and still most common name to the great hole."[37] Gypsies arriving in the area— a "houling Wilderness," according to Defoe (p. 44)—naturally sought whatever shelter they could find, and hence arose the specific regional association between gypsies and the Devil.

Jonson knew all this. In the opening act of *The Devil Is an Ass* (1616), when the devil Pug claims to be "of *Derby-shire* . . . about

37. J. H. Brooksbank, "Castleton: Its Traditions, Sayings, Place-Names, Etc.," *Transactions of the Hunter Archaeological Society*, III (1929), 43.

the *Peake*," he is asked whether "That Hole Belong'd to your Ancestors," and his answer is "Yes, *Diuells* arse, Sʳ" (HS VI, 172: I.iii.34–35), and later on Pug is introduced as "*Diuel, o' Darbi-shire*" (p. 241: IV.iv.187). We even have a hint or two that Jonson at some point did his usual research job on the subject. In *The King's Entertainment at Welbeck* (1633) he introduces Father Fitz-Ale as the "Herald of *Darbie*," "the learned *Antiquarie* o' the North," who has at his finger tips "all the written, or reported *Wonders* of the *Peake*." And the wonders include "*Satans* sumptuous Arse…" (HS VII, 794–795: ll. 88–93, 96).

As Jonson's words suggest, he could have turned both to oral tradition and to printed sources to find information on the Devil's Arse. Furthermore, it just may be that he could draw on personal experience. According to a poem by Francis Andrewes, Jonson went touring more than once in the Derbyshire Peak District. Andrewes claims that when he himself went to see Pool's Hole (another "wonder" not far from the Devil's Arse), his guide said,

> I'le tell you heare came on a tyme
> A Big fatt man, that spake in Ryme.
> Wee had much a-doo, to drawe him in,
> ffor hee at first stuck by the chin. . . .

*   *   *

> An other yeare this Man came hyther,
> Then hee had studied it [n.b.] I gather.
> And then I heard him plainely speake,
> Both of this Hole, and that i'th Peake.
> That Hole, the Diuells Arse I meane,
> So cal'd (quoth hee) t'is in my sceane.
> Because Cock-Lawrell to a feast
> Did him invite. . . .[38]

The number of Jonson's visits and their chronology in relation to his writing are impossible to determine, but we may say at least that the Derbyshire wonders struck his imagination sufficiently for him to visit the region and allude to it a number of times in his work, and also, most pertinent at this point, that he was well aware of such lore as was associated with the Devil's Arse.

All in all, the cave was a fine meeting place for rogues and vagabonds, and it is not surprising that the seventeenth century regarded

38. Reprinted in HS XI, 387–389.

it as such. It is therefore worth observing that *The Gypsies Meta-morphos'd*, which presumably draws most of its *dramatis personae* from this setting, displays a thorough intermingling of masque and antimasque elements. The gypsies who appear at Burley have all swarmed forth from the Devil's Arse ("Right so as bees out swarmen from an hyve," says Chaucer's Summoner, describing the exodus of friars from the "develes ers"),³⁹ and from thence they present themselves boldly before the King himself. Far from being symbolically annihilated or even abashed by the quasi-divine glory of the King, they rattle off some patter, dance, and go about their usual business of telling fortunes. In other words, Jonson achieves a potent merging of two rather different worlds which tempers and qualifies both of them. Burley-on-the Hill and the gypsy encampment inside a hill, both presided over by Buckingham-as-Captain, are different aspects of a single literary entity. More broadly, they are different aspects of a single and very complex historical fact with which James had to cope. James was much pleased by Buckingham's Burley; it was Jonson's challenge, while working for Buckingham himself, ironically, to intimate that Buckingham had other "headquarters" elsewhere.⁴⁰

To help convey the nature of Buckingham's offstage base, Jonson linked it with the famous rogue Cock-lorrel. In fact, as we have seen earlier, he made Cock-lorrel the gypsies' founder, their *"first lord"* (B 801).⁴¹ Quickly though this word "lord" is sounded, then silent, it has a special spark in the gypsy masque, for the present "lord," the current incumbent arch-rogue, is none other than Buckingham himself. "Lord" and "lorel" are terms which seem often to have been used together in early times, doubtless partly because of their mutual alliterative attraction, and partly because of their polar connotations. (The *OED* cites More's *De Quatuor Novissimis* [1522], "while the lorel playth the lord in a stage playe.") Jonson uses the terms not merely as contrasts, however, but also as ironic complements. The word "lorel," which lay so conveniently at hand for Jonson, designates a worthless person, a rascal, rogue, or blackguard, everything that a "lord" should not be; and when one adds to "lorel" the prefix-word "cock," which has traditional connota-

---

39. "Summoner's Prologue," ll. 1693–94, in *The Works of Geoffrey Chaucer*, ed. F. N. Robinson (Boston, 1957), p. 93. Would anyone question that Chaucer intended this touch to be not only comic but satiric?

40. This topic is pursued further in Chap. IV.

41. See pp. 58–60.

tions of vain pride and means, among other things, chief, leader, or ruling spirit, the result is a name that is perfectly splendid for Jonson's purpose. For good measure, one might further confirm the appropriateness of the name "Cock-lorrel" in Jonson's ballad by turning back to a passage in the *Fable of Ferdinando Jeronimi*; George Gascoigne, some thirty-five years earlier, had written there of "a peéce of Cocklorels Musike . . . such as I might be ashamed to publish in this company. . . ."[42]

Implications regarding the relationship of setting, naming, and theme in Jonson's masque may be pursued still further. If King James is a most proper and honored guest at Buckingham's Burley, who would be equally proper and honored at the Captain's gypsy retreat? Jonson gives the answer in his Cock-lorrel ballad. In doing so, in fact, he provides a little myth, always fair game for interpreting and especially in this instance because Jonson has presented Cock-lorrel as a sort of mythopoeic predecessor of Buckingham. Since it is the custom of masques to use mythic materials, and since there was little such material on gypsies, we should note with particular care the nature of Jonson's invention here. Who is the *deus ex machina* (he comes in a coach!) of gypsydom? The ballad opens thus:

> *Cock-lorrel would needs have the Devill his guest,*
> *And had him once into the Peak to dinner,*
> *Where never the Fiend had such a feast,*
> *Provided him yet at the charge of a sinner.*

> (B 821–824)

Jonson borrowed the name "Cock-lorrel" because it was already associated with roguery. He capitalized on its fame and then proceeded to dye it a still darker color by saying, with jocular good humor, that Cock-lorrel is so sunk in sin and on such familiar terms with evil that he invites the Devil himself to dine. It is tempting to think Jonson knew that one meaning of "lorel" was "devourer."[43] Fortuitously or not, however, we have the ballad-story of a devourer who invites the arch-devourer to dinner, serving such delicacies as sheriffs and sergeants, panders and promoters. The tone of comic play here is an effective hedge against the demonic savagery that Jonson has in view. It helps to soften our awareness that, as the Flanders and Swann song has it, "Eating people is *bad*."

42. In *The Whole Woorkes of George Gascoigne* (1587), p. 206.
43. John Bullokar, *An English Expositor* (1616), K2ᵛ.

So far as anyone knows, the inset story of the banquet is Jonson's own invention. In the old mystery plays, of course, one source of comedy had been that the devils treated the bodies of sinners more or less like those of animals. And Jonson doubtless was aware that just the preceding year the Devil had danced at the palace of Denmark House in Middleton and Rowley's *World Tost at Tennis* (1620). He himself, in *News from the New World* (1620), had alluded to a pamphlet which described how the Devil had been feasted recently by certain witches up in Derbyshire.[44] And he himself had created a character (Fitzdottrell, in *The Devil Is an Ass*) who wanted to acquire a devil so as to become richer and more prestigious. In other words various kinds of diabolical building blocks lay more or less close at hand. Nevertheless, Jonson must be given full credit for concocting the ballad of Cock-lorrel's feast for the Devil.[45]

In his own century it was to become the best known of his songs.[46] The name Cock-lorrel became so closely associated with the feast

44. Though Jonson had no occasion to mention items on the menu, he knew abundantly well that Great Britain's witches had precedent from classical witches for dining on human flesh.

45. Raoul de Houdenc's *Songe d'Enfer* in the twelfth century and Rabelais' *Pantagruel* are suggested as analogues by Herford and Simpson (X, 629–630).

46. Two tunes have been associated with the text. The one most frequently linked with Jonson's words is the traditional "Packington's Pound," which is thought to have appeared first "in an ascertainably datable form in 1596" (Alan L. Levitan, "The Life of Our Design: The Jonsonian Masque as Baroque Form," unpub. diss., Princeton, 1965, p. 240). Levitan suggests that the traditional nature of this piece, "robust and folk-like in melody and rhythm" (p. 243), would have helped to point up "the distinction between the 'popular' tradition behind this masque and the more serious classical traditions underlying most of Jonson's other masques; a difference in the *kind* of music required by different subject-matter would not be hard to justify" (p. 241).

The other tune, called "An Old Man Is a Bed Full of Bones," may be found in John Playford's *The English Dancing Master* (1651), p. 76. See J. Woodfall Ebsworth, ed., *The Roxburghe Ballads* (Hertford, 1890), vol. VII, pt. 1, pp. 217–221, and Claude M. Simpson, *The British Broadside Ballad and Its Music* (New Brunswick, N.J., 1966), pp. 129–133.

Later verses inspired by Jonson's tended to be strongly political. For instance, Marchemount Needham put out a broadside in April, 1661, called "The Cities Feast to the Lord Protector. To the Tune of *Cooke Lorrell*." The rhyme-words of the first stanza are the same as those in the opening lines of Jonson's ballad:

SIR Mayor invites his Highnesse his guest,
And bids him to *Grocers-Hall* to dinner,
There never was Saint at so great a Feast
Provided him at the Charge of a Sinner.
  With a ran tan the Devil is dead.

(Reprinted in *Rump: or an Exact Collection . . . Relating to the Late Times* [1662], I, 374.) One should not forget, however, that comic, satiric, and political elements were interwoven in the Cock-lorrel ballad from the time when Jonson first wrote it.

which Jonson had him give for the Fiend, in fact, that normal human clumsiness led some later men to call the rogue *Cook* Lorrel. In some cases the metamorphosis of "Cock" to "Cook" may have resulted from a normal human disinterest in accurate spelling, but one may hope that laughter was the motive in *Grobiana's Nuptials* (ca. 1640), a grossly comic play in which the character of Lorrell is actually a cook.

Towards the close of Jonson's ballad one learns that it was in the Peak, after he had feasted, that the Devil let loose the tremendous fart which caused the place to be known ever after as the Devil's Arse. The Arch-Fiend and his factors had been associated for centuries with foul air. More recently, in Jonson's own *Devil Is an Ass*, the titular hero had disappeared at the end leaving

Such an infernall stincke, and steame behinde,
You cannot see S^t. *Pulchars Steeple*, yet.
They smell't as farre as *Ware*, as the wind lies,
By this time, sure.

(HS VI, 268: V.viii.132–135)

In Gervase of Tilbury, moreover, Jonson might have read about the strong wind which blows from the entrance of the cave in question as if through a pipe, to the astonishment of all who go there: ". . . et in monte caverna foraminis, quae velut fistula ventum pro tempore validissime eructat. Unde tanta prodeat aura miratur populus. . . ."[47] Whatever his stimulus in the matter, however, Jonson took the name of the cave as a given, and proceeded to invent a mock-genesis for its inspiration. It may even be that such infernal creation as he relates is to be regarded as a grossly comic inversion of the divine creative *afflatus* as set forth in Holy Writ. According to Genesis 2:7, "the Lord God formed man . . . and breathed into his nostrils the breath of life"; and Psalms 33:6 records that "By the word of the Lord were the heavens made; and all the host of them by the breath of his mouth." Jonson was not unaware of the doctrine. In one of his *Underwood* poems he wrote that man is but "a thing,

---

47. "De Antipodibus et Eorum Terra," in *Radulphi de Coggeshall Chronicon Anglicanum*, ed. Josephus Stevenson (1875), p. xxxi. Though I have found no early reference to the matter, gypsies everywhere tend to link wind with the Devil—especially with his sneezing (Jean-Paul Clébert, *The Gypsies*, trans. Charles Duff [New York, 1963], p. 154). King James himself pointed out that the Devil in Scripture is called the Prince of the Air (*Daemonologie, in Forme of a Dialogue* [Edinburgh, 1597], p. 47; Ephesians 2:2.

blowne out of nought."[48] Whether he had the concept in mind at the time he wrote of the comic creation of the Derbyshire cave, however, is a matter one can neither prove nor disprove. One may simply note that the breath of God and the wind of the Devil are elements as diverse as most men can conceive, and that Jonson has nevertheless attributed to the latter such creative power as is usually reserved to the former alone.[49]

With the Devil a guest of the first gypsy captain in Derby and with God's viceroy a guest of the present "Captain" in Rutland, we need critical blindness out of the ordinary to miss Jonson's fine use of comparison and contrast. The one guest loves bacon and the other despises it. The one is a *"wencher"* (B 836) and the other, to say the least, is not ("no great wencher" is the Captain's discreet phrase [B 262]). At Windsor Jonson added the idea that the stench made by the Devil in Derby was supposed by the learned to be the scent of tobacco, an obvious allusion to James's aversion to that "wicked weede" (W 948). On the one hand we have Buckingham at Burley, feasting and flattering the royal guest ("I aime at the best," he says as Captain, "and I troe you are hee" [B 251]); on the other hand we learn that the Captain still continues Cock-lorrel's tradition of feasting at his "famous Palace of the Peak" (B 218). Though there is only an indirect allusion to any recent visit there from the Devil (W 970–971), we are given several details relating to the gypsies' current mode of Derbyshire entertainment. They dance at their feasts (as they will presently at Burley), they set forth the praises of the current reigning strumpet (a neat contrast to the flattering fortunes about to be assigned to the ladies at Burley), and when they dine on such occasions they regard as "wholsome" only those "viands" that are stolen (B 222). The Captain's Derbyshire world, in short, appears to be what one of Jonson's characters elsewhere calls an *"Arsie-Varsie"* version of the Captain's Burley world (*Tale of a Tub*, HS III, 41: III.i.2). Jonson habitually played with such parallels in his work, not only in his masques and antimasques, but in his satirical comedies as well, where values are purposefully in-

48. "An Epistle to a Friend, to Perswade Him to the Warres," HS VIII, 163: l. 32.
49. It may be worth a footnote to observe that the measureless distance traditionally stretches between God and the Devil is disconcertingly closed by the word said to be used by English gypsies for God, viz., "Devel"—or, alternatively, "Dibble," "Dubble," or "Duvvel." See George Borrow, *Romano Lavo-lil: Word-book of the Romany or, English Gypsy Language* (1923; reprint of 1st ed., 1874), pp. 28, 29, 30.

verted. The ideal is delineated and advocated by a portrayal of what is flawed, "the giddy world turn'd the heeles upward," as Jonson has Nose say in *Time Vindicated* (1623; HS VII, 662: l. 219). His purpose in this is plain. By singing "a rare blacke *Sanctus*, on his head," a man may tell "Of all things out of order" (ll. 220–221). If one considered only casually "all things" in the gypsy masque, perhaps one would be willing to say that the Captain/Buckingham figure, like Faustus, has a good angel and a bad, the Devil and the King. One of the intriguing problems raised by *The Gypsies Metamorphos'd*, however, is precisely that the ideal world of the masque has been infiltrated by representatives from the Adversary.

To say all this is to acknowledge that the ballad of Cock-lorrel is quite as important to the masque as commentators, sympathetic or otherwise, seem always to have sensed it to be. It is to add, moreover, that its significance reaches well beyond the fact that Jonson epitomizes in it the raucous fun of the masque as a whole—or its disgusting coarseness, if one is of that persuasion. In other words, the ballad is important not merely for what one might term its tonal purposes, for its more or less superficial comic and satiric elements; it is even more important on basic thematic grounds. Not only does it present a memorable bit of diabolical myth which suggests an inversion of all that which James's court should represent; it also casts a lurid, lambent light on some of the other less obviously figurative elements in the masque.

The possibility that Buckingham's two roles, gypsy and lord, are in some way validated by the power of the two guest/masters of the masque is strengthened when one considers that King James—Burley's primary guest and the masque's primary auditor—was very much persuaded of the reality of the Devil. Though James might find occasions on which to laugh wholeheartedly at a "*farce*" (the word is Jonson's [B 818]) about the Devil's Arse, his basic stance on the subject is simply this: "*Those that denies the power of the Deuill, denies the power of God. . . .*"[50] (As a matter of fact the Devil was also convinced of James's existence. When asked pointblank in an interview why he hated the King so much, the Devil replied, "by reason the King is the greatest enemie hee hath in the worlde. . . .")[51] To forearm the readers of his *Daemonologie* James had even taken the trouble to explain some of the Devil's devices, and certain com-

50. *Daemonologie*, p. 53.
51. *Newes from Scotland* (1591), B2ʳ.

ments which he attributes to his interlocutors may surely be brought to bear on any persons so obviously the Devil's factors as gypsies. For instance, relevant to fortune-telling, James writes that "Prophecie proceedeth onelie of GOD: and the Devill hath no knowledge of things to come."[52] Nevertheless, the Devil continues to

> make his schollers to creepe in credite with Princes, by foretelling them manie greate thinges; parte true, parte false. . . . [There is] no man doubts but he is a thiefe, and his agilitie . . . makes him to come with suche speede . . . [and] in like maner he will learne them manie juglarie trickes at Cardes, dice, & such like, to deceiue mennes senses thereby: and such innumerable false practicques. . . .[53]

James had even devoted some time to pondering that portion of the Devil's anatomy which gave its name to the gypsies' Derbyshire headquarters. Instead of with gypsies and rogues, however, he associated it with another reprehensible sort of being. The witches' mode of adoration, he wrote, is "kissing of his hinder partes. Which though it seeme ridiculous, yet may it likewise be true. . . . So ambitious is he, and greedie of honour . . . that he will euen imitate God in that parte, where it is said, that *Moyses* could see but the *hinder partes of God*. . ." (p. 37). At the risk of being anachronistic, one may be glad that when Jonson turned to such matters he knew he was writing comically.

The devil-witch connection was a very real matter both to James and to some of Buckingham's other guests on that August night at Burley. The King was by no means so uncritical on the subject as some have thought, and yet his belief in witches had been reinforced from time to time, for example when he learned that some thirty-nine of his subjects had met with the Evil One at the old haunted church of North Berwick for the purpose of overthrowing himself. That had been about thirty years ago, and now the Devil was continuing to make contact with British witches. During the year of the gypsy masque he made at least seven recorded visitations in

52. *Daemonologie*, p. 3. Spoken by Philomathes, the learner. Epistemon qualifies this, saying the Devil knows *part* of the future, but lacks "prescience" (p. 4).
53. *Daemonologie*, p. 22. On the other hand, James told Sir John Harington that he himself "had soughte out of certaine bookes a sure waie to attaine knowledge of future chances. Hereat, he namede many bookes, which I did not knowe, nor by whom written; but advisede me not to consult some authors which woulde leade me to evile consultations" (*Nugae Antiquae*, sel. by Henry Harington and arr. by Thomas Park [1804], I, 369-370).

Scotland,[54] while down in England his most famous subject of the year was Elizabeth Sawyer ("the witch of Edmonton"), hanged at Tyburn in April.[55] As a matter of fact, Buckingham's own in-laws at Belvoir had themselves had a terrifying time in recent years with three female retainers who turned out to be witches.[56] These women —a fiery-eyed mother and two daughters—had sealed a pact with the Devil, and the Earl of Rutland's oldest son, Henry, Lord Roos, thereafter became sick and died (1613). The second son, Francis, Lord Roos, suffered severe torments, then also died (1619). And the Lady Katherine, who was to become Buckingham's bride in 1620, became perilously ill. It is altogether possible that Jonson refers to this horrible and prolonged series of events when he has the Third Gypsy read the palm of the bereaved mother, the Countess of Rutland: "You will find it from this night/ Fortune shall forget her spight..." (B 394–395).

The devil-witch connection is worth pursuing thus far because it helps to close the circuit between the devil and gypsies, on the one hand, and, on the other hand, witches and gypsies. Because of their skill at legerdemain it was readily supposed by some that gypsies, like witches, had the aid of familiar spirits. Moreover, it takes no great imaginative leap to realize how the midnight roistering of gypsies in a wild, secluded place, with fires snapping and wavering in the wind, might be confused with a witches' *Sabbat*.[57] In Jonson himself we have seen how the story of gypsies who invited the Devil to dinner in Derby was preceded just a year by his reference to a story of Derbyshire witches who did the same. However, Jonson's own most direct merger of traditions comes in *The Sad Shepherd*. Here the shape-shifting witch Maudlin (the mother of an uncouth swineherd named Lorell!) describes to her daughter the magic belt which plays such an important part in the plot:

54. George F. Black, *A Calendar of Cases of Witchcraft in Scotland 1510–1727* (New York, 1938), pp. 34–35.

55. Henry Goodcole told the public "*of the Divels Accesse to Her, and Their Conference Together*" (from the title page of *The Wonderfull Discoverie of Elizabeth Sawyer* [1621]).

56. *The Wonderful Discoverie of the Witchcrafts of Margaret and Phillip Flower, Daughters of Joan Flower Neere Bever Castle: Executed at Lincolne, March 11. 1618. Who Were Specially Arraigned and Condemned ... for Confessing Themselves Actors in the Destruction of Henry L. Rosse, with Their Damnable Practises Against Others the Children of the Right Honourable Francis Earle of Rutland ...* (1619). See the discussion by C. L'Estrange Ewen, *Witchcraft and Demonianism* (1933), pp. 231–234.

57. Clébert, who makes this observation (p. 54), notes also that real gypsies regard it a mark of special favor to be a witch (p. 158).

A Gypsan Ladie, and a right Beldame,
Wrought it by Moone-shine for mee, and Star-light,
Upo' your Granams grave, that verie night
Wee earth'd her, in the shades; when our Dame *Hecat*,
Made it her gaing-night, over the Kirk-yard,
With all the barkeand parish tykes set at her. . . .

(HS VII, 31: II.iii.39–44)

To be sure, anyone familiar with the gypsy masque knows that it is rollicking and high-spirited, not dark and grim. Whatever he tried to say within the piece, Jonson never forgot that he was working through the medium of a court entertainment, not a sermon. Still, the wonder is that he dared at all to depict a rather gypsy-like royal favorite *as* a gypsy, and that he then took the further step of linking his gypsy courtier with the Devil. In addition to the links already noted, one might also point out that when the gullible Puppy asks if the Captain will let him join the gypsy band, Jonson's imagery totters between that of a guildsman's contract and a devil's pact. At first Puppy asks, "will your Captaine take a prentice Sir?" (W 957), but just a breath later he is saying, "I would binde my selfe to him, bodie and soule, either for one and twentie yeares, or as many liues as he would" (W 958–960). As a matter of fact, Puppy previously had asked the Patrico what "*sort or order of Gipsie*" he might be (B 785), and it was the answer to this question which provided the lead-in for the ballad of Cock-lorrel: the Patrico, like all his companions, is "*A Divells Arse a Peakian*" (B 788).[58] The overtones of such passages should not be oversimplified, and Jonson, whatever his high concept of the poet as *vates*, should not be mistaken for a seer. Nevertheless, the fact remains that a relatively short time after he wrote this masque, Buckingham really *was* viewed by some as "The divell's factor."[59] In 1626 a paper appeared on a post in Coleman Street which read in part:

Who rules the kingdom? The King.
Who rules the King? The Duke!!
Who rules the Duke? The Devil!!![60]

58. There is also a trace here of the old "fraternity" of vagabonds. When Cock-rell refers to "a Gipsie in ordi'narie" (W 983), furthermore, one is made aware briefly of the hierarchy of positions at court.

59. An "Epitaph" in Frederick W. Fairholt, ed., *Poems and Songs Relating to George Villiers, Duke of Buckingham* (1850), p. 65.

60. Fairholt prints this on his title page. Quite different was the claim in the preceding favorite's reign that the King was ruled by Robert Carr, and Carr by Sir Thomas Overbury.

By attributing to Jonson not prescience but simply intelligent awareness of such matters as they stood in 1621, one might think that he
tried to adumbrate them in his masque. If he did, it is not surprising
that he also chose to camouflage them with a good deal of bluff and
burly good humor.

To understand the darker side of the brightest star at James's
court, one should know something of the astrologer and fortune-
teller John Lambe. Not only was Lambe thought to inspire Buckingham's worst actions; he was known popularly as "the Duke's devil"
(after Buckingham's elevation, of course), and said to be the means
by which Buckingham was leagued with *the* Devil. Truth to tell,
Lambe was no fine fellow. As early as 1608, well before Buckingham's rise, he had been indicted for practising "execrable arts." In
and out of prison after that, he found himself eventually in the
King's Bench Prison, London, but life must have been no great hard-
ship for him there because he still was allowed to see his "clients."
Moreover, since he could not only predict the future but also
raise apparitions from a crystal glass, he gained a certain renown.
Jonson had one of his Gossips in *The Staple of News* speak of
Lambe's skill at conjuring devils (HS VI, 303: first Intermean, ll.
50–52).

In view of the fortune-telling theme of Jonson's 1621 masque, as
well as the one which followed (*The Masque of Augurs* [1622]),
it would be interesting to know when Buckingham first sought
Lambe's aid. We do not have this information, but we do know that
Buckingham consulted him on the presumed insanity of his brother
John, whose mental problems had come to the fore in 1620. We
know also that in June, 1623, while still in prison, Lambe violated an
eleven-year-old girl. Then we are thrown back on conjecture again.
Apparently Buckingham's influence and, significantly, his interest
in the case were great enough to gain Lambe his freedom even after
a jury had convicted him. Not even Buckingham could free Lambe
of public hatred, however. After leaving the Fortune Theater one
June day in 1628, with his crystal ball on his person, Lambe was
assaulted by a mob in Finsbury. Trying to escape, he sought haven
in a series of taverns and even succeeded in enlisting the aid of four
constables, but the crowd persisted, beat him down, and finally
knocked one of his eyes from its socket. The next morning he died,
taking with him, one supposes, a good many secrets. It is in the
nature of the situation that we cannot know much now about the

real relationship between the astrologer and the royal favorite. We can do little more than catch glimpses of people's attitude toward it. Surely it is significant, though, that two months after Lambe's death, when Buckingham himself was assassinated, the mood of the mob found expression in the line, "For want of Lambe the Wolfe is dead."[61]

Even allowing for the exaggerated reports which frustration, hate, and envy may be relied on to spawn, it is clear that in Buckingham the English public had a real cause for grievance. He continued to become yet worse in the years that followed the gypsy masque, until finally verbal attacks gave way to bloody violence, but even in 1621 he was eminently worthy of much of the criticism he received. The truth is that no royal proclamations could prevent men from criticizing either Buckingham or his satellites.

An interesting and pertinent parallel to Jonson's satire on Buckingham appeared in a sermon delivered just a couple of years after *The Gypsies Metamorphos'd*. Its very existence helps to illuminate and perhaps corroborate the hypothesis that is offered here regarding the masque. The sermon, too, was presented directly to the King, and it, too, made one of the King's chief officials a sort of Devil's disciple. In fact its victim, Lionel Cranfield, was a man who had risen so spectacularly from his merchant background that the Villierses, as we have seen, snapped him up for one of their kinswomen. It turns out that Cranfield did much to check waste in the various departments where he held high posts, and the King, with cause, was impressed. In 1620 Cranfield became a member of the Privy Council, and in 1622 he was created Baron Cranfield of Cranfield and Earl of Middlesex. His ride on fortune's wheel kept taking him higher and higher until finally he dared to question some of Buckingham's policies. Then in May, 1624, he was charged with corruption as Master of the Court of Wards. Naturally found guilty, he was stripped of his offices, fined, and sent to the Tower.

The sermon in question is described by Arthur Wilson, who reports that the King reacted to this particular attack on one of his servants with a tolerant amusement. Wilson's words are all the more

61. Cited by Sidney Lee, *DNB* (Oxford, 1921–1922), XI, 443. Perhaps it should be observed that the relationship between the two men was not always smooth. In 1625 Buckingham was irritated with Lambe for his involvement with Lady Purbeck (John Villiers's wife), who apparently had obtained some charms from him. Buckingham acknowledged then that "Lambe has hitherto, by . . . shifts, mocked the world and preserved himself" (*Calendar of State Papers, Domestic . . . 1623–1625*, ed. Mary Anne Everett Green [1859], XI, 476).

striking because he was an eyewitness of the event and because we know the King's private attitude to have been rather different. He writes:

> ... about this time one of his [James's] own *Chaplains*, preaching before him at *Greenwich*, took this *Text*, 4 *Mat.* 8. *And the Devil took Jesus to the top of a Mountain, and shewed him all the Kingdoms of the World, saying, All these will I give*, &c. He shewed what power the *Devil* had in the World at that time, when he spake these words, and from thence he came down to the power of the *Devil* now. And dividing the World into four parts, he could not make the least of the four to be *Christian*, and of those how few went God's way? So that he concluded the *Devil* to be a great *Monarch*, having so many Kingdoms under his command, and no doubt he had his *Vice-Roys*, *Council* of *State*, *Treasurers*, *Secretaries*, and many other Officers to manage, and order his affairs; for there was *order* in *hell* it self; which after he had mustered together, he gives a *character* of every particular *Officer*, who were fit to be the *Devil's servants*, running through the *body* of the *Court*, discovering the *correspondencies* with *Jesuits*, secret *Pensions* from Foreign Princes, betraying their Masters Counsels to deserve their Rewards, working and combining to the prejudice of God's people. And when he came to describe the *Devil's Treasurers* exactions and gripings, to get mony, he fixt his *eye* upon *Cranfield*, then Lord *Treasurer* (whose marriage into the house of *Fortune*, and Title of *Earl*, could not keep him from being *odious* to the people) and pointing at him with his hand, said with an *Emphasis*, *That man* (reiterating it) *That man, that makes himself rich, and his Master poor, he is a fit Treasurer for the Devil.* This the *Author* heard, and saw, whilst *Cranfield* sat with his hat pulled down over his eyes, ashamed to look up, lest he should find all mens eyes fixt upon him; the King, who sat just over him, smiling at the quaint *Satyr* so handsomly coloured over.[62]

In connection with James's complacent reaction, at least in public, it is tempting to ponder the earlier statement of Jonson to Drummond that if he "might have favour to make one Sermon to the King, he careth not what yʳ after sould befall him. . ." (HS I, 141). It is fruit-

---

62. *The History of Great Britain* (1653), pp. 151-152.

less to conjecture what Jonson might have said had he ever been given such an opportunity, but since he seems to have thought of it as involving some danger, we may suppose he had not forgotten that the traditional label for Horace's satires was *Sermones*.[63]

The satirical Greenwich sermon which compared specific officers of the Devil with those of the King is parallel in several significant ways to the gypsy masque. Equally striking for its infernal parallels, though, and providing us with a referent prior to the masque, is Thomas Dekker's *Villanies Discovered by Lanthorne and Candle-light*. That Jonson knew some form of this pamphlet there can be no doubt. It has been noted here previously as a source for some of his gypsy material. No one appears to have seen, however, that Jonson may be indebted to it in other ways as well.

As the pamphlet opens it is term time in Hell and Don Lucifer, Prince of Darkness, is summoning his followers to a meeting in his great hall for the purpose of considering a letter from Belzebub of Barathrum. Naturally Lucifer has agents at work in all kingdoms everywhere, and naturally their purpose is "to win the subiects of other Princes to his obedience. . ." (B2ᵛ). At the moment Belzebub's letter has raised the problem that the Bel-man of London (in an earlier Dekker pamphlet) has jeopardized the Devil's disciples by exposing their methods among men. When no action can be agreed on, the court breaks up and a common council is called. Now a fiendishly clever plan is accepted whereby a spirit skilled in shape-shifting is to infiltrate various earthly places in disguise. He is to win new converts and thereby bring forth fruit "fit to be serued vp to Don Lucifers Table, as a new banqueting Dish. . ." (B4ʳ). (Here, possibly, is a preview of that bill of fare which Jonson has Cock-lorrel furnish the Devil.) The secret agent of Darkness is ordered to frequent such places as taverns and theaters, and especially to "creepe into bosomes that are buttoned vp in Sattin. . ." (B4ʳ). Once in London, he seeks advice from a woman named Pride, who says that the next thing he must do is "put himselfe in good cloathes, such as were sutable to the fashion of the time, for that here, men were look'd vpon only for their outsides. . ." (B4ᵛ). Thus the "Stigian traueller" is metamorphosed—Dekker's word is "translated"—"into an accomplished Gallant. . . ." He is now "Our Caualier" (C1ᵛ).

63. Cf. Jonson's *Poetaster*, HS IV, 243: III.i.26. It is necessary to add that the King tried ineffectually to intercede on Cranfield's behalf. Though Buckingham was to have his way, James thought he was making a rod with which to scourge himself.

Hence we have the image of a new-made cavalier ready to operate at top efficiency for his Prince—not James, however, England's royal sun, but Lucifer, Prince of Darkness.[64]

One should neither belabor nor magnify the Dekker-Jonson parallels, for the comparison between the underworld of rogues and that of devils was a commonplace. Neither would it be wise to forget Jonson's own concern with similar material in *The Devil Is an Ass*. In the latter play the devil Pug is so impressed by the evil afoot in England that he exclaims, "why, *Hell* is/ A Grammar-schoole to this!" (HS VI, 241: IV.iv.70–71).[65] Still it is possible that Jonson found rather more illumination in *Villanies Discovered by Lanthorne and Candle-light* than is usually assumed. He found gypsy material here, as has long been recognized, but it would seem important, too, that the gypsies he found were placed in a setting which was, like that of his masque, specifically and rather comically diabolical.[66]

iii. *Diablerie and the Hunting Theme*

> *Man should not hunt Mankind to death,*
> *But strike the enemies of Man. . . .*
>   Jonson, *Time Vindicated*[67]

The subject of setting (Burley and the Devil's Arse, one present "onstage," and the other implicit there but existent only "offstage") has brought us to a variegated consideration of the masque's dia-

---

64. Of course the idea is not new. In the *Ludus Coventriae* cycle the devil appears as a gallant.

65. Presumably Jonson was influenced here by Dekker's *If This Be Not a Good Play, the Devil Is in It* (1611). In Dekker's play Pluto orders Rufman, a devil, to take a courtier's shape on earth, even though "aboue vs dwell,/ Diuells brauer and more subtill then in Hell" (I.i, in vol. III of *The Dramatic Works* . . . , ed. Fredson T. Bowers [Cambridge, 1958], p. 126). Rufman's job is to bend the monarch of Naples to evil. Though he had planned to spend his days virtuously, the king now says,

> What man soeuer (strange or natiue borne,)
> Can feast our spleene, and heigthen our delight,
> He shall haue gold and be our fauorite.
> Tilts, turneys, masques, playes, dauncing, drinking deepe
> Tho ere noone all *Naples* lye dead-drunke a sleepe.

(I.ii, p. 135) He assures Rufman, "Thou hast our fast embraces" (II.i, p. 151).

66. Dekker, it might be noted also, describes gypsies as "tawny Diuels" (*Villanies* [1620], F2ᵛ).

67. HS VII, 673: ll. 532–533.

blerie. The subject could be overemphasized. Jonson clearly uses
diablerie as a means of adding darkness and bite to his gypsies, but a
danger of exploring it at all thoroughly is that one may be thought to
have misconceived his sense of proportion, as well as, indeed, the
satirical limits to which he might go. With this caution in mind, let
us proceed yet a bit further and single out for consideration a thematic motif in the masque in which the Devil plays a part. Stated
most baldly, it is this: the Devil shares his taste and talent for hunting
with both the gypsies and the King.

Early in James's life it had been clear that he had weak legs. His
walk was always to be awkward and undignified (he had to be carried to the Parliament of 1621), but on horseback this particular
physical shortcoming could be minimized. On horseback, though his
seat was never more than "indifferent good," he could move with
relatively greater assurance and authority, and hunting became one
of his chiefest joys.[68] On the way down from Scotland in 1603
James borrowed a pack of hounds at Burley from Sir John Harington, "and with these he hunted the timid hare all the way to Belvoir
Castle. . . ."[69] As early as June that year, before he was even crowned
King of England, Thomas Wilson was writing to Sir Thomas Parry
that "Sometymes he comes to Counsell, but most tyme he spendes
in the Feilds and Parkes and Chases. . . ."[70] And Osborne, who calls
him "this Sylvan Prince," rather disgustedly leaves "him dres'd to
posterity in the colours I saw him in the next Progresse after his
Inauguration, which was as *Greene* as the grasse he trod on, whith
[*sic*] a *Fether* in his Cap, and a *Horne* instead of a Sword by his
side. . . ."[71] Years after the fact, a gentleman of his court recalled
how the King "did so ouer stok his forist, & restrain the inhabitance
from disturbing the deere, thow found in the corne or thair medos,
as if hunting had bin a caling, rather than a recriation, & uenison the

68. Whatever glories James later shed on Buckingham, none was more important
to their personal relationship than the appointment as Master of the Horse. When
the gypsy masque opened at Burley, it was doubly appropriate that two horses
should be led before the company. Not only was the horse an animal closely associated with gypsies, but the master of the gypsies was also Master of the King's
Horse. In *Neptune's Triumph* (1624) Jonson refers to Buckingham with the epithet
"loyall HIPPIVS" (HS VII, 686: 1. 154).

69. "Sabretache," i.e., Albert S. Barrow, *Monarchy and the Chase* (1948), p. 72.
This first visit of James to Belvoir must have gone well, for on the morning of his
departure he is said to have made forty-six knights before breakfast (Irvin Eller,
The History of Belvoir Castle [1841], p. 58).

70. Quoted by Elizabeth Burton, *The Jacobeans at Home* (1962), p. 35.

71. *Historical Memoires on the Reigns of Queen Elizabeth, and King James*
(1658), p. 54.

richest Commodity of his Kingdom. . . ."[72] It is no wonder, then, that Jonson, in a birthday masque for James, celebrated him as *"the best of Hunters*, Pan."[73] In addition to hunting parks at St. James's, Greenwich, and Theobalds, James early in his reign established places to hunt at Royston and Newmarket, where he would retire for as long as two months at a time, making it known that he wished to be bothered by no more government business than necessary.[74] Out in the country frequent orders were issued to local residents to protect the game, keep down the hedges, and repair the roads. Almost comically sad is a proposal of 1611 "for repairing during the winter the highways to Royston and Newmarket, five miles round London, and afterwards the roads throughout England."[75] As a matter of fact, on 31 July 1621, just three days before the gypsy masque, some letters and a warrant went out to various Norfolk men announcing the imprisonment for example's sake of one of the chief offenders among the "common distroyers of his Majestie's game in that countrie."[76]

James justified his hunting on the grounds that it was good for the kingdom. This obviously required some rationalization, but James was equal to the challenge. Jonson was merely following a beaten path, therefore, when he had the gypsy Captain observe that the King hunts "not so much for the food,/ As the weale of your body, and the health of your blood" (B 256–257). For one thing, James's favorite dish was not venison but sheep's head (boiled in wool, flesh removed, served with butter). For another, as Jonson dared mention in the gypsy masque (W 1180), James suffered from gout, and by some means had come to have faith in the efficacy of bathing his

---

72. Anon., "The True Tragi-comedie Formerly Acted at Court & Now Revi[v]ed by ane Eie Witnes" (*ca.* 1654), 10ʳ; British Museum Add. MS 25348.

73. *Pan's Anniversary*, HS VII, 535: l. 180. James also referred to himself as Pan (Craigie, II, 193).

74. The French Ambassador divined that these frequent absences resulted from the fact that, beneath all show to the contrary, James felt incapable of managing state affairs properly (report from the Comte de Beaumont of 22 October 1604, in Frederick Von Raumer, *History of the Sixteenth and Seventeenth Centuries*, trans. from the German [1835], II, 209). Beaumont reported that "the only means to obtain converse with him" was to join him in the chase (II, 201). The sugary A. D. B. (whose initials might be taken as an anagram describing his book) notes, regarding hunting, that "those Courtiers doe not misse the marke, which indeuour to imitate their Prince in so famous and worthy a recreation, and with all diligence vse it, and take especiall delight in it" (*The Court of the Most Illustrious and Most Magnificent James, the First* . . . [1619], p. 112).

75. *Calendar of State Papers, Domestic* . . . *1611–1618*, ed. Mary Anne Everett Green (1858), IX, 91.

76. *Acts of the Privy Council of England 1621–1623*, ed. J. V. Lyle (1932), p. 30.

feet "in every bucks and staggs bellie in the place where he kills them, which is counted an excellent remedie to strengthen and restore the sinewes."[77] But most important, James claimed that since hunting was the means to his better health, it was also good for the kingdom. What was good for the "weal" of his body was good for the commonweal.

Setting its excessiveness aside, James rested assured in knowing that, according to age-old traditions, hunting suited his royal station. In the handbook on kingship which he wrote for Prince Henry he commended recreation on horseback, and especially hunting. "I cannot omit here the hunting," he said, "speciallie with running hounds, which is the moste honorable and noblest sorte thereof. . . ."[78] He frankly told Parliament, after referring on one occasion to venison, partridge, and pheasant, "I doe not thinke such Game and pleasures should be free to base people."[79] Therefore Thomas Dekker was but reflecting the royal view of hunting in *Villanies Discovered by Lanthorne and Candle-light*, the pamphlet we have noted here earlier in connection with both Jonson's gypsy material and his theme of a shape-shifting cavalier on the loose in society; Dekker says that "Hunting is a Noble, a manly, and healthfull exercise. . ." (C4ᵛ). According to Dekker, those who hunt "the long-liued Hart, the couragious Stag, or the nimble footed Deere: these are the noblest hunters, and they exercise the Noblest game: these by following the Chase, get strength of bodie, a free and vndisquieted minde, magnanimitie of spirit, alacritie of heart. . ." (C4ᵛ). Jonson himself, in *Time Vindicated* (1623), put similar thoughts in verse:

> *Hunting it is the noblest exercise,*
> * Makes men laborious, active, wise,*
> *Brings health, and doth the spirits delight,*
> * It help's the hearing, and the sight:*
> *It teacheth arts that never slip*
> * The memory, good horsmanship,*
> *Search, sharpnesse, courage, and defence,*
> * And chaseth all ill habits thence.*
>   (HS VII, 672–673: ll. 516–523

77. *The Letters of John Chamberlain*, ed. Norman Egbert McClure (Philadelphia, 1939), II, 249.
78. *Basilikon Doron* (Edinburgh, 1599), p. 144.
79. *Workes of the Most High and Mightie Prince, James*. . . (1616), p. 547.

The main fact to note at this juncture, however, subsumes the nobility of hunting and reaches on to the metaphorical usefulness of hunting. The passage immediately following the one just cited from *Time Vindicated* constitutes the final admonition of Jonson's Chorus and brings his masque to a close thus:

> *Turne Hunters then,*
>> *agen,*
>> *But not of Men.*
>> *Follow his ample,*
>> *And just example,*
> *That hates all chace of malice, and of bloud:*
>> *And studies only wayes of good,*
>>> *To keepe soft Peace in breath.*
> *Man should not hunt Mankind to death,*
>> *But strike the enemies of Man;*
>>> *Kill vices if you can:*
>> *They are your wildest beasts.*
> *And when they thickest fall, you make the Gods true*
>> *feasts.*

(ll. 524–537)

Obviously the end in view here lies far beyond either hunting per se or the virtues which hunting is normally supposed to develop. The goal of the ideal hunter is to kill *"the enemies of Man . . . vices. . . ."* Virtue lies in hunting vices. In hunting of this kind, moreover, the hunter imitates that *"ample,/ And just example"* of Christ and King James, each of whom is a Prince of Peace and Champion of Good.[80]

In the gypsy masque, where other themes and modes prevail, the King hardly may be said to provide an "example" of how to drive "vices" out of the land. Quite the contrary. He is a genial monarch who happily suffers gypsies to read and even kiss his royal hand. For all Jonson's attention to James's hunting in this masque, the King is presented as a mere hunter of stags. Here, alas, is a rather real James, a fair reflection of the King who justified his excessive hunting on the grounds that what was good for his own body was good for the body politic. One may hold, to be sure, that hunting is a noble exer-

80. Obviously it is not altogether satisfying to cite the explicit symbolism of a later masque to explain the implicit symbolism of an earlier one, but the fact is that the later does appear to shed light on the earlier. For a discussion of Jonson's use of hunting as a symbol, see W. Todd Furniss, "Ben Jonson's Masques," in *Three Studies in the Renaissance: Sidney, Jonson, Milton* (New Haven, 1958), pp. 112–113.

cise, but Jonson knew there was more important game to be hunted than stags.

The more pervasive, effective, and meaningful hunting in the masque is carried on entirely by the opposition. Again we find Jonson working by means of contrasts, again we must be willing to think figuratively, and again we may turn to Dekker's *Villanies Discovered by Lanthorne and Candle-light* for a parallel and precedent —in fact, it might be argued, for a source. Dekker's third chapter, in which he sings the praises of hunting, comparing it with wars from which the victor returns "crowned with honour and victorie" (C4ᵛ), is called "Of Ferriting." Ferrets are weasel-like animals kept to drive rabbits out of their burrows, and hunting with ferrets (i.e., "Ferriting") is simply a kind of cony-catching. Thus Dekker veers easily into the subject of hunting human dupes and gulls. It turns out that his main purpose for praising hunting and hawking, both "noble games, and Recreations," is to contrast them as strongly as he can to their basest opposite, for "nothing can be more hurtfull" than the hunting of men (D3ᵛ). And *this* is the means by which Dekker introduces various types of rogues, including, finally, gypsies. In other words, the subjects of noble and debased hunting are meaningfully juxtaposed in Jonson's major source. In the masque itself, however trippingly the word may have come off the Second Gypsy's tongue, "hunters" can have only negative implications when applied to the gypsies themselves (B 68).

Naturally the range of game which gypsies hunt is different from that of the King. To take up the subject where Jonson does, we find in the first sentence of the masque, a stage direction, that the gypsies enter with "*stolne poultry &c.*" strapped to the back of one of their horses, and later we learn that this wording includes geese and pigs. Such birds and beasts as were actually cast to perform in the masque were squalling and squirming at Burley, we may suppose, making themselves very much more startlingly apparent to the masque's original auditors and viewers than to a modern reader. Here, indeed, was a lively image of hunting! In Jonson's source, Dekker tells how the gypsies, "damnable Hunters after flesh" (F3ʳ), go after "the very heart blood of those whom they kill" (F2ᵛ), and Jonson says later that their range of prey includes mutton, lamb, veal, chick, capon, and turkey (B 219–220).

Jonson took care to include pigs, too, not merely because real gypsies stole them but especially because the King hated pork. Beyond the fact that the appearance of this particular quarry in Burley's marbled halls was bound to provoke some grins and guffaws, there also may be a morsel of food for thought in the idea that these same stolen pigs which were common "grunters" when stalked by gypsies are destined to be transformed to "Kings game" (wild boars, perhaps?) when hunted at "Saint Jamses, Greenwitch, Tibals" (B 67, 76, 73). The King's bounty and influence, operative everywhere, it seems, are effective even when it comes to the nature and titles of animals. The King's acorns will "change" the stolen pigs in "both kind and name" (B 75). Such a reordering in the porcine realm might be thought to provide a slight but comically provocative preview of the major metamorphosis which is advertised in the title. Eventually the very gypsies themselves are to be *"chang'd"* (the word is Jonson's, B 928) while carrying on their trickery within the royal sphere of influence. But are they changed in essence? Changed utterly? If it may be supposed that the pigs change more in "name" than "kind," and that a pig by any other name would smell as sweet (there is no hint of a substantial Circean metamorphosis), then perhaps we have here a bit of precedent for saying that even after the gypsies have "changed," they are emphatically courtiers with a past.

As hunters of domesticated animals, of course, the gypsies are really preying on the people who own those animals. This is made vividly clear in a figurative way in the Cock-lorrel ballad when the first gypsy captain serves human meat for the Devil's dinner. The gypsies' ultimate victims are always people. Herford and Simpson assumed that the very children who enter riding on that first horse have been kidnapped (HS II, 315). Perhaps they were misled by Jonson's phrase *"bound in a trace of scarffes"* (B 30), but the "trace" is intended merely to keep the tots from tumbling off, and the first speech of the masque identifies them as gypsy offspring. They are misbegotten, to be sure, but no less "counterfeit Egyptians" for that. Gypsies simply had a custom of loading several children on a single horse—as Jonson could have learned from Dekker. Jonson's gypsies do consider kidnapping some of the fine ladies at Burley, and they do plan to "Strike faire at some jewell" (B 175). Nevertheless, the only "hunting" specifically required during the action of the piece occurs when the gypsies meet the clowns. Ironically it is the country folk themselves, woodcocks all, who strike up some music in order to lure the gypsies closer. Not that there is any confusion as to who the hunters are and who the hunted. The bumpkins are a little like

poor Faustus trying to conjure up a devil. The gypsies, like Mephis-
tophilis, could have found their way thither without any enticement
by their prey.

Since gypsies are dangerous and predatory, they themselves are
proper objects to be hunted. Thinking of the historical reality, not
at all of Jonson's masque, Simson writes of them thus: "Like stags
selected from a herd of deer, and doomed to be hunted down by
dogs, these wanderers were now [i.e., after the passage of the 1609
Act] singled out, and separated from the community, as objects to
whom no mercy was to be shown."[81] In Jonson's masque the language on the matter is tinged not with sentimentality, however, but
mock-admiration. In Jonson the gypsies are "goodly game," more
specifically a "covy" (B 500, 499), lively and attractive birds of a
feather. Playing with the canine connotations of Puppy's name,
Jonson has him ask who "sprung" the gypsies (B 652), only to have
Townshead point out that Puppy himself "quested last" (B 655).
The passage comes clear when one knows that "sprung" is a term
from fowling which means made to fly up or rise from cover, and
"quest" is a verb used for the peculiar bark of hunting dogs on sight-
ing game. Most definitely any gypsies who are guilty of crimes (and
what gypsies are not?) are game that should be hunted, if not by
Townsheads and their Puppies, then certainly by constables and
magistrates. Puppy will "stand to't, that a wise Gypsie (take him at
time o'th' yeare)"—a gamesome figure, surely—"is as politicke a
piece of flesh, as most Justices in the county where he maunds [i.e.,
begs]" (B 578–581).[82] At Windsor Jonson went on to have one of
the country fellows guess from the Patrico's manner that he is not
the sort to "be taken in the trap of authoritie by a fraile fleshlie constable" (W 1061–62), but the others think he might be caught with
the right bait, and Cockrell imagines how "he would chirpe in a
paire of stockes" (W 1065: also B 887). Jonson's avian metaphor
surfaced previously, also, when the Patrico dispersed the gypsy
flock by saying, "Away birds" (B 639), and warned that Beck-
harman (the constable) might come to hunt them and strike them
"all dumbe,/ With a noyse like a drum" (B 642–643). The language
is indirect, but the meaning plain: the constable might shoot them

81. Walter Simson, *A History of the Gipsies*, ed. James Simson (New York,
1866), p. 116.
82. "Politicke" is a striking word to assign a gypsy. Whatever connotations we
decide it has, however, it is clear that the gypsy and the justice stand on different
sides of the law. Each belongs to a different hierarchy, a different "nation" (B 216),
and hence each has different allegiances.

because, in the sight of the law, gypsies are not only birds of prey, but "fair game."

Jonson's metaphor calls to mind his greedy birds in *Volpone,* the vulture, crow, and raven, and also his rascally cozeners in *The Alchemist.* "What sort of birds were they?" asks the newly returned Love-wit, and Mammon replies, "A kind of Choughes,/ Or theeuish Dawes, sir, that haue pickt my purse. . ." (HS V, 403–404: V.v.59–60).

The bird imagery in the masque is also rather startlingly reminiscent of a metaphor which the King himself used earlier in 1621. On 10 March James appeared unexpectedly in the House of Lords in response to the recent tumult "touching delinquents upon patents granted by me." He made it clear at this time that, "Bycause I am the giver of all patents, yt can not but reflect on mee." This was true enough, and, because the subject of patents led more or less directly to that of Buckingham, he took pains to give specific praise to Buckingham's administration. On the other hand, he concluded by qualifying the royal sanctuary which his favor afforded this particularly splendid bird. If anyone should accuse the favorite, said James,

> I desire you not to looke of him as adorned with theise honours as Marquess of Buckingham, Admirall of England, Master of my Horse, Gentleman of my Bed Chamber, a Privie Counsellor and Knight of the Garter, but as he was when he came to me as pore George Villiers and if he prove not himselfe a white crow he shalbe called a black crow.[83]

Buckingham, the quondam "pore George," at this point fell to his knees for all eyes to see, and committed himself to James's grace. It was a good symbolic exchange and must have had a dramatic effect. As occasionally was his lot, however, James was hoist with his own metaphor. A rare bird indeed is the crow that is not black.

83. Zaller, who relays the incident, explains how James happened on this unfortunate choice of language: " 'White Crow' was a snipish reference to one of the precedents cited by Coke before the Lords on March 8: 4 Henry IV, the case of Brangwyn or White Crow. Coke was accused of having falsified this precedent" (pp. 67, 70, 204). On 13 March, in order to justify himself, Coke "brought an old Statute booke where the statute is against those Courtiers that begg suites soe importunatly of the kinge, is intitled, Brainguyn" (*The Belasyse Diary,* in *Commons Debates 1621,* ed. Wallace Notestein, Frances H. Relf, and Hartley Simpson [New Haven, 1935], V, 36). It is helpful to know that "*Brangwyn* . . . in the British Tongue signifies *White Crow.* And he was called a Crow because he was oftentimes calling and acquiring. And White because he had *aulica et candida vestimenta*" (Notestein, p. 36).

Though the constables' hunting of malefactors, of "vices," is an idea which Jonson raises, not an action he depicts, it yet may be regarded as a sort of satiro-realistic parallel to the much nobler sort of hunting which the King, farther up the scale, should be practising. Unfortunately the King's attention is focused elsewhere. The real King James was willing to chase a single stag for eight days, but still, paradoxically, his interest in hunting was too limited. Whereas the gypsies are functioning in a way quite proper to gypsies, the same may not be said for the King, either in the masque or out of it. Therefore Jonson has taken it on himself to warn James that the rich, ripe fruits of the court have attracted some dangerous birds. And in this he spoke true as a gun.

The next point is perhaps not so obvious: if the high-level version of the constables' hunting is the rightful job of the King, the high-level version of the gypsies' hunting is ultimately the job of the Devil. As the King wrote in his *Daemonologie*, the Devil "vses al the meanes he can to entrappe [men] ... in his snares" (pp. 6–7). Surely one needs no specific source, however, to argue that the Devil's job is to prey upon men and to bag as many souls as he can. We may assume also that just as God and Christ have their agents (the chief of whom is the King), so the Devil has his. Hence it is that when the Devil comes to dine with Cock-lorrel, this arch-rogue and gypsy lord serves up a usurer and a lecher, a justice and a jailer ... and *"A Constable sous'd with vinegar"* (B 874). The Devil is only too glad to devour as many mortals as he can.

As a matter of historical fact the King could have taught George Villiers a good deal about hunting stags. He actually did provide him riding lessons for a while. George-as-gypsy, however, George in his antimasque shape, dapper as a crow, is acting out the precepts of the hunter-monarch of quite another realm. All this leads to a very simple point: granted that predatory stalking is a characteristic gypsy skill, a chief danger of gypsies turned to courtiers is that now they may hunt without hindrance.

iv. Cupiditas *Again: The Thievery Theme*

> All the world is ours to winne in.
>
> *The Gypsies Metamorphos'd* (B 107)

The hunting theme in *The Gypsies Metamorphos'd* is only partially separable from the *cupiditas* theme, which manifests itself mainly as thievery. The two work together and to much the same end. The theme of hunting is the more metaphorical and hence the safer for Jonson's purposes; the *cupiditas* theme is the more awkward to handle, yet beautifully unavoidable and useful because thievery is a means to subsistence for the gypsy race, a *sine qua non* of gypsy-dom.

Most simply, Jonson's problem was how to get away with de-picting Buckingham and his relatives and friends as thieving knaves. There was no really perfect solution, so he handled the problem as disarmingly as he could by emphasizing their liveliness and charm and by denying their dangerous qualities—which he nonetheless managed to mention elsewhere. Most notably and awkwardly he had the gypsies return the various articles which they have stolen during the course of the masque. Then he took the added precaution of having their chief spokesman, the Patrico, assure the clowns that the gypsy Chief is by no means a thief. Whatever Jonson gave with one hand, however, he ambidextrously took away with the other. When the clowns ask the Patrico how one may become a gypsy, he tells them that one must be able and willing to steal. After all, as the Third Gypsy has explained (in mock-heroic couplets), the gypsies' "*Magna Charta*" provides that "no viands [are] wholsome that are bought" (B 222). With one hand Jonson made gestures to protect his gypsies (and himself, of course) from criticism. With the other he repeatedly pointed to the fact that these rascals are guilty of thievery.

The Gypsies Metamorphos'd, like all masques, is an entertain-ment designed in part to appeal to the eyes, and Jonson placed some spoils of thievery on view at the very outset. We have noted here earlier that before a single word is uttered the stage directions call for the Second Gypsy to enter leading a horse "*laden with stolne poul-try, &c.*" At first the audience had no sure way of knowing that this "*poultry, &c.*" was stolen, but given the common reputation of gypsies such a conclusion would be perfectly natural. Furthermore, Jonson's inclusion of the adjective "*stolne*" in his very first sentence is for *readers* a specific and unmistakable clue. As a matter of fact, in case there is doubt in the matter, Jonson proceeds at once to have the Jackman specify in the opening speech of the work that these *are* stolen goods. He speaks obscurely, in canting terms, observing that gypsy children normally ride with the "cheats" (that is, with the stolen goods) until they are themselves old enough to "nip a jan" (that is, to steal a purse).[84] But how necessary are any words at all? Even Puppy and Townshead, two clowns, are bright enough to know and say that gypsies are thieves. Even though this band is better looking than most, the country folk warn one another in advance that while in the gypsies' company they had better "look to" their "pockets and purses" (B 543). From the beginning it is clear that these gypsies are underworld characters, and soon we find that Jonson even dares have them assure their Captain they "never yet did branch of statute break,/ Made in your famous Palace of the Peak" (B 217–218). In other words, they are emissaries faithful to the statutes of an *"Arsie-Varsie"* world. Charming they may be, but in James's world they are thieves.

Thievery is talked of in various places in the masque, but demonstrated explicitly only in the "scene" where the rustics are introduced. At first the rustics are so impressed by the gentlemanlike air of the gypsies that they wonder if indeed they can be gypsies. Cockrell wonders if they really can "mill" (steal). Are they masters in their art? Townshead thinks they must be bachelors: "they cannot have proceeded so farre, they have scarce had the time to be lowsie yet" (B 511–514). It turns out, though, that however comely they may be, these gypsies are proficient thieves. Anyone who thinks that Jonson has done everything possible to whitewash his "fine fingered Gypsies" (B 689) should recall that in this scene he has them demonstrate their professional skill. Considering the importance of pantomime in Jonson's works, we should not be misled by the jolly words that they speak; the original audience *saw* that these gypsies have the ability to steal without being caught. Moreover, while the gypsies relieve the bumpkins of their trifling treasures—thread, nutmeg, purses, and pins—they are acting precisely as Harman, Dekker, Rid, and everyone else including the clowns knew they would. What, then, is one to make of the fact that before the scene ends they return all they have taken? What is one to make of gypsies who say, *"We scorne to take from yee,/ We'had rather*

---

84. "Cheats" is a term which often means merely "thing" or "article," and since it comes immediately after the word "convoy," Brooke and Paradise gloss it as "baggage" (*English Drama 1580–1642* [Boston, 1933], p. 628). The context suggests, however, that Jonson uses the word to mean a "product of conquest or robbery; booty, spoil," for which meaning the OED cites W. Adlington (1566), Robert Greene (1592), Philemon Holland (1600), and Jonson's teacher, William Camden (1610). The "cheats" may *be* baggage, but if so they are, more specifically, *stolen* baggage. Jonson has just given two synonyms for stealing, and in the next line notes that, riding thus, the children will be "Out of clutch of" the constabulary.

spend on yee" (B 770–771)? Perhaps a better question is, how could Jonson have solved his problem any better? The explanation for the gypsies' return of their loot is that Jonson dared go so far and no farther. It should be noted, moreover, that in the very process of exonerating the gypsies he has the Patrico bend over backwards far enough to implicate them in yet another way. While protesting the innocence of the gypsies, the Patrico tries to throw their thievery on the shoulders of their victims. He returns Clod's half-pennyworth of nails to Townshead, and Frances's blue thread to Prudence, saying, "*If any man wrong yee,/ The thiefe's among yee*" (B 772–773). Rather than letting such roguery vex them, though, the bumpkins express still more admiration for the gypsies. After they importune a bit, therefore, the Patrico in the Windsor version goes so far as to talk of giving these "*country boyes*" (B 817) some lessons in thieving.

When the gypsies engage in fortune-telling at a higher social level, namely among the personages present from court, no stealing is specified. Conceivably some took place, since the Patrico issues orders for it; but more likely it did not, since the script does not call for it. In either case a certain excitement must have been generated by the fact that the gypsies speak of the *possibility* of stealing even here. This standard accompaniment to fortune-telling is brought to the fore when the Patrico informs his fellows, "Here faire is, and market" (B 151), a fine pun to suggest that this is a proper place to ply their normal trades. Undaunted by surroundings or persons, they may play at "fast, and loose" (B 153) and other "legerdemaine" (B 185) because here there is no "Justice Lippus" (B 194).[85] Were a justice present it would be otherwise, for no matter how dashing they may look, a justice would put them in fetters or the stocks (B 196), or perhaps have them stripped and whipped (B 197–198).[86] Here is a point worth pondering: the gypsies assume that no one at Burley will bother to enforce the law. Though

85. I do not recall seeing it noted that Jonson is punning here on the name of the great Belgian humanist Justus Lipsius.

86. Or worse. In his handbook for justices William Lambard mentions counterfeit gypsies when discussing both rogues and felons (*Eirenarcha, or Of the Office of the Justices of Peace* [I have used the 1619 ed.]). Even the least culpable variety of rogue was to be "punished by whipping, and boring through the grissell of the right eare with a hot yron an inch in compas" (John Cowell, *The Interpreter* [Cambridge, 1607], Mmm2ᵛ). A second offense made one a rogue of the "second degree" and subject to death as a felon.

the source of power, the King himself, is present, here they have nothing to fear. Indeed, such is their luck that their thievery need not even be small in scale. Do not bother "diving the pockets" (B 168) and fishing in purses here (B 171), says the Patrico, but "Strike faire at some jewell,/ That mint may accrue well. . ." (B 175–176). At Windsor this advice was intensified to a yet more startling form. Speaking of the Lord Keeper of the Great Seal the Patrico says, "Theres a purse and a seale/ I'haue a great minde to steale. . ." (W 194–195).

In the courtly fortune-telling scene there is even a parallel to the gypsies' accusation that the bumpkin victims may engage in some stealing of their own. This time, of course, any aspersion on the customers is more dangerous, since the palms that are read belong not to dramatized caricatures but to real people. To begin with, the Patrico merely tells the Jackman not to worry about their own gear while working at Burley because he himself will keep an eye on these (possibly thieving) gentlefolk. Probably most readers would agree that this is good-natured badinage. Of course Jonson has had to set up the whole business so that one may view it as such. The point, however, is that probably it is not *merely* badinage. It accords too well with what he says in *Timber*: "*The great* theeves of a State are lightly the officers of the Crowne; they hang the lesse still; play the Pikes in the Pond; eate whom they list. The Net was never spread for the Hawke or Buzzard that hurt us, but the harmelesse birds, they are good meate" (HS VIII, 603). Again the officers of the law appear as fowlers, the malefactors as birds.

It is here in the courtly fortune-telling scene that we find the most direct and devastating criticism in the masque. Buckingham's mother, the ambitious matriarch of the Villiers clan, was the perfect type of grasping, domineering woman from whom (in the Windsor version) Jonson has the Patrico (the gypsies' "priest") bless the King's sight: "A smock rampant . . . that itches/ To be putting on the britches. . ." (W 1135–36).[87] D. H. Willson rightly calls her "a rapacious and predatory old termagant."[88] One can scarcely read as merely "merry," therefore, her fortune as told by Jonson's Fourth Gypsy:

87. Dol Common is called a "smock-rampant" in *The Alchemist* (HS V, 400: V.iv.126).

88. *King James VI and I* (1956), p. 387.

Your pardon Lady, here you stand
(If some should judge you by your hand)
The greatest fellon in the land
    Detected.

                                (B 421–424)

Of course many gypsies *were* felons. The Countess, however, both
as constant manipulator on behalf of the Villiers family and also as
mother of their Chief—the realities of the masque world and the
actual world are inseparable—has proved herself to be the "greatest
fellon" of all. Her fortune continues:

I cannot tell you by what arts,
But you have stolne so many hearts,
As they would make you at all parts
    Suspected.

                                (B 425–428)

Quite clearly expressed here is the subject of illegitimate acquisitiveness, veiled only by a wisp of flattery (conventional in that it is all
right for a fair lady to steal hearts). "I cannot tell you" is nicely
ambiguous because one never can number the ways of graciousness
nor tell in public the machinations of this particular woman. What
examples of "stolne . . . hearts" could Jonson have had in mind?
Perhaps the passage alludes generally to the Countess's acquisition
of swarms of followers who properly owed allegiance not to her
but the King.[89] Or perhaps the reference is more personal. Gossip
had it that once when she was pressing the match between George
and Katherine Manners, she detained the girl at George's lodgings
in Whitehall. Katherine stayed overnight, the court was aghast, the
King was angered, and the favorite's marriage to the heiress followed.[90] Or what about the marriage of her troubled son John,

89. For another reference to this sort of heart-stealing see the passage quoted
from Wither on p. 177. The Spanish Ambassador, Gondomar, "jested that he did
not despair of England's conversion when he saw more prayers and oblations
offered to the mother than to the son" (cited by Willson, p. 387).

90. It is difficult to ascertain the truth of this matter. Perhaps the young lady
was merely taken ill and kept by Buckingham's mother in her own apartment. One
contemporary view is reflected in the following anonymous lines:

When Buckingham had got his kate
her father seemed to fret his galle
but when the preest co[n]cluded her fate
he was content to paye for all

(MS Ashmole 38, 229ʳ, Bodleian)

which had been forced on Frances Coke? Or the marble-fronted impudence she displayed in trying to find a bride for the unattractive Christopher? For good measure one may even toss in the rumor about her own attachment to George's friend John Williams, the new Lord Keeper of the Great Seal. Not that a specific solution to the problem is necessary. Whatever specific "arts" the Countess may have practised, her acquisition of "hearts" has brought her under general suspicion.

The Gypsy proceeds thus with his reading:

Your very face . . . [is] such a one,
As being view'd, it was alone
Too slippery to be look'd upon,
    And threw men. . . .

(B 429–432)

The lady's face is treacherous, and to describe it Jonson turns, as he did on a couple of other occasions, to a passage he remembered from Horace: "vultus nimium lubricus aspici," meaning "very dangerous when it is looked upon."[91] Given the setting they have in the gypsy masque, the words may hardly be construed as mere flattery.

Nevertheless, a thread of silvery flattery does glisten among the other elements of the Countess's fortune, or Jonson never would have dared say as much as he does. The most scintillating bit of all—and also the blackest—he saved until last. How could he summarize all that the Countess is? How could he explain her success? Whatever the ethic of her methods, she is "Still blest in all you thinke, or doe," which immediately suggests these next lines: "Two of your sons are Gipsies too:/ You shall our Queene be. . ." (B 437–439). Until the Fourth Gypsy has begun to tell her fortune, this lady has been merely one among the courtly spectators of the masque, but as soon as he takes her palm to read, she becomes one of its subjects. This much, of course, may be said of each of the seven other persons whose palms are read. This is what makes the masque so completely and complexly topical. As the Gypsy concludes the Countess's fortune, however, the world of the masque is expanded so as to include her in a very special way. The Gypsy's words suggest that in a couple of senses she is the gypsy who really takes precedence here. Her sons are gypsies *too*. The wording gives her primacy. Moreover, she shall be "our Queene." The only English

91. Herford and Simpson (X, 285) trace this to Horace's *Odes* (I, xix, 8).

Queen at the English court should be the consort of the King, but
Queen Anne had been dead since 1619. The Countess of Buckingham, by standing firm and close behind her George, was as much
a "Queen" as England had. All the more shocking is it, then, to
realize that such a one is here made the *gypsy* queen. (The first
queen of the counterfeit English gypsies was presumably Kyt Calot
—Kate Harlot.) A matriarchal figure at the head of a tribe, she is
part of a hierarchy which runs counter to all that King James represents, and one which we eventually find is supported by the Devil
himself. Yet here she sits in honor in the midst of James's court.
Further than this Jonson could not be expected to go.[92]

The thievery theme runs throughout *The Gypsies Metamorphos'd*
and manifests itself in various ways, but nowhere does it appear
more dark than in this reading of the Countess's palm. A more characteristic indication of the sort of tonal balance demonstrated by the
masque as a whole is found in the Patrico's advice to the gypsies. It
is short and efficient: "Be merry, and cruell" (B 174). This would
do well for a gypsy motto, having something of the quality of the
Golden Rule turned cheerily inside out. When first we stop to
analyze it in terms of the masque's probable effect on a viewer,
doubtless the first of the two adjectives—"merry"—stands out as the
one more obviously dramatized; but everything "merry" in the
masque is qualified by something "cruell," and a steady look at the
masque finally reveals so many signs of thievery and fraud that one
may wonder how Jonson has dared say so much.

Considering that he has brought a band of thieves before the King
and had them display their skills, one might be inclined to wonder
what would become of a real rogue who attempted a performance
at court without the backing of Buckingham. The answer is not

92. Among real gypsies the "*phuri dai* is the feminine version of the tribal chief.
She is generally a very old woman, whose power, however unofficial and concealed
it may be, is not less real. . . . In the role of *phuri dai* very clear traces are found of
the old Gypsy matriarchy" (Clébert, p. 128).
   The fortune which follows that of Buckingham's mother is that of Lady Purbeck,
John Villiers's wife. The Second Gypsy charges her with deceit, murder, and theft
(B 455, 458), but in so pleasant and Petrarchan a way that at first it hardly seems
to constitute evidence of the sort we are concerned with at the moment. In fact,
the contrast between these two fortunes is emphasized because the Countess is
made Queen of the Gypsies, and her daughter-in-law, Queen of Love. Even if
Jonson means to say nothing pejorative about Lady Purbeck, however, it is significant that his praise of her is expressed in imagery related closely to one of the
masque's pervasive themes. In a way its conventionality helps to cushion what he
says about thievery elsewhere; at the same time, it weaves Lady Purbeck into the
essential fabric of the piece.

hard to find. A few years earlier when an actual cutpurse named John Selman attempted a small theft at Whitehall in the presence of the King, he was apprehended immediately and executed. His theft took place on Christmas day, 1611, and his execution followed on 7 January. Jonson was at court and knew all about it. On the day before the execution he arranged to have Robin Goodfellow in *Love Restored* refer to "the *Christmas* cutpurse" (HS VII, 380: ll. 119–120); and later he remembered and had Nightingale sing of the incident in *Bartholomew Fair* (HS VI, 76–77: III.v.120–128, 146–156). The Selman business is a very small fact of history, but probably we who are so far removed from the Jacobean scene should try not to lose sight of it, or of the frame of mind which shaped its outcome.

Likewise, perhaps, we should try to recapture some of the fainter overtones in those devil-may-care notes of merriment that are sounded so insistently by the thieves in *The Gypsies Metamorphos'd*. According to the Patrico, the gypsy tricks are done *"gratia risus"* (B 730), and, to be sure, Jonson's gypsies have some of the tone of his ballading Nightingale, who performs his song of cutpurses while his "secretary" Zekiel is busy cutting purses. Jonson is not without admiration for expert rogues. Little wonder is it, then, that his gypsies have some of the *élan* of Shakespeare's Autolycus. They, too, are high-spirited canters and carolers, inveterate snappers-up of unconsidered trifles. The whole business, however, is double- (or perhaps triple-) sided. The gypsies are lively and attractive, but they are also reprehensible. Furthermore (and here the third side comes in) the trifles which these particular gypsies are snapping up include some of the finest prizes in England.

v. *The Nature of Jonson's Gypsies*

> Ile avouch it a man would not desire to haue his purse pickt in better companie.
>
> *The Gypsies Metamorphos'd* (W 975–976)

In considering the setting of the gypsy masque and some of its themes we have had occasion to touch frequently on the nature of Jonson's gypsies. As we turn more directly to this subject, we might ask first whether Frank Aydelotte is correct—or, better, in what way he is correct—in maintaining that Jonson completely confused gypsies with English rogues.[93] In the light of what we know about Jonson's general methods, we may think it less likely that he was confused than that he chose to mix traditions. Lord Frampull in *The New Inn* reflects, if nothing else, something of Jonson's characteristic intellectual curiosity when he claims that he has made a study of gypsies (among other low-life types) because "to these sauages I was addicted,/ To search their natures..." (HS VI, 487: V.v.91–100). Then again, Jonson, like Frampull, was fallible.

Perhaps one should begin by recalling that Jonson makes a fictive Tudor rogue, Cock-lorrel, the founder of the English gypsies.[94] It has been suggested here that he probably did so because Cock-lorrel afforded a bit of tradition which was appropriately enhanced by an aura of lighthearted revelry and lawlessness. Probably Jonson had been reminded of the name by reading that confusing scrap of gypsy history in Rid, where passages on English gypsies and rogues are intermixed. It is doubtful that Jonson was confused, however. Had he followed Rid exactly, he would have had to give his founding father the rather obscure name of "Giles Hather," and one may credit him with sensing at once the greater appeal of "Cock-lorrel," a connotative name with which nearly everyone was familiar. Either way his Captain would be English, and Jonson took no pains to skirt the matter.

As for the Jackman, Jonson may have realized that the term really should be "Jarkman." Within the gypsy masque itself, at any rate, he uses the word "jarke" (B 60), which in the language of rogues means "seal." With seals and signatures affixed to their licenses, vagrants of various sorts were allowed to wander and beg through the villages and countryside. A different kind of license was issued to habitual travellers such as bearwards, peddlers, jugglers, and (a common shape for a gypsy) tinkers. Both kinds of licenses, we may safely assume, were in considerable demand, legitimate and otherwise. Hence, presumably, the rise of the "jarkman." Hence also, it appears, Jonson's reference to this character as a *"clarke"* (B 811). In Awdeley's words—and the misprint in his text is probably the ultimate source of the name of Jonson's character—a "Iack man" is a rogue who is able to "write and reade, and somtime speake latin." A sort of scholar gone to seed, "He vseth to make counterfaite licences which they [the rogues] call Gybes, and set to Seales, in

93. *Elizabethan Rogues and Vagabonds* (Oxford, 1913), p. 19.
94. See pp. 59–60.

their language called Jarkes."[95] A few years later, however, Harman was denying that the ranks of real vagabonds included such a type. Whether they did or not, the denial was insufficient to keep later men from writing about jackmen. Real or not, therefore, the jackman has had to be noted in the annals of English roguery. Again, then, as with Cock-lorrel, we may say that Jonson has brought to his masque an element which is consonant with gypsydom, but, so far as we know, not part of it.

The picture is different when we turn to the Patrico. Jonson's depiction of a Patrico as the "Priest of the game" (B 128) is quite in keeping not only with some of his sources but also with his own usual practice.[96] It may even be that the idea of "priest" lingers faintly in the first part of the word, with its suggestion of "pater" or "patter" (cf. the mysterious Latin of the clerics); and possibly the last part of the word is related to Romany "cova" or "covo," meaning "that man."[97] The problem is, whose word was it? Aydelotte reminds us that in Awdeley's *Fraternitye of Vacabondes* the Patrico (or "Patriarke Co" [Aiii^r]) appeared as

> a sort of hedge-priest—who performed marriages which should hold until death did part the married couple. This meant that whenever they were tired of living together they could be divorced over the body of any dead animal they found in the road, by shaking hands and parting, the husband on one side of it, the wife on the other. Simson, who published a *History of the Gypsies* in 1865, claimed that a similar form of divorce was practised by them in Scotland at the time he wrote, with only the difference that instead of looking for a dead animal in the

95. *The Fraternitye of Vacabondes* (1575), Aiii^r.

96. In both his poems and plays Jonson often uses religious imagery to highlight the reprehensible qualities of those who have, as Partridge puts it, "so lost their sense of the right true way of living that they love what normally they should hate" (*The Broken Compass* [1958], p. 65). Previously, in *Bartholomew Fair*, Jonson had applied the term facetiously to Justice Overdo, who is called also the "Patriarch of the cut-purses" (HS VI, 60: II.vi.149–150). Carrying connotations of greatness and venerability, "patriarch" was the title of early Christian bishops and hence, perhaps, may also do duty as a sort of comic heightening of "priest." Later on, in *The Staple of News*, Jonson made "Patrico" more or less synonymous with "*Arch-priest o' Canters*" and "*primate metropolitan* Rascall" (HS VI, 347: IV.i. 45–46).

97. Eric Partridge gives as variants "patriarcho," "patriark(e)co," "patriark co," "patri-coe," "pater cove," "patring cove," and "patryng cove" (*A Dictionary of the Underworld* [3rd ed., 1968], p. 498); and suggests that the source is "pater + co(ve)," "cove" meaning man, companion, chap, fellow—and rogue (*A Dictionary of Slang and Unconventional English* [6th ed., New York, 1967], pp. 609, 184).

road, the husband killed his best horse and over its body parted from his wife. This may be only a semi-humorous rogue custom borrowed by the gipsies, and still surviving, but Simson attempts to identify it with a Hindu ceremony for divorce. . . . The hypothesis that the custom belonged to the gipsies rather than to English rogues is still further confirmed by the fact that Harman denies that any such custom existed among the rogues and that there was any such name as Patrico, while Borrow, on the other hand, gives Patrico as a gipsy word. Awdeley's description of the Patrico is probably a bit of gipsy lore which he picked up somewhere and included in his pamphlet on vagabonds. But the gipsies and the English rogues were two different classes.[98]

Where does this little summary leave us? Since there is such confusion as to whether the Patrico derives from traditions of English rogues or gypsies or from someone's fertile imagination, it is perhaps unwise of us, at least on this subject, to point an accusing finger at Jonson.

The most important idea to derive from these several facts and conjectures may be that even if we can spot some traces of genuine gypsy lore in Jonson's gypsies, the English elements in them are dominant. In fact, no matter how much Jonson "searched" before composing the gypsy masque, he included in it no elements not explicable by the fact that all of his gypsies, including the Patrico, really are Englishmen in disguise. On this point there should be no confusion. Even if Jonson himself was personally confused (this is a less important matter), he chose precisely the right course to keep that sort of ambiguity out of his masque. He has the Jackman announce with perfect clarity in the very first song that the success of these gypsies depends in part on "bacon" and "rinds of walnuts." These are "olive-coloured spirits" or "yellow" or "tawny" or "*browne*" (B 486, 366, 110, 814) not because of their racial background but because they have applied a special ointment to their skin. The range of color words here reflects the simple fact that the varied complexions of the performers were bound to react variously to "Master Woolfs" ointment, and Jonson could achieve some verbal variety by being faithful to that phenomenon.[99] Whether one

---

98. Aydelotte, pp. 19–20. The George Borrow reference is to *Romano Lavo-lil*.
99. Jonson says the ointment was "Made and laid on by Master Woolfs appointment,/ The Courtes *Lycanthropos*, yet without spelles,/ By a meere barbor. . ."

chooses to regard Jonson's gypsies per se or the players who portrayed them, their coloring could be washed off.

What is one to do, then, with all the references to Egypt? If they constitute a problem, it is easily resolved: the gypsies' talk about Ptolemy is part of their patter. In the Jackman's first speech we are told that those five children who enter on the horse are "the five Princes of Ægypt," "the off-spring of Ptolomy, begotten upon severall Cleopatra's in their severall countyes. . . ." Genuine gypsies likewise, from the time of their first appearance in Europe, had claimed to be princes, dukes, and earls because doing so made life easier for them. It follows that in order to be good counterfeits, English gypsies would have to make similar claims. Hence Jonson's borrowing of this genuine gypsy tradition may be viewed as a result of his English rogues' intent—a comically blatant one—to dazzle and deceive their auditors.

Life being what it is, there were doubtless good gypsy imitators and bad among real English rogues, a few who aimed to be convincing counterfeits and more who were neither intelligent enough nor energetic enough to make anything more than a halfhearted effort. Thus the actual historico-sociological situation provided Jonson with an excellent base. (The reader may recall that that base has been sketched here previously in Chapter II, in a discussion of Tudor and Stuart gypsies.) Once Jonson decided to depict counterfeit English gypsies, he was free to use or modify any traditions or terms which seemed most useful for his masque, whether they derived ultimately from English rogues or Romany, or even from pamphleteers with lively imaginations.

This last comes close to saying that Jonson did not even feel compelled to make his courtiers behave like genuine counterfeits. Part of the fun, part of the point, is that he did not. He was not creating that sort of mirror. Utilizing but moving well beyond both Romany and rogue traditions, he created his own special breed of gypsies for this masque. He created English gypsies who are ragged yet courtly. The countryfolk are much impressed by the fact that these gypsies are "gentleman-like" (B 503). It is thematically significant that (in Cockrell's phrase) these are gypsies "*of quality*" (B 781).

(W 1280–82). It should be noted that in this reference to the King's apothecary, Johann Wolfgang Rumler, Jonson not only puns on lycanthropy but also suggests its alliance to witchcraft. This fits well with the darker shading he has given his gypsies all along. Having planted the idea of "spelles," however, he retreats to safer ground.

Jonson's Buckinghamian gypsies, it turns out, are not only purveyors of praise but fit subjects for it as well. We may finally decide that it is right to succumb to their Pied Piper appeal, as King James did, but before joining the procession we should recall what Alexander Sackton has told us about the paradoxical encomium.[100] In his little study of adoxography, the praise of the unworthy, Sackton points out that Lucian was the major classical contributor to the adoxographic tradition as a vehicle for irony. No stranger to Jonson, Lucian was among other things the author of a mock-encomium on the parasite, and one might argue that Jonson was the author of something similar not only in *Volpone* (III.i.1–33) and elsewhere but also in *The Gypsies Metamorphos*... weighing the complimentary elements in the atmosphere Jo... ...tes for his gypsies we ought to know Sackton's conclusio... ...lays of Jonson offer richer examples of the paradoxical... ...O... than those of any other Elizabethan dramatist" (p. 94... ...en o... son's bumpkins find the gypsies "gentleman-like," the... ...he c... has his gypsies themselves create an alluring air of me... ...s true n... ht do well to recall his technique in, say, Volpone's h... ...sed with Ve might also recall some of the techniques of that oth... ...also beca... t who, a hundred years earlier, wrote in praise of f... ...ir words... read him, and read him well.

For those of us who can never see the masque proper... , and one i... the major clues to the gypsies' nature now lie in their... ...hought. Edsimply in what that language says but also in what it... ...ys, Jonson Furniss has pointed out that basically the diction of Jons... ...s." In the is that of the English court. "The single exception," he... ...mbolical-their occasional use of the jargon of gypsies and thiev... ...*Metamor-*Jonson makes no effort to catch the real gypsy *patois.* I... ...ways of dismays us with an occasional spray of roguish gibble-g... ...had had counterfeit gypsy terms—"bene bouse" for "good drink,"... ...ues and for "sleeping place," and "Room-Morts" for "fine ladies... ...hes can 64, 141). Had he insisted on using many more such terms, his... ...nunicawould have become intolerably obscure. As it is... ...nphasis

100. "The Paradoxical Encomium in Elizabethan Drama," *Studies in English*, XXVIII (1949), 83-104. See also Henry... doxical Encomium with Special Reference to Its Vogue in *MP*, LIII (1956), 145-178, and G. J. Weinberger, "Jonso... 'Celebration of Charis,'" *Genre*, IV (1971), 305-328. Though Jonson, Rosalie L. Colie's *Paradoxia Epidemica* (Princeton, 19... general work on the Renaissance tradition of paradoxy.

101. "Ben Jonson's Masques," in *Three Studies...*, p. 143.

his stand on the matter at any particular time he was always too clever not to capitalize on the visual aspect of masquing. Perhaps his musing about costumes for masques reinforced his concern for costume in his public plays. Or perhaps it was the other way around. Either way, there is reason to suppose that Jonson was concerned with the appearance of his gypsies, as well as with that of the courtiers they become. As a matter of fact, since he designed the masque to require nothing special in the way of scenery—deep in the country, at Burley-on-the-Hill, he let a room at Burley be the main scene—the costumes of the masquers must have had a relatively greater emphasis than usual.

Although nothing is known about the individual costumes in the gypsy masque, we may draw a number of inferences about the general appearance of the performers. Most important is the fact that Buckingham and his crew *were* dressed as gypsies. According to Dekker's *Villanies* this would mean that "Their apparell is old, and phantastick," and that they wear "Scarfes of Callico, or any other base stuffe" (F2ʳ). The reference to calico is slight but interesting: like true gypsies, true calico came originally from India. As for the "Scarfes" themselves, Jonson says, as we have seen, that the gypsy children are bound with "*a trace of scarffes*" (B 30). The word "phantastick" which Dekker chooses is regrettably vague, but in all likelihood it encompasses the turban-like circlet of cloth (a special sort of "scarf"?) which from early allusions and pictures appears to have been the single most definitive item of gypsy clothing.[106] Jonson knew that Skelton had depicted Eleanor Rumming in a gypsy turban.[107] As a matter of fact Jonson felt sufficiently comfortable

106. A splendid sixteenth-century sketch of a gypsy woman wearing a turban has turned up in the municipal library of Arras. Written on it in an old hand is an inscription which, translated, reads, "The Egyptian woman who by medical art restored health to the King of Scotland, given up by the physicians" (Angus M. Fraser and François de Vaux de Foletier, "The Gypsy Healer and the King of Scots," *JGLS*, 3rd series, LI [1972], 1–8). The authors conjecture that the king was James V. A book that Inigo Jones is known to have used, Boissard's *Habitus Variarum Orbis Gentium* (1581), depicts a gypsy woman in a huge, flat variety of turban (p. 61). See also the pictures included by Vaux de Foletier in "Iconographie des 'Egyptiens': Précisions sur le Costume Ancien des Tsiganes," *Gazette des Beaux-Arts*, ser. 6, LXVIII (1966), 165–172.

107. The Patrico tells the clowns in the Windsor version that to be a gypsy

You must be bene-bowsy
And sleepie and drowsie
And lazie and lowzie....

(W 996–998)

Skelton, shortly before describing the turban, had used these same three rhyme-

with the word to use it metaphorically in *Epicoene* (1609), where old Morose is said to wear "a huge turbant of night-caps" (HS V, 169: I.i.144–145). Furthermore, the probability that this exotic article of dress was associated with counterfeit gypsies is suggested by the earliest known picture of them. The illustration for the broadside ballad called *The Brave English Jipsie* (1626 or earlier) provides a crude but recognizable representation not only of a gypsy in a turban, but also of six children riding on a single horse like so many green geese to market.[108]

We know for sure that the clothes of the Burley gypsies were ragged—and properly so. Dekker speaks of gypsy clothes as "full of rents" (F2r), and Jonson's Jackman sings of the matter:

Be not frighted with our fashion,
Though we seeme a tatter'd nation;
We account our ragges our riches,
So our tricks exceed our stitches.
(B 100–103)

Of course their tricks will exceed their stitches even after they become courtiers. Hence the danger of their presence at court. This point would be especially emphasized if, as seems plausible, the actors appeared in their own bravest clothes during the final moments of the masque.[109] During most of the piece, in any case, they are clad in tatters, some of which, perhaps, were yellow. There is reason for

words in his description of Eleanor, written about 1515. She is

Droupy and drowsy
Scuruy and lowsy
Her face all bowsy

(From *Here After Foloweth Certayne Bokes, Cōpyled by Mayster Skelton* [1545?], Cvir; turban mentioned Cviir.)
Jonson himself, in *The Fortunate Isles*, wrote of Eleanor thus:

Her face all bowsy,
Droopie, and drowsie,
Scuruy, and lowsie....

(HS VII, 720: ll. 374–376)

108. See Plate No. 5 and pp. 61–62. Such headgear may have been a true relic of the gypsies' Indian heritage. The picture also gives a crude suggestion of the characteristic gypsy cloak, fastened on one shoulder and passing beneath the opposite arm. See Henry Thomas Crofton, "The Former Costume of the Gypsies," *JGLS*, N.S. II (July, 1908–April, 1909), 207–231.

109. After all, they appear at the end as courtiers. One must exclude from such conjecture the professional actors brought along to help perform the show. They were simply catalytic agents who helped make the whole affair possible.

thinking that yellow is particularly a gypsy color, and Jonson does, in passing, allude to the gypsies' fondness for "saffron'd linnen" (B 106). Though the ice is thin out here, it may be permissible to wonder if the satiric edge of Jonson's symbolism is particularly acute in this matter, for, as Linthicum reminds us, "Drama followed the generally recognized attribution of certain colours to persons of certain status. Followers of the Court wore yellow in part of their costume. . . . ,"[110] and Cockrell claims that *"the King has a noyse* [band] *of Gypsies"* (B 783). These gypsies are, after all, King James's. All we may say with certainty, however, is that yellow is the only color which Jonson mentions in such a way that one may associate it with the gypsies' "tatter'd" clothes.[111]

Whatever the color or colors of the clothes, they are clean. Towns-head assumes that the gypsies "have scarce had the time to be lowsie yet," and Puppy responds: "I would be acquainted with them while they are in cleane life, they'll doe their tricks the cleanlier" (B 514–517). In other words, the gypsies' costumes, like their diction, were apparently far less foul than would have been the case had they spent the previous night in the Devil's Arse or under some hedge between there and Burley. Cockrell puts the matter nicely: "a man would not desire to haue his purse pickt in better companie" (W 975–977). Furthermore, we know that the Patrico is sufficiently conventional to wear hose (W 515).

We know also that Jonson's gypsies are adorned with what Dekker refers to as "toyes, to intice the countrey people. . ." (F2ʳ). Included among the "toyes" Jonson specifies are cockle shells, nut-shells, and ribbons (B 105–106). The cockle shells (Cock-lorrel shells?) may have been an especially happy hieroglyphic touch. In the first place a cockle or scallop shell had through long centuries been the badge of a pilgrim, especially one who had been to Com-postela, and in these present roguish wanderers we have a perfect

110. M. Channing Linthicum, *Costume in the Drama of Shakespeare and His Contemporaries* (Oxford, 1936), p. 24.

111. In view of its context the word "saffron'd" is not likely to mean "yellowed with usage"; it may mean "dyed with saffron" (see Linthicum, p. 2) or it may simply mean "yellow." Perhaps one should recall the passage in *The Devil Is an Ass* where Fitzdottrell babbles, "*Yellow, yellow, yellow, yellow*, &c.," and Sir Poule comments, "That's *Starch*! the *Diuells* Idoll of that colour" (HS VI, 266: V.viii.74–75). Yellow was also a compulsory color for many Jews—another outcast people. With such diversity of meaning available and with such slender evidence at hand in the masque, one probably should not press any particular reading too hard. See also p. 168.

type of anti-pilgrim.[112] In the second place cockle shells figure prominently in Buckingham's coat of arms. Since gypsy leaders often decked themselves with gold and silver trinkets, and since Buckingham's arms contain five golden cockle shells, one is tempted to ask whether Buckingham himself wore cockle shells—perhaps gold or gilded ones—in his gypsy masque. The suggestion may seem far-fetched to a modern reader who finds heraldry as exotic as the writing in a Ptolemy's tomb, but we might do well to heed the words of an expert in the field, who finds Jonson "mightily cunning in the armorial lore of his age," and says that "he employs his heraldic learning chiefly in the way of satire."[113] Though the surviving evidence is only circumstantial, Buckingham's guests that August probably would have had no trouble in finding cockle shells rampant at Burley. Heraldry was a very important element in house decoration, and J. Alfred Gotch writes that "Nothing is more usual than to find the owner's arms carved over his front door, and on his principal chimney-pieces. . . ."[114] Virtually the only concrete source that we can turn to, moreover, the York House watergate—all that survives of Buckingham's magnificent town house in London—proves to be prominently adorned with huge cockle shells. One must keep the matter in perspective, of course, keep the microscope in focus; on the other hand, Jonson's fleeting reference to cockle shells may be related to his major point in the gypsy masque. If Jonson arranged to have Buckingham himself adorned that evening with cockle shells, he thereby signalled the radical identity between Buckingham's roles as gypsy and lord.[115]

We know for sure that Jonson's gypsies tinkle and jingle merrily as they move, and especially when they dance. The Patrico observes, "We ring you no knells/ With our Ptolomys bells. . ." (B 555–556). In Dekker's pamphlet Jonson had read that gypsies customarily hang

---

112. In his next masque, *The Masque of Augurs*, Jonson not only returned to his successful fortune-telling motif but also included an antimasque of straying and deformed pilgrims.

113. Oswald Barron, "Heraldry," in *Shakespeare's England* (Oxford, 1932; 1st ed., 1916), II, 84–85. See also Arthur Huntington Nason, *Heralds and Heraldry in Ben Jonson's Plays, Masques and Entertainments* (New York, 1968; 1st printing, 1907).

114. "Architecture," in *Shakespeare's England*, II, 69.

115. Apropos of such a possibility it may be of interest to note again that Frances, Lady Purbeck, is assured by the gypsy who reads her palm that "Venus here doth Saturne move/ That you should be Queene of Love" (B 451–452). Most readers are likely to think this merely a conventional compliment, but it is especially adroit because Lady Purbeck's personal seal was a crowned heart.

"their bodies like Morris-dancers, with belles..." (F2^r), which would have been a clue that he might have the masquers at Burley attach bells of various sizes and tones to their ankles, knees, and waists—treble, mean, tenor, bass, and double bells. Clod's first line is "They should bee morris dancers by their gingle, but they have no napkins" (B 489–490).[116] Nor do they have a Maid Marian, a Friar, or a Fool. "Unlesse," says Clod, "they be all fooles" (B 496). At which point he is informed by Townshead that the newcomers are gypsies. No connection between Jonson's gypsies and morris dancers should be pursued too insistently. Jonson's gypsies wear bells because gypsies wore bells. If Jonson had not known the fact previously, his major source told him. It may be worth remarking, nevertheless, that the word "morris" comes from "Moorish," and that it perhaps began to be applied to such dancers as it did because of their custom of blackening their faces and hence of making themselves look like Moors. Jonson's gypsies may have looked for a moment like morris dancers not merely because of their bells, but because of their artificially darkened faces.

With specific regard to the morris fool, furthermore, it may be worth mentioning also that fools are associated with disorder. The fool's parti-colored costume is commonly regarded as a visible manifestation of his disjunction from order. Therefore, with a hint from the clowns in the present masque (Clod wonders if the gypsies "be all fooles"), we might view the gypsies' tatters as another form of motley. In fact Clod's innocent conjecture looks very much like an allusion to the joke often made by the morris fool immediately after the six morris dancers arrived: "Here we be, masters! Six fools and"—with a gesture to himself—"one dancer."[117] Gypsies are anything but foolish, of course. The point is that they, like the fool, are public entertainers who operate within society but against its grain.[118]

Briefly pursuing the matter of folk traditions, we might note also some of the parallels between Jonson's gypsies and the vice. In an attempt to speak earnestly through figures which on the surface were divertive, Jonson had a variety of dramatic precedents, but

116. In *The Staple of News* Jonson spoke later of "gingling *Gipsies*" (HS VI, 347: IV.i.52).

117. Cecil J. Sharp and Herbert C. MacIlwaine, *The Morris Book*, Part I (1912; 2nd ed.), p. 28.

118. "Fools," remarks Willeford, "induce chaos by violating ... rules" (*The Fool and His Scepter* [Evanston, Ill., 1969], p. 101).

most striking of all in connection with his gypsies' rather diabolical affinities is the traditional vice.[119] Both in the old moralities and other plays as well, the vice (whose "Dad," according to some sources, was the Devil) was supposed to be physically nimble, the better to dance and caper (as Jonson's gypsies do). His costume probably varied from play to play, but probably also, as Craik concludes, its essence was "reckless disreputability," evidently (as with Jonson's gypsies) a "grotesque combination of the flashy and the shabby."[120] A vice was likely to rattle on about fantastic events (such as we find in Jonson's Cock-lorrel song) and perhaps to speak a mock prophecy (as certainly is the wont of these gypsies). In fact, he was likely to be assigned the important task of opening the play in which he appeared (like the Jackman in Jonson's masque), giving a jocular speech designed to establish rapport with the audience. He was certainly supposed to be nimble-tongued, like the main gypsies here, and to be capable of playing upon words, again like the Devil's disciples in Jonson's masque. He could be expected to speak verses that sometimes made sense and sometimes did not—as do the gypsies here with their jargon. What is more, he customarily spoke in tumbling verse, such as Jonson revived for the vice in his *Devil Is an Ass* and, perhaps not coincidentally, such as he sometimes assigns to his gypsies.

One may not argue on such grounds that Jonson's gypsies are all *ipso facto* latter-day vices, any more than one may argue on the grounds we have seen earlier that they are witches or devils or morris fools. Such parallels should be suggestive, not restrictive. And there would seem to be a provocative and artistic appropriateness in the fact that Jonson's gypsies speak and act with some of the carefree, conscienceless good humor of the old morality vices. There would seem to be cause to note in particular, therefore, that it is only in his manner that a vice is comic. His effect is always serious. In Spivack's words, "He laughs as he bites. . ."; though the vice is sometimes capable of good acts, "The heart of his role is an act of seduction. . . ."[121] In other words, even if no one would wish

---

119. The vice, who originally may have entered the drama via the popular festival, was apparently established as a clown even before he appeared in the morality plays. See Francis Hugh Mares, "The Origin of the Figure Called 'the Vice' in Tudor Drama," *HLQ*, XXII (1958–59), 11–29.

120. T. W. Craik, *The Tudor Interlude* (Leicester, 1967; 1st impression, 1958), pp. 71, 72.

121. *Shakespeare and the Allegory of Evil* (New York, 1958), pp. 193, 152.

to say that Jonson's "*Divells Arse a Peakian*" (B 788) gypsies *are* vices, there are reasons enough to say that they are in many ways *like* them. As so often is the case with Jonson, we have grounds here for holding that his complex theme is not merely conveyed but reinforced by his form.

It is almost startling to observe how well Jonson's gypsies blend in with (and perhaps, therefore, are derived from) certain dramatic or quasi-dramatic traditions. The merriment of the gypsy, like that of the fool and the vice, is self-qualified by its cruelty. The fool and the vice, as well as the gypsy, are by nature irresponsible. All are expert dancers. In short, all are attractive nuisances who, like Falstaff, must be firmly rejected if the Hals of the world are ever to function properly. In view of Jonson's probable aim in the masque, it may even be worth remarking that the morris fool in particular always aimed his fooling *against* somebody, and that he nearly always tended to be abusive. If this seems to be flying high, at least it is generally true to our experience that the man dressed as a clown or gypsy gets away with saying and doing more outrageous things than does the average man in the street. Jonson grasped this idea and used it.

One of the special and important twists in *The Gypsies Metamorphos'd* is that the language he uses is not merely the language he assigns to his gypsies, but the complexly parabolical figure of the gypsy itself. It is helpful to glean such details as we can about the speech and appearance of Jonson's gypsies, and to consider some of their predecessors in English tradition, and yet the main thing to bear in mind is the fundamental fact that his performers *do* appear and act like gypsies. Hence words and clothes alike reinforce one another in at once obscuring the performers' everyday personae (the faces they prepared to meet the faces that one meets) and externalizing at least one major aspect of their inner essence. As Orgel puts it, "The basic identity of the courtier and his mask—the dancer and the dance—had been asserted . . . even by the early Tudor disguisings. This was a constant and central idea for the masque."[122] Jonson brilliantly turns tradition upside down, however, by concentrating on the antimasque characteristics of his masquers. Once committed to work by means of the gypsy figure, he had to work at some remove from literal reality. He could not present Buckingham in filthy

122. *The Jonsonian Masque* (Cambridge, Mass., 1965), pp. 33–34. I hazard repeating this idea again because it is so important to my thesis.

rags in his own masque, and he could not give him genuine gypsy (or even counterfeit gypsy) dialogue to speak. He could not write such language, no one in the court could speak it, and probably no one at Burley could understand it. But he did call for the gypsies to wear rags, he did assign them some rogue jargon, and he did attempt to convey a sense of their recklessness (which was qualified, to be sure, like their language and clothes). Thus he was working closer to life—at both surface and deeper levels—than any of those who earlier had attempted to put gypsies in a courtly show.[123] When we weigh his gypsies against all that is known of actual sixteenth- and seventeenth-century gypsies and counterfeit gypsies, the wonder is that he was able to make use of as many of their historical character-istics as he did. Furthermore, the adoxographic prettying up which he indulged in merely drew his characters closer to the speech and manners of their courtly parallels. Jonson could not lose. Softening some of the realities of gypsy life merely helped close the gap be-tween dancer and dance.

vi. *The Players in the Masque*

> Then all did say when they beheld him dance,
> He grac't the *English*, foil'd the Court of *France*. . . .
>
>   Flecknoe on Buckingham[124]

As a rule the speaking parts in masques were taken by professional players. It was the King's Men, Shakespeare's old company, who spoke Jonson's lines in *Love Restored*, *The Irish Masque*, *Mercury Vindicated*, and *The Golden Age Restored*. As Orgel remarks,

---

123. We have noted earlier the appearance of elegant gypsies before Henry VIII in 1520 (see pp. 48–49). From the first year of Edward VI we have a description of certain masquing garments which include "2 frocks or und' garments for Egipcyans of tawny tilsent [tinsel] co^th sleves; two shorte mantells for Egipcyans of crymson golde bandkyn, [a rich embroidered stuff . . .] fringed w^tb colen [Co-logne] sylver," etc. (F. G. Blair, "The Costume of Gypsies in the Masque," *JGLS*, 3rd series, XXXIII [1954], 75). From the Scotch and English court of James himself I know of only two tantalizing glimpses: one in Alexander Montgomery's "Cartell of the Three Ventrous Knichts" (1579), in which an Egyptian appears; and one in *The Ayres That Were Sung and Played, at Brougham Castle in Westmerland* (1617; performed 1617), by George Mason and John Earsden. We have neither libretto nor description for the latter, but the verses which survive call for the appearance of "Egyptians" (D1^r).

124. *Heroick Portraits* (1660), D8^v.

"The single, obviously anomalous, exception is *The Gypsies Metamorphosed*, which caters to Buckingham's histrionic talents."[125] Not only did Buckingham dance for his King this time—and he was one of the best dancers at court, a man of "strenuous Agility"[126]— but this time he spoke as well. To be sure, professionals must have been called in as usual to take the roles of the Jackman and Patrico, but Buckingham spoke aloud some sixty lines. Neither Jonson nor Buckingham misdirected his effort in this business. One of the sixty was an untaxing, "Well, dance another straine, and we'le think how" (B 232), and the remaining fifty-nine were all addressed directly to "James the just" (B 301). One supposes that Buckingham's charms never shone to better advantage. Immediately following Jonson's finest lyric in the masque ("The faiery beame upon you, / The starres to glister on you. . ." [B 237–246]), the favorite went up to the King, spoke words of winning carelessness, kissed the royal palm, and told the royal fortune. There is every reason to think James was delighted. As for Jonson, he could exult in the moment not only because he had put Buckingham on target ("I aime at the best," says the Captain [B 251]), but also because he had so beautifully hit his own.

The only problem attached to Buckingham's role is that the Second Gypsy refers to him as Charles (B 81). It has been suggested that this is a vestige of Jonson's intent at some time to give the role to the Prince, and one cannot ignore such a possibility. The difficulty is that it conflicts with many elements in the masque as we have it. In fact it conflicts at so many points that one is hard put to imagine an *ur*-text of the piece in which such a use of "Charles" would fit. External evidence lacking, perhaps some conjectures are in order, even though to entertain such conjectures one perforce must seem to look with the microscopic eye of Pope's fly. Perhaps also one may hope that the viewing has a bit of additional justification in the array of incidental details it affords.

Why is the Captain called "Charles"? First off, on grounds of decorum and sensibility it might be suggested that Jonson never would have tried to bring out the talents or inner essence of a proper, prudent, reserved, refined, decorous, devout, and rather cool young

125. Introduction, *Ben Jonson: The Complete Masques* (New Haven, 1969), p. 5.
126. David Lloyd, *The States-men and Favourites of England Since the Reformation* (1665), p. 660.

prince by casting him in the role of a gypsy chief.[127] Judged on the basis of all we know, Charles would have been distinctly uncomfortable in such a role. He had made his public debut as a dancer several years earlier in Jonson's *Pleasure Reconciled to Virtue* (1618), but that work had had an obviously suitable theme, required him to speak no lines, and enabled him to perform in a suitable costume—a satin outfit of crimson and pale blue with silver-spangled lace, blue and silver roses on his shoes, and a fair white plume on his head. One might add that it was this masque which occasioned James's most famous bit of masque criticism. When the dancers began to tire, he shattered the decorum of the occasion by calling out, "Why don't they dance? What did they make me come here for? Devil take you all, dance." Whereupon not Charles but Buckingham leapt forth (quite literally) and cut a score of capers sufficiently high, precise, and spirited to mollify the King. Others tried to follow the favorite's example, but "none came up to the exquisite manner of the marquis." Charles kept good time and "excelled them all in bowing," but Buckingham stole the show.[128] Even some three years or so later, at the time when Charles attended the gypsy masque, the only named character he is known to have played in a masque was Truth in Jonson's *News from the New World* (1620). Here he had been able once again to display his dancing skill under circumstances which were obviously suitable for a prince. Furthermore, in view of his problem with stuttering, it was just as well that Jonson could arrange to depict Truth at James's court as silent. Jonson was not the man to relish entrusting his well-wrought lines to any speaker, royal or otherwise, who "some times could hardly get out a word." True enough, Charles on occasion could "speak freely and articulately," but giving such an undependable per-

127. Charles was a complex person and not without spirit, but all these adjectives may be illustrated and documented. A letter from Dr. George Carleton, for instance, written in February, 1615, speaks of him as "shy, grave, swete in speache, very admired, without any evil inclinations" (cited by E. Beresford Chancellor, *The Life of Charles I. 1600–1625* [1886], p. 34). In 1621 the Venetian Ambassador described him as an exceptionally taciturn person (*Calendar of State Papers . . . Venice . . . 1621–1623*, XVII, 168).

128. *Calendar of State Papers . . . Venice . . . 1617–1619*, ed. Allen B. Hinds (1909), XV, 113–114. The King rewarded Buckingham with "marks of extraordinary affection, patting his face." Godfrey Davies observes that by comporting himself thus, James "had publicly affronted the nobility of England, including the Prince of Wales, . . . and openly shown his partiality for an upstart quite unknown four years before" ("The Character of James VI and I," *HLQ*, V [1941–42], 61).

former a significant number of lines in a courtly show, when many nimbler tongues were about, was a problem that nearly any man— prince or poet—would have been glad to avoid.[129]

Buckingham, on the other hand, had appeared before the King as an actor in a play just the preceding year.[130] He is not known to have had a speaking role in a masque before 1621, but certainly he was gifted with a careless assurance and natural *sprezzatura* which were beautifully complemented and drawn forth by the anapestic impudence of the gypsy role. Besides, even if gypsies are left out of the picture, what could have been more natural than for Buckingham to play the captain of the courtiers at the end of the masque? He was the observed of all observers at the English court. He was the King's "cheiffest Man." So well does the masque cater to his position and "histrionic talents," in fact, that one might well be inclined to pose this question: if Charles had been cast as the Captain, what role would have been left for his host?

At least for purposes of discussion, we may assume that Jonson never meant the Captain's role for Prince Charles. Certainly there is no hint but the name that he might have. Certainly the gypsy role was radically inappropriate to the Prince and appropriate in every imaginable way to Buckingham—appropriate because of its overall nature, because of the place where it was to be performed, and because of the occasion of the performance. One might pursue the point by adding that the role was made more Buckinghamian still in the earliest form of the masque because the gypsies there tell the courtly fortunes of five (six, if we include the Countess of Exeter) of Buckingham's female relations: mother, wife, mother-in-law, sister-in-law, mother of sister-in-law, and (the late-coming sixth) wife of sister-in-law's grandfather. Aside from these women, only the King and Prince are assigned fortunes.

It is also worth noting that were we to view the name "Charles" as a vestigial indication that the Prince was once to play the Captain, we should have to confront the problem of its remarkable survival during a thorough revision of the masque. Provided we might im-

129. The quotations here are from William Lilly's *Life and Death of Charles I*, in *The Lives of Those Eminent Antiquaries Elias Ashmole, Esquire, and Mr. William Lilly...* (1774), p. 183.

130. He acted in a comedy performed 5 August 1620 at Salisbury (Allen B. Hinds, ed., *Calendar of State Papers and Manuscripts ... Venice ... 1619–1621* [1910], XVI, 390).

agine that Jonson ever devised an earlier form of the gypsy entertainment to set off the talents of the retiring Prince, we would have
to imagine also that in revising it he inserted Charles's present fortune (which gives no indication of being patched in) and recast
the major fortune of the masque, that of the King (the Jackfellow-
like tone of which would have been most inappropriate for the
Prince), and, more difficult still, that he undertook the general
rewriting necessary to give the masque its present bold ambiguity
(which certainly seems part of the original fabric of the work and
definitely would have been unseemly as a verbal setting for the
Prince). Furthermore, we would have to confront the fact that
while a "normal" single-word error might slip through a couple of
revisions, the chances of survival must decrease greatly for an erro-
neous use of the name "Charles" in a Jacobean masque.

All things considered, it is most natural to assume that Buckingham approached Jonson to prepare some sort of masque to entertain
James and the Prince when the royal progress paused at Burley, that
Buckingham anticipated taking part in it, and that Jonson had the
exciting inspiration of presenting the dashing and altogether gypsy-
like lord as a gypsy. Or conceivably (the irony is no less) the
idea to use gypsies was Buckingham's. In any case, Jonson would
then have proceeded more or less directly to write the masque as
it was first performed—paid for by Buckingham, starring Buckingham, and, with wonderful wit, satirizing Buckingham.

Yet the name "Charles" occurs in the text as we have it. Could it
actually have been spoken at Burley? With a prince named Charles
in the audience, the name would have sounded striking, indeed, if
applied to another man. Is it possible that Jonson meant something
by it? The Jackman begins the speech next following the prob-
lematical one by saying, "If here we be a little obscure, it is our
pleasure, for rather then we will offer to be our owne interpreters,
we are resolv'd not to bee understood. . ." (B 84–86). Then he goes
on to mention the obscurities of canting, and the exact referent of
his remark is allowed to remain "obscure."

Three tentative solutions may be offered for this problem. Each
takes the Jackman at his word and assumes an intentional vagueness
on Jonson's part. More particularly, each assumes that the use of
"Charles" is a sample of Jonson's occasionally oversubtle handling
of names. Gabriele Jackson has made the provocative observation
that in Jonson's works, "Repeatedly, apparent inconsistency in

naming . . . reveals itself as meticulous distinction";[131] and to this one might add that Jonson was sometimes misled by his own ingenuity. At the beginning of James's reign, for instance, in *The King's Entertainment* (1604), he had a speaker observe that the then Lord Mayor was "As worthy, as he's blest. . . ." The line sounds perfectly conventional, and most of its original auditors, one may reasonably suppose, probably thought it nothing more than a standard bit of flattery. In the printed version of the *Entertainment*, however, Jonson explained what he had meant: "Aboue the blessing of his present office, the word [blest] had some particular allusion to his Name, which is *Benet*, and hath (no doubt) in time bin the contraction of *Benedict*."[132]

Granted Jonson's long-lived interest in names and especially in communicating by means of them, and recalling that the speech with "Charles" in it is followed immediately by one which refers to the intentional obscurity of the passage, it may, indeed, be proper to ask what meaning "Charles" could have. If the name is not an error, one might suggest, first, that conceivably it is a device used to parallel the head of the gypsies with the head of the court. The King's first name was really not James, but Charles. Jonson had previously sported with this fact in *For the Honour of Wales* (1618). Does the name here, then, suggest a unity of friend with friend? Love between man and man, one's other self, was, after all, a renaissance ideal.[133] More negatively, there might be a certain point and satis-

131. *Vision and Judgment*, p. 61.
132. HS VII, 93. A few further samples of Jonson's ingenuity may be in order. For *The Haddington Masque* (1608) the setting "was a high, steepe, red cliffe, aduancing it selfe into the cloudes, figuring the place, from whence (as I haue beene, not fabulously, informed) the honourable family of the RADCLIFFES first tooke their name. . ." (HS VII, 250: ll. 23-27). It is a commonplace that in his comedies Jonson proved capable of inventing many allusive names, e.g., Pertinax Cob, Lady Centaure, Abel Drugger, and Sir Epicure Mammon. Even in his full-dress memorial poem to Shakespeare he included the now-famous puns on "sporting *Kid*" and Shakespeare himself, who seems "to shake a Lance" in his "true-filed" lines (HS VIII, 391-392: ll. 30, 68-69). Not surprisingly, the King and his court approved this sort of thing. When James first heard a sermon by Dr. Richard Field, Chaplain in Ordinary to Elizabeth and later to himself, he is said to have exclaimed that here, indeed, was a Field for God to dwell in (William J. Thoms, ed., *Anecdotes and Traditions* [1839], p. 13). See T. Meier, "The Naming of Characters in Jonson's Comedies," *English Studies in Africa*, VII (1964), 88-95.
133. An apposite literary manifestation of name-linkage occurs in *Edward the Second* when the monarch, addressing his minion, identifies himself as, "Thy friend, thy self, another Gaveston!" (I.i.142, in *The Plays of Christopher Marlowe*, ed. Roma Gill [Oxford, 1971], p. 262).
One should not expect to prove anything in such a matter, but as peripheral evidence one might consider also the following anonymous poem, apparently

faction in using such a "linking" name to emphasize the nature of the two quite different (if not really antithetic) realms which are represented in the masque, each of them headed by a Charles. Or, to come at the same suggestion from yet another direction, perhaps assigning Buckingham the name of the King could be viewed as a commentary on the King's sharing of too much royal power. As Jonson's patroness the Countess of Bedford put it in 1623, "those that are nearest the well-head know not with what bucket to draw for themselves or their freinds."[134] In other words one presumably might have wondered which of these "Charleses" really was "Captain."

Then again, and more obviously, the name "Charles" could have been a means of linking the favorite and the Prince, James's two very different "sons," his "sweet boys, and dear venturous knights," as he called them a couple of years later.[135] James was known to call Buckingham his bastard brat, and Buckingham often addressed James as "Dad." Thomas Middleton, viewing the situation from a distance in his *Game at Chess*, referred to the favorite and the Prince as "Two Princelye Peices."[136] Equally to the point, the young men's own gestures toward kinship are suggested by the names they chose when starting out on Charles's courting expedition into Spain. Both donned false beards and called themselves Smith—Tom and John. The friendship which developed between them grew greater still, of course, with the passing of the years, but in 1621 Charles already felt close to George. "I defy thee," he wrote in November, "in being more mine than I am, Thy constant, loving friend...."[137] Already

---

written somewhat later in James's reign and making a mockery of the idea of a unifying love between James and his favorite:

To the Duke of Buckingham

The king loves you, you him;
Both love the same;
You love the king, he you;
Both Buckingham.
Of sports the king loves games,
Of games the duke;
Of all men you; and you
Solely, for your looke.

(Fairholt, p. 5)

134. *Calendar of State Papers, Domestic . . . 1619–1623*, ed. Mary Anne Everett Green (1858), X, 569.
135. Halliwell-Phillips, II, 166.
136. IV.iv.104, ed. R. C. Bald (Cambridge, 1929), p. 106.
137. *The Letters Speeches and Proclamations of King Charles I*, ed. Sir Charles Petrie (New York, 1968; 1st ed., 1935), p. 6. Charles's relationship with George,

it was obvious that England probably would be left someday in the hands of this strongly contrasting pair of "princes." Furthermore, viewing the same point from a still more negative angle, one might say that well before 1621 Buckingham had become a sort of "Charles" (and therefore to some extent displaced the Prince) by commanding the King's deepest love and taking into his own upstart hands a variety of powers which were certainly princely in everything but name.

A third suggestion becomes possible if we combine the first and second ones here. In being called Captain Charles, Buckingham was linked to both the royal father *and* the royal son (one a "Captain," the other a "Charles"), who had themselves been linked by Jonson as "Charleses" in his Welsh masque. Deplorable as the matter may be, Buckingham's real position was something like that of a triumvir. If Jonson had some such subtle point as this in mind, then he has implied a very great deal, indeed.

The foregoing are only suggestions, however. The fact is that the presence of the name "Charles" in the masque remains a problem to be solved. Though the point has not been recognized, it is a problem which lingers even if one takes the conventional route of believing that Jonson originally meant the Prince to play the gypsy Captain, for in order to believe this one must overlook the fact that the role was better suited to the man who played it than to any other man then alive. One well might suggest that since Jonson was the man he was, the correspondence between Buckingham and his role, between dancer and dance, is not likely to have been a coincidence.[138]

Information concerning the rest of the players in the masque is fragmentary, but the main point to bear in mind is that the cast consisted chiefly of Buckingham, his family, and his friends.

The Second Gypsy was played by William, Baron Feilding, the husband of Buckingham's sister Susanna. Though he had married Susanna at a time when the prospects of neither were great, Nichols

---

however, still had its ups and downs. In July, shortly before the masque, the two men quarreled over the appointment of a new Bishop. Before the month was over, fortunately, the great peace-maker managed to restore peace between them.

138. With Charles as an auditor, by the way, there is no problem in the otherwise problematic lines from Song 2 (after the gypsies metamorphose) which go thus: "Vertue! his kingly vertue which did merit/ This isle intire! *and you are to inherit* [italics added]" (B 948–949). To give this visual meaning the Jackman needed only to bow toward the Prince, or perhaps step over to where he sat in honor at the edge of the playing area.

reports, doubtless accurately, that Feilding had his alliance with the Villiers family to thank for his elevation to the Barony in 1620 and to the Earldom of Denbigh in 1622.[139] As a gypsy Feilding was entrusted with telling not only the important fortune of Prince Charles, but also that of Lady Purbeck, the beautiful young wife of his brother-in-law John. In fact it turns out that his verbal energies, like those of Buckingham, were reserved mainly for telling fortunes. Otherwise he spoke a scant four lines, two before the metamorphosis (by means of a horse-whore's pun he told what lay in Jack Cockrell's future) and two afterward.

The Third Gypsy was Endymion Porter. Appointed as a boy to the post of page in the house of the great Conde de Olivares, Porter had been reared in Spain. In Wilson's words, he acquired the language of that land, "but found no other *Fortune* there, then brought him over to be Mr. *Edward Villers* his man, in *Fleet-street*, . . . before either the Marquess or his Master were acceptable at *White-Hall.*"[140] After serving Edward, one of Buckingham's half-brothers, for several years, Porter entered the favorite's own household in 1617 or early 1618. Then in 1619 he married Olivia Boteler, daughter of Sir John Boteler and Buckingham's half-sister, Elizabeth.[141] According to one of his biographers, "Thanks to Buckingham, Endymion's new relations formed or were to form an influential group. His father-in-law was made a baronet in 1620 and, eight years later, was raised to the peerage," though "Sir John's only distinction . . . lay in his having married Buckingham's sister." [142] Porter himself diplomatically named his first child George and continued to advance. Some time in 1621 he was chosen to enter the service of Prince Charles as a Groom of the Bedchamber, and in 1623—doubtless partly for his knowledge of Spanish—he accompanied the Prince and the favorite when Charles went courting in Spain. Certain dates are hard to come by in Porter's career, but it is of interest to find that for a while during his attachment to Buckingham's household he served as the favorite's own Master of the Horse, no insignificant post considering Buckingham's involve-

139. John Nichols, *The Progresses, Processions, and Magnificent Festivities of King James the First* (1828), vol. IV, a part of vol. III, p. 688. "Sue" is named by the Fourth Gypsy in the fortune spoken to her mother (B 442).
140. Wilson, p. 225.
141. Gervas Huxley, *Endymion Porter: The Life of a Courtier 1587–1649* (1959), p. 42, says 1619; Dorothea Townshend, *Life and Letters of Mr. Endymion Porter* (1897), p. 14, says 1619 or 1620.
142. Huxley, p. 42.

ment with horses. He even managed some of Buckingham's finances. Despite the fact that he himself finally died a bankrupt, it is pleasant to learn that many years after his master's death Porter charged his sons in his will (he died in August, 1649) to "respect the children and family of my Lord Duke of Buckingham, deceased, to whom I owe all the happiness I had in the world."[143]

A witty fellow who found himself involved in Buckingham's entertainments, Porter took on the third most demanding role in the gypsy masque (the other two being those of the Patrico and Jackman). Not only does it appear that he had nearly twice as many lines as any of the other non-professionals; he was also the first of the courtier gypsies to speak. To Porter were assigned the third and fourth fortunes. After the King's and Prince's hands had been read, Porter's part required him to honor Buckingham's Kate and then her stepmother Cecily, Countess of Rutland, the first rather jocularly and at considerable length, the second more briefly and sedately.[144]

In addition to taking a prominent place in the masque, Porter may have been called on to speak still other lines by Jonson during this same royal visit to Burley. Always printed along with the masque, the welcoming *"Speech at the Kings Entrance at Burly"* is clearly not part of the dramatic entertainment given on the evening of 3 August. By that Friday night the King had been feasting and hunting at Burley for several days, and it would have been absurd to bid him then to enter Buckingham's house. Modern students have noted this point, but they have been singularly incurious about it. Surely the speech was written to be delivered when the King first arrived, but who spoke it? The address concludes, "You'l find within, no thanks, or vowes, there shorter, / For having trusted

143. Quoted by Townshend, p. 236.
144. In Kate's fortune we have another instance of Jonson's witty allusiveness. When he has the gypsy address her as "Face of a rose" (B 344), a modern reader is likely to see no more than a conventional compliment, unless he happens to know that Katherine had particular cause to be proud of her Ros or Roos blood. For about two hundred and fifty years her home, Belvoir Castle, had been held by the Roos family. In 1508, on the death of Edmund, Lord Roos, the family estates went to Edmund's sisters and co-heirs, and it was not until Eleanor, the elder, married Sir Robert Manners that Belvoir came into the hands of the Manners family. Naturally Roos continued to be an important name in the family. As we have seen earlier, both of Kate's brothers had, at the time of their death, borne the title Lord Roos.

Jonson's special care for such matters was in part a reflection of the interest of his time. It is likely to be more than coincidence that Katherine Manners herself bore the Christian name she did; the arms of Belvoir are *azure* with a catherine-wheel *or* (see W. A. Carrington, "The Early Lords of Belvoir," *Journal of the British Archaeological Association*, N.S. VII [1901], 299–326).

thus much to his [Buckingham's] Porter" (B 26–27). Does "Porter" mean "porter"? Perhaps it does, but one might suggest also that Jonson is telling us here, by means of a pun, what was perfectly obvious to those who heard the lines, namely, that they were delivered by Buckingham's favorite and best-known Porter, Endymion. For what it is worth, we find Jonson indulging in precisely this sort of name-play within the text of the gypsy masque. Ludovick Stuart, the son of James's early favorite, was now Lord Steward of the King's Household, and Jonson has the Fourth Gypsy conclude his fortune at Windsor thus: "To proue a false Steward you'll find much adoe, / Being a true one by blood and by office too" (W 466–467).[145] Furthermore, the position which Porter held or recently had held in Buckingham's household made him a thoroughly appropriate spokesman to be stationed at the outer gate—perhaps near the porter's lodge—with a few words of warm welcome.

The Fourth Gypsy—the one who steals Puppy's purse—may have been Buckingham's brother John, Viscount Purbeck. Orgel regards such a matching of player and role as "very far from being demonstrable" and "at most a convenient hypothesis," and yet still, after exploring the matter as best he can, he accepts the hypothesis.[146] There are several causes for uncertainty. Aside from Buckingham himself, the other "son" of the Countess to whom the Fourth Gypsy himself refers could presumably be any one or another of Buckingham's brothers, including the Countess's son-in-*law*, Feilding. Furthermore, that "son" could have played either the Fourth or Fifth Gypsy, or the Second (if he were Feilding), or, conceivably, a gypsy who had no lines or number at all. Nevertheless, when it comes to conjecturing who played the Fourth, John seems the

---

145. Of course one has other evidence that this sort of wit is by no means unique. In December of the same year, after the Commons had written its Protestation, the Privy Council sent for Sir Edward Coke (Lady Purbeck's father), deprived him of his place at the Council table, and sent him to the Tower. Catherine Drinker Bowen notes that "He was locked in Lord Cobham's old quarters. One of the rooms had been used as a kitchen; as Coke approached with his guards he saw something scrawled on the door: 'This room wants a cook' " (*The Lion and the Throne: The Life and Times of Sir Edward Coke* [Boston, 1957; copyright, 1956], p. 454).

Another example, also culinary, appears in Aston Cokayne's *Masque Presented at Bretbie* (1640; pub. 1658), in which a satyr is given an invitation to leave his cave and join the Bretbie household. He replies, in part, that he would indeed enjoy "the stately Banquets"; hence he says, "Spite of the Fates, and *Grecia*'s best Protector,/ I'le be *Achilles*, and o'recome by *Hector*" (p. 122). A marginal note explains that Hector is "*The Cooks Name*." Clearly the allusion is so intimate that Cokayne feared it would be missed even by contemporaries.

146. *Complete Masques*, p. 495.

brother who most readily fits what we know of the case, and perhaps not least because his wife and mother-in-law were present. This "perhaps" is particularly sensitive. However proper it may have been for Sir John, his wife, and Lady Hatton to appear together at Buckingham's house, it should be remembered that the younger lady had been virtually sold to the Villierses by her ambitious old father, Sir Edward Coke, over the objections of both ladies.[147] John proved to be a devoted husband, but he was some ten years older than the Lady Frances, and in 1620—the year before the masque— he had had the first of his intermittent bouts with mental illness.[148] On the other hand, it should also be noted that the Fourth Gypsy is given but a single fortune to tell, that of the Countess of Buckingham, the one lady present who might be presumed to have most sympathy for any one of Buckingham's brothers; and with her fortune spoken by one of her boys (John, let us say), that lady was less likely to notice that hers is the only one laced liberally with dubious compliments. The Fifth Gypsy, to be sure, speaks still fewer lines than the Fourth, and no writer or casting director would have chosen to put John's mind under too much pressure, but the Fifth Gypsy's role, the smallest speaking part in the entire masque, consists almost entirely of Lady Hatton's fortune. No matter what the words of that fortune might be, they are not likely to have had their best effect if spoken to her by Viscount Purbeck. All in all, we may do well to fall back on the hypothesis that Purbeck played the Fourth Gypsy.

The role of the Fifth may have been intended for a lord named Gervase. Who he was or whether he played the part we do not know. All we can say for sure is that in the same passage in which Jonson refers obscurely to some service done for the King by

147. Lady Hatton (who still used her first husband's name instead of Coke's) made no bones about her marital strife. Strong-minded and rich, she is told by the Fifth Gypsy, "Others fortunes may be showne,/ You are builder of your owne. . ." (B 473–474).

148. One reason for doubting John's ability to perform in the gypsy masque is that in October, 1621, we find Chamberlain remarking that "Viscount Purbecks witts be out of the way" (II, 402). The chronology in the case is obscure, but Lady Purbeck certainly had a lover later on. To Robert Howard, fifth son of the first Earl of Suffolk, she bore a son in October, 1624. (As Jonson has the Second Gypsy tell Lady Purbeck, "You will turne all hearts to tinder" [B 467].) She was brought before the Court of High Commission and, in her first trial, sentenced to public excommunication. In her second trial she was fined £500 and ordered to do public penance (walk barefoot in a white sheet from Paul's Cross to the Savoy, and stand on view before the church). Instead, she managed to disappear from sight for a while.

"Captaine Charles," he alludes also to "Gypsie Gervice" (B 80). Perhaps he tosses the name out as an allusion to be caught by the knowing, or perhaps there really was a gentleman named Gervase who entered presently in the Captain's entourage. Orgel, in any case, has offered for consideration the name of Sir Gervase Clifton, Bart. (1587–1666).[149] Clifton would have been a suitably well-born neighbor of Buckingham (he lived some twenty-five miles from Burley, seventeen from Belvoir), and he certainly was known to both James and Charles. A spirited, red-headed fellow, he is said to have been sound of body, cheerful, and facetious—altogether a good masquer, one might suppose. It argues well for his spirit that by the time he reached old age he was noted not merely for his courtesy and generosity, the usual virtues of a virtuous baronet, but also for marrying seven wives. If he did appear as the Fifth Gypsy, though, apparently he was the only one in the group who lacked familial ties with Buckingham. On the other hand, with only twelve lines *in toto*, his role scarcely would have been large enough to dim the fact that most of the gypsies are essentially Buckinghamians. And, after all, even No. 5, whoever he was, danced under Buckingham's captaincy.

Though the unifying effect of Buckingham's captaincy is obvious enough, it is tempting to step off the path just a moment at this point in order to consider how such an effect might have been enhanced by the unifying effect of the dance on the players. The Burley performers doubtless demonstrated their skills in several ways in their several dances, but group dances in general tend to smooth out the individual characteristics of those dancing them. This is one way they achieve some harmony. Now, if one takes seriously a hint which Jonson drops early in the masque, one might suppose that the gypsies are likely at some point to have performed a version of the dance known as the "brawl" (B 226). If in fact they did, Jonson would thereby seem to have demonstrated once again the value of his painstaking concern for details. Readers must miss any such effect or merely guess about it, but in a brawl or bransle (the word comes from the French *branler*, to sway from side to side) the dancers imitate their leaders as in the game follow-the-leader. If in fact James's gypsies did dance the brawl—a dance much in

---

149. *Complete Masques*, pp. 496–497. Some interesting biographical information appears in "An Humble Oblation to the Pretiouse Memory of . . . Sʳ: Gervas Clifton Knᵗ: & Baronet," in MS Ashmole 36, 205ʳ–206ʳ (Bodleian).

vogue then at Whitehall—there is no doubt whatever that the main leading dancer, setting the pattern for all the rest, showing the way, would have been Buckingham as Captain. It would be very like Jonson to make a popular dance symbolic, and it may be that he has done so here.[150]

Having taken notice of Gypsies Nos. 1 through 5, we now must face the fact that the total number of gypsies in the masque is something of a problem. To begin with the known, we are told that the Captain dances in with *"sixe more"* besides himself (B 93; W 86). If, as seems probable, we may trust this statement, then some of the gypsies never speak a line (a plausible assumption in a masque), and appear merely to dance and fill out the scene. If this stage direction is accurate, furthermore, the probable meaning of *"more"* is *"more than* the two gypsies who have opened the show," since those two are already "on" when the Captain and his six *"more"* companions enter. In other words, despite some puzzles in the numbering of the gypsies and the labels of their speeches, the Patrico and Jackman may probably be regarded as (though they are not so termed) an Eighth Gypsy and a Ninth.

With or without numbers, the two performers who played the Jackman and Patrico were together responsible for speaking or singing nearly half the lines in the masque.[151] If we may infer the nature of their talents from the demands of the script, they must have made a pleasant and striking contrast to each other. Except for the first and third speeches—important ones, obviously—it appears that the Jackman was required only to sing. After asking for his guitar, which he soon begins to play, and calling for his "Chiefe" to enter (B 90–91), the Jackman expresses himself entirely by means of a wide variety of songs. In order to be successful, the player who

150. All this is highly conjectural, but one reason the dance may have seemed appropriate for gypsies is that the English word "brawl" had connotations of rowdiness. There is considerable variation possible within the brawl, however; Thoinot Arbeau (anagram for Jehan Tabourot) is said to list twenty-four varieties in his *Orchésographie* (1588). See Jeffrey Pulver, *A Dictionary of Old English Music & Musical Instruments* (1923); Mabel Dolmetsch, *Dances of England and France from 1450 to 1600* (1949); and Willi Apel, *Harvard Dictionary of Music* (2nd ed., Cambridge, Mass., 1969). I am assuming here, of course, that it is not necessary to argue for the symbolic aspect of at least some dances in masques. As a sample piece of evidence one might cite the dance in *Hymenaei* which the performers *"ended in manner of a chaine, linking hands,"* upon which Jonson had Reason observe, *"SVch was the Golden Chaine let downe from Heaven"* (HS VII, 221: ll. 317-320).

151. According to my estimate the Patrico has 271 lines; the Jackman, 181; the Third Gypsy, 100; Puppy, 75; and Buckingham, 60.

took this role would have had to be both an instrumentalist and a vocalist, and one wonders if indeed he was, as George Watson Cole suggests, Nicholas Lanier.[152]

According to Roger North, Lanier was a composer, singer, and lutanist, altogether "a very Ingenious vertuoso."[153] Moreover, Buckingham paid him £200 on 6 August, the day after the Belvoir performance.[154] It has been assumed that this very large sum was a payment for composing the music of the masque. Possibly it was, but possibly also this is not the whole truth. For one thing, Robert Johnson, who had been contributing to court masques at least since Jonson's *Masque of Queens* (1609), has been credited with writing at least some of the music for *The Gypsies Metamorphos'd*.[155] Since there seems to be no reason to doubt that Johnson contributed something here, we are faced with the question of whether Lanier would have been paid so much as £200 for writing just a part (even most) of the music for the masque. It was an era of lavish spending, but even in his heyday as a favorite under Charles I, Lanier's total income, including livery, is said to have been only about £272 a year.[156] One might reasonably suspect, therefore, that he also wrote

152. Thinking that Lanier probably appeared *somewhere* in the show, Cole also makes the less plausible suggestion that he may have taken the Patrico's role (p. 9). This would have necessitated finding someone else (someone more appropriate than Lanier?) to take the role of the musical Jackman.

153. From MS notes published as *The Musicall Gramarian*, ed. Hilda Andrews, foreword by Sir Richard Terry (1925), p. 19. North records how Lanier, in the reign of Charles, would sometimes sing a favorite song for his King, while Charles "stood next, with his hand upon his shoulder" (p. 20).

154. Not 21 July, as a hasty glance at the head of the account sheet might suggest (Public Record Office, State Papers, July–Sept., 1621, CXXII, 32).

155. See John P. Cutts, "Robert Johnson: King's Musician in His Majesty's Public Entertainment," *Music and Letters*, XXXVI (1955), 110–125, and "Robert Johnson and the Court Masque," *Music and Letters*, XLI (1960), 111–126. In the former Cutts affirms that the Johnson song settings which survive come mainly from the period 1607–17; "these show distinctly, moreover, that during this time Robert Johnson was writing incidental music continuously for the Blackfriars productions of the King's Men Company of Players, and for this company only" (p. 110). Hence Johnson's association with masques seems the more natural. Also a lutanist, Johnson served in The King's Musick from 1604 to 1633 (Walter L. Woodfill, *Musicians in English Society from Elizabeth to Charles I* [New York, 1969; 1st printing, 1953], p. 301). His setting of "From the Famous Peak of Darby" (sung just after the Captain and "*six more*" gypsies enter) is scored for *cantus* and *bassus* duet, however, and Ben Jonson's text calls for a solo from the Jackman. Presumably the song could have been shared in performance by the Jackman and Patrico, or it could have been set twice by Johnson (once, perhaps, subsequent to the performance). At present it is impossible to say whether or not this version was the original. On the other hand, Johnson is credited also with the last of the five dances in the masque. Cf. Levitan, pp. 239–245.

156. Woodfill, p. 180.

some other music for the King's 1621 visit to Burley. A good deal of music was performed at great banquets and ceremonial events, and even if ready-made music were suitable for most of these, a royal visit such as the present one might well require that some be new. There is also reason to think that other special entertainments besides Jonson's masque were performed during the several days of James's stay. Some of these may have called for additional original music.[157] Perhaps still more important for us at the moment, however, is the fact that Lanier was a singer. Most notably, he had performed in Jonson's *Lovers Made Men* (1617), where he sang, according to Jonson, "(*after the Italian manner*) Stylo recitativo."[158] Even after the facts are all drawn together, it must be confessed, they are too few for us to see or say with certainty in this matter, but it may well be that the £200 which Lanier received that August—when Jonson received half as much—reflects the favor accorded not merely to a skilled composer, but to a skilled performer as well. Granted our present state of knowledge, in short, it is possible to suppose that Nicholas Lanier, the lutanist, singer, and composer—"a very Ingenious vertuoso"—did, indeed, take the role of the guitar-playing Jackman, a character who expresses himself almost entirely by means of song, and one whom Jonson in his text describes as a "sweet singer" (B 121).

The contrasting part of the Patrico calls for skills that are, on the one hand, more strictly verbal and, on the other, more pantomimic. It is the Patrico who oversees the robbing of the clowns as well as, by "*legerdemaine*" (B 775–776), the nimble return of the pitiful loot. At Windsor he may have attempted more. After the Patrico has described some particular gypsy feats, Townshead exclaims, "Admirable trickes, and he do's hem all *se defendendo*. . ." (W 1060–61), which sounds as though "he do's hem all" before the very eyes of clowns and audience alike. As for verbal skills, he not only speaks a good many trickily intricate lines but he also delivers the inserted ten-line fortune of the late-comer, Frances, Lady Exeter ("Madam, we knew of your comming so late,/ We could not well

157. Chamberlain says that during the visit there "was great provision of playes, maskes and all maner of entertainment" (II, 396).
158. HS VII, 454: ll. 26–27. According to Emslie, what Lanier is more likely to have written for Jonson's masques—this one and others in the 1614–22 period—is not recitatives as we know them but declamatory "ayres." ("Nicholas Lanier's Innovations in English Song," *Music and Letters*, XLI [1960], 22). As further evidence of Lanier's virtuoso qualities, one might note that Jonson says he designed the scenery for *Lovers Made Men*.

fit you a nobler fate/ Then what you have ready made. . ." [B 408–410]). It appears that he even sang a bit. We must have a case here, then, of a talented, quick-witted actor playing the part of a talented, quick-witted rogue. Jonson, in fact, draws attention to the Patrico's verbal responsibility as well as to his place in the gypsy scheme of things when he has the Patrico define himself as the

> . . . bringer
> Of bound to the border,
> The rule, and recorder,
> And mouth or your [the gypsies'] order. . . .
>   (B 124–127)

Though the new Bishop of London, George Montaigne, was at Burley that night, we have seen already that the Patrico was pointed out as the "Priest of the game,/ And Prelate of the same" (B 128–129). Hence the appropriateness of the Windsor addition which had him pronounce the blessing on James. Hence, too, the fact that all along he has been allowed to function as a sort of master of ceremonies. If one has the impression that the role calls for something of a good-natured father figure, a skilled professional who really was at least somewhat older than the other performers, that impression is not diminished when Puppy exclaims, "Say you so old Gypsie? 'slid these go to't in rime, this is better then canting by t'one halfe" (B 572–573). But the relative age of the performer is conjectural; his ripeness is all.

Raising the apparent total of gypsies to fourteen were the children who entered at the opening of the masque. To fill these non-speaking roles the casting director needed only to round up five children who were attached in some way to the Buckingham clan. We do not know who they were. Buckingham had no offspring yet, though his doting Kate was pregnant. As a matter of fact, Jonson had the Third Gypsy refer to her current task of tending the "fruit" of her "belly" (B 379), and James himself during his visit wrote a *Votum* wishing that his two favorite Villierses might soon be blessed "with fruit delicious sweet & fayre."[159]

Of the children who appeared in the masque, one in particular was singled out as the son of "a kinsman of our Captains," "one o' the blood" (B 41–42, 56–57). This child proves to be the subject of some twenty-four or more lines in the very opening speech of the

159. Included in Craigie, II, 177.

masque. He therefore is important. Although a few of the things we are told about him are obviously meant to be illustrative of the children as a group, Jonson chose to give a miniature biography of *this* child. How much of it is facetious? He is said to have been born in Flintshire, Wales. Is this because many gypsies were supposed to come from Wales, and Flint afforded Jonson an easy pun on striking a spark? The child's mother, who is said to have run away with a relative of the Captain, is supposed to be the daughter of a man who at that time was sheriff of the county, but who now is a justice. The father disapproved of the match, pursued the runaways to the marches, caught up with them in Chester, and finally was reconciled with them there. Now their child is seven years old, and apparently because he has been rather sickly (he has not "thriv'd"), he looks as if he is not yet five.

At the risk of seeming hopelessly literal-minded, one might wonder which, if any, of these details may really point to a particular child "o' the blood." What is the purpose of specifying that a gypsy seven-year-old is the size of a five-year-old—it does not do much to create a "gypsy" atmosphere—unless the performer was really a normal-sized five-year-old or a puny seven-year-old? What is the point of mentioning these ages if he actually were ten or four? Probably the child performer *was* about five or about seven, and more probably the former, since Jonson is not likely to have insulted a seven-year-old scion of the kindred by saying that he looked merely five.

Jonson gives a good many hints here which someone sometime may follow to a sure conclusion. Meanwhile the most likely nominee would seem to be a boy whose father took the significant role of the Second Gypsy, and whose mother was referred to by name in the text (B 442). His older brother was about thirteen, too old to be tied by scarves "in the infants equipage" (B 61), but he himself was five—the "right" age—in 1621. Moreover, he bore the Christian name not only of his maternal grandfather, but also of his powerful uncle, the host and Captain, George Villiers. Young George Feilding, second son of Buckingham's only full sister, was very probably an important little person, indeed a "famous impe" (B 49), at Burley on the night of 3 August 1621. The following year, on 22 November, at the age of six, he was raised to the peerage: he was created Baron Feilding of Lacaghe and Viscount Callan. Then three years later, when still but a child, he was made a Knight of the

Bath.[160] All in all it now appears hard to imagine a more appropriate
child to function as, so to speak, the Captain of the Children.[161]

Whoever the various children were, Jonson did well to include
them. It was pleasant for their parents to see them playing in costume before the King, and for Jonson's thematic purposes they
were a wonderful means to achieve an air of multeity. The texts do
not indicate their exit, but probably it comes early, at the point
where the Jackman requests "roome for our Chiefe" (B 90–91).
Probably this line was a cue to clear the floor for the dance which
immediately follows. Within the space of a few moments, in any
case, the acting area at Burley displayed nine or so adult gypsies,
five child gypsies, two horses, and miscellaneous stolen farm animals
and fowl. Hence the force of the line, "Thus the'Ægyptians throng
in clusters" (B 99).

The text itself of the Windsor version tells us that the hobbinolls
of the masque were played by knights, and the wenches by pages
(W 1112–15). Together they provided a contrasting village or
country milieu in which Jonson could display his gypsies at work.
We know the names of none of these performers. The names they
assumed—and Jonson usually thought about such things—may suggest the youth of the men who played Cockrell and Puppy. As a
matter of fact, a few informed guesses might be made about their
identities, but they would be no more than guesses, finally, and they
would not advance our case here. That they were not clods we
may be sure. *Their* inner essence was not at stake. (Jonson, by the
way, had years before had Catiline equate "clods" with "the people" [HS V, 490: III.648].) They were simply humorous touch-
stones to indicate the quality of the invading band, the principal
masquers. Jonson's interest in the clowns is indicated, nonetheless,
not only by the care with which he created their parts, but also by

160. See *Collins's Peerage of England*, augmented by Sir Egerton Brydges
(1812), III, esp. p. 275.

161. A pursuit of the Welsh clues in the boy's background leads in a different
direction. May we safely forget that his mother is said to be a Flintshire girl (as
Susanna Villiers was not), daughter of a man who was sheriff at the time of her
"elopement" and "now" is a justice? The only man who fits the latter description
was Sir John Trevor, Sheriff of Flintshire in 1613 and Justice in 1621. And Trevor
had four daughters—Magdalen, Mary, Margaret, and Dorothy. But here the trail
cools. Unlike her sisters, Dorothy appears to have married into a family with court
connections, but Sir John Hanmer came from Flintshire and was unrelated, so far
as I can tell, to the favorite's family. The Trevor-Hanmer union did produce a son,
Thomas, who later was a page at the court of Charles, but in 1621 he was about
nine, a bit old for the imp in the masque. (For information on the four bridegrooms
of Trevor's daughters, and especially on young Thomas, I am grateful to Mr. A. G.
Veysey, County Archivist, Flintshire.)

the attention he gave to revising them. Though the matter seems lightly spontaneous, not labored, we have here as leader of the "clods" one Townshead. As thorough a clown as the rest, Townshead yet bears up his part by venturing "the poore head o'th' towne" (B 626–627) and by balancing the facts that we have also the "head" of the gypsies and the "head" of the court and, hence, the head of all England. That is to say, each group with which we are concerned in the masque has its leader, reminding us unobtrusively but consistently of the concept of hierarchy. Jonson's interest here is shown in other ways, too. Even to begin with, the actor who played Puppy was given more lines than Buckingham. Perhaps Jonson in creating Puppy recalled with some fondness the character he had called Puppy in *Bartholomew Fair* or even, though it raises the problem of chronological priority, that other Puppy in his *Tale of a Tub*, a constable's man whose language likewise savors of the cart. In any event, the actor who played Paul Puppy of the gypsy masque (it is *Ball* Puppy in *The Tale of a Tub*) became a spokesman for all the goodhearted innocents of England's countryside when he said,

> I ha' lost my purse too, and more in it then
> Ile speak of, but e're I'de crye for't as
> thou dost— Much good doe 'hem with all
> my heart, I doe reverence 'hem for't.
> (B 670–673)

Masked here in more nut-brown mirth than Jonson usually cared to muster is one of his principal points. As Marston put it in *The Malcontent*, "God made honest fools to maintain crafty knaves" (II.v. 98).[162] For our present purposes we need to know only that the clowns and wenches were played by Englishmen.

vii. *The Metamorphosis*

> *It is not pould'ring, perfuming, and euery day smelling of the taylor, that conuerteth to a beautiful obiect: but a mind, shining through any sute, which needes no false light either of riches, or honors to helpe it.*
> *Cynthia's Revels*, dedication[163]

Most ordinary Englishmen, the Puppies and Clods of the realm, are likely to remain ordinary forever. Jonson's bumpkins entertain the

162. *The Malcontent*, ed. M. L. Wine (Lincoln, Neb., 1964), p. 55.
163. HS IV, 33.

idea that they might turn gypsies, and the gypsies speak of working on some of their courtly auditors so as to make *them* turn gypsies, but neither of these ideas comes to anything. Both are peripheral. The titular emphasis on the gypsies' change is reinforced within the masque.

The fact remains, though, that the word "metamorphosed" calls attention to a change which Jonson is at no great pains to explain.[164] One is inclined to ask, why the discrepancy between action and explanation? Why do the gypsies metamorphose? Herford and Simpson say in their essay on Jonson's masques that "Dramatic reason, in truth, there is none; but [the lords] . . . were wanted for the Main Masque, and the actual situation emerged through the thin woof of fiction" (HS II, 315). Jonson's epilogue, tacked on to the Windsor version of the masque, gives his editors a reason for this view. Jonson says there that the cause of the metamorphosis is "a thing not touchd at by our poet" (W 1275). Nevertheless, a token dramatic reason *is* given in the masque. The Patrico, who has already impressed the clowns with his legerdemain, says he can do better still. Since his victims have proved to be an appreciative audience, he will show them a yet more remarkable *gypsy trick*. Not only will he show them the King and Prince; he will make "*The Gypsies were here,/ Like Lords to appeare. . .*" (B 902–903). The thinness of dramatic motivation is notable, nonetheless, and all the more so insofar as Herford and Simpson are correct in saying, earlier in their masque essay, speaking of *The Hue and Cry after Cupid* (1608), "Jonson was obviously bent upon eliminating the crude unmotivated sequences of so many royal entertainments" (HS II, 277). Jonson's practice was not consistent, however, and Herford and Simpson themselves make the still surer point that his practice in creating courtly entertainments "is so free from the vices of system and the grooves of habit that his technique is hard to grasp" (II, 334). It would be wrong, then, to say too quickly that Jonson was "regressing" in the matter of motivation in the gypsy masque. If he was not, though, what was he doing?

The question of why the gypsies change may well have arisen both during and after that first performance at Burley, and perhaps at rehearsals as well. Furthermore, some of the more acute listeners, possibly some of the performers, may have put the question to the one

164. The form of the title which I have used is that in Greg's version, the conjectural "original." See Cole, pp. 5–6.

man who could answer it, much as Prince Henry had asked for some light on Jonson's learned allusions after *The Masque of Queens* had been performed. The best reason for thinking that some of Jonson's auditors were curious is that the various elements in a good masque were supposed to mean something; and the best reason for thinking that someone really did express his curiosity in this particular instance is that something moved Jonson to add a handful of explanations for the metamorphosis in the Windsor epilogue. If his aim in the masque was anything like the critical one delineated in the present study, he could not have given a straight answer. Besides, it is a poet more rare than Jonson who would be quick to give his public a flat statement of what he has already said figuratively and to the best of his ability in verse. On the other hand, Jonson did address himself in the epilogue to the question, Why do the gypsies change? He even drew attention to the fact that in the masque itself he had left the matter obscure. "Good Ben slept there," he suggested, "or else forgot to shewe it" (W 1276). One of the most careful writers of his own or any day, and a man who took extraordinary pride in his craft, has presumably neglected to think of a reason for the gypsies' change, or, if he did think of one, then he "forgot to shewe it"! Despite the shadow here of a comparison with Homer (*quandoque bonus dormitat Homerus*), this is witty, self-deprecatory evasion. Its very ineptness calls attention to the fact that Jonson probably knew perfectly well what he was doing.

In the epilogue he expresses three basic answers to the problem. The first, weakest, and most elaborately expressed is simply that the transformation was effected by a ball of soap (to wash off the walnut stain) and a change of costume. This gets us nowhere, as Jonson well knew. It is just a bit of information as to how the performers put on the show. A second answer is that the transformation, aided by "a barbor and a taylor" (W 1290)—the makeup man and costumer—has been effected by the "power of poesie" (W 1289). But how convincing is this? Such an explanation might be fine for some masque concerned with Apollo and the muses, but poesy is not a subject of *The Gypsies Metamorphos'd*. It is only a vehicle, and therefore akin to the walnut juice and costumes. Nor is the great classicist likely to have used "power of poesie" to allude to the powers afforded by poetic license. This second answer, then, is a second witty evasion. The third answer which Jonson offers is much the best, and yet even it is insufficient by itself to carry the weight of the whole piece: the gypsies change, says Jonson, because it is their normal custom to "disguise ... habit and ... face" (W 1287). Of course they are aided this time by a barber and tailor, but any and all gypsies are *supposed* to be able to change forms. Even Clod knows they are called moon-men. For some reason the Patrico, as we have seen, goes so far as to imply that he would be willing to take personal credit for making the gypsies "appear" like lords, and as their "priest" perhaps he is the obvious one to oversee any "transubstantiation" which occurs. But one should not confuse miracles with gypsy tricks. Despite the Patrico's patter, disguise is an everyday aspect of gypsy "magic." In other words, the Patrico's prior explanation (it is all a gypsy trick) is quite close to this third answer (it is a matter of gypsy disguise). But the more important point to notice is that the gypsies are said to remain gypsies even after gypsy trickery has been expended to make them seem otherwise. A metamorphosed gypsy, says the epilogue, "takes on a *false person*" (W 1288; italics added). If there is any allegorical point here, it lies near the surface and is close to what Spenser is getting at in *The Faerie Queene* when he asks,

> What man so wise, what earthly witt so ware,
> As to discry the crafty cunning traine,
> By which deceipt doth maske in visour faire,
> And cast her colours died deepe in graine,
> To seeme like truth, whose shape she well can faine,
> And fitting gestures to her purpose frame;
> The guiltlesse man with guile to entertaine?
>
> (I.vii.l)

All things considered, this third answer, that crafty gypsies have assumed a fair new guise, is a very bold one. It has considerable appropriateness and takes us close to one aspect of Jonson's complex truth. If we did not know as much as we do, it would have to suffice.

Jonson was constrained to write obscurely, but the problem we face may be put quite clearly: if something more than cunning and craft were necessary to complete the gypsies' change, what might that something be? The answer most likely to be correct is so conventional that one should be permitted to echo Buckingham's question to the King:

Could any doubt, that saw this hand,
Or who you are, or what command
   You have upon the fate of things,
Or would not say you were let downe
From Heave'n. . . ?
(B 288–292)

Jonson had been writing variations on this theme ever since the beginning of his career as a masque-writer—even before then, if one include the effect of Queen Elizabeth's presence on Macilente in the court production of *Every Man Out of His Humour* (1599).[165] In *The Masque of Blackness* (1605), his first formal masque, he had presented James with a group of Ethiopian ladies whose problem was that they had been turned black by the fires of the sun. Never one to minimize his capabilities, the Sun of Britain was doubtless glad to have Jonson inform the court that James's own "beames" were

. . . of force
To blanch an ÆTHIOPE, and reuiue a *Cor's.*
His light scientiall is, and (past mere nature)
Can salue the rude defects of euery creature.
(HS VII, 177: ll. 254–257)

This was saying rather much. As Dolora Cunningham points out, such a transformation of blackness to beauty "is analogous to that Christian transformation of fallen human nature which was traditionally accomplished by the grace of God, whose special agent the ruling monarch was generally acknowledged to be...."[166] At a less exalted level one might say, with Meagher, that the King's favor "does make a difference: those on whom it shines may meet a gracious reception far beyond the desert of their defective natures, and may be beautified with the honors which James bestowed so freely."[167] *Beautified with honors*: the idea is quite intriguing. Cunningham and Meagher are both correct, of course, and whether one take the high road or the low, the major thing to know is that

165. Jonson's justification of his handling of Macilente is worth remarking: "*There was nothing (in his examin'd* Opinion) *that could more neare or truly exemplifie the power and strength of her Inualuable* Vertues, *than the working of so perfect a* Miracle *on so oppos'd a* Spirit" (HS III, 602–603).
166. "The Jonsonian Masque as a Literary Form," *ELH*, XXII (1955), 123.
167. *Method and Meaning in Jonson's Masques* (Notre Dame, Ind., 1966), p. 111.

probably it *is* the royal presence which provides the masque with its major transforming power and glory. Thus it is, for example, in Jonson's *Masque of Beautie, The Vision of Delight*, and *The Irish Masque*. In the last of these, where there is no such reason as in the gypsy masque to be obscure, the "bard" is quite explicit on the point:

> It is but standing in his eye,
>   You'll feele your selues chang'd by and by,
> Few liue, that know, how quick a spring
>   Workes in the presence of a king. . . .
>   (HS VII, 404: ll. 177–180)

Thus informed, we are better able to catch the implications of a fleeting allusion which Jonson allows himself in the very epilogue of *The Gypsies Metamorphos'd*. In discussing reasons for the metamorphosis and immediately after he has referred to his forgetfulness, he writes, "But least it proue like wonder to the sight/ To see a Gipsie, as an Æthiop, white . . ." (W 1277–78)—and thus invites us to recall any white Ethiopes we may have known. The most famous, of course, appears in that wonderbook of Heliodorus, the *Aethiopica*. Far more germane, however, are the Ethiopes in Jonson's own first masque, those black beauties changed to white by the power of King James.[168] "Good Ben" was about as forgetful this time as an elephant.

One advantage of printing the Porter/porter's welcome to the King with the gypsy masque is that it helps to clarify the quasi-divinity of the King's role as conceived by Jonson. Part of the speech goes thus:

> Welcome, O welcome then, and enter here
> The house your bounty'hath built, and still doth reare,
> With those high favours, and those heap't increases,
> Which shews a hand not griev'd, but when it ceases.
> *The Master is your creature* [italics added]; as the place;
> And eve'ry good about him is your grace. . . .
>   (B 12–17)

At Windsor, where the speech could not be used, the same important idea was, significantly, added to some of Buckingham's lines:

---

168. Herford and Simpson note that the idea of blanching an Ethiopian is based on an ancient proverb (X, 453–454).

And may your goodnes euer finde
In mee, *whome you haue made* [italics added] a minde
  As thanckfull as your owne is large.
(W 316–318)

James had indeed showered Danaean favors on the Villiers family, and as Volpone's Mosca says—Jonson writing the words—gold "transformes/ The most deformed. . . ." In fact, as Volpone himself observes, "Who can get thee [gold],/ He shall be noble, valiant, honest, wise. . . ." At which point Mosca summarizes, "And what he will, sir" (HS V, 25: V.ii.100–101). The pity is that the magnifico and his parasite come so near to voicing the truth. It is all very well to be told that the King "Can salue the rude defects of euery creature," but it is something of a letdown to suspect that worldly goods and positions—"gold"—are the main means of manifesting his power. The welcoming speech at Burley and the gypsy masque reinforce each other, however, in saying as clearly as Jonson could that the master of the house as well as the very house itself is a creation of the King's "bounty" and "favours." (It is more certain that the King created Burley than that the Devil did the Devil's Arse.) A barber and tailor might contribute such ingredients as color and costume, and gypsy tricks might beguile both country and court, but the only alchemist capable of transforming gypsies to courtiers is the King himself.

If we leave gypsies out of the picture, James himself would not have boggled at being assigned transforming or even creative powers. He was King of the realm and could—as he reminded the Commons earlier in 1621—"impart honor to whom he pleases and in what extent he pleases and no man to Question him."[169] Precisely here is one of Jonson's most important points in the gypsy masque. The Lord Chancellor Bacon had spoken of the royal power as *primum mobile*.[170] For better or worse, James was in a position to create. Furthermore, he took particular delight in transforming certain of his subjects into something higher than they had been, much as though he really were scattering some of those sparkles of divinity

---

169. "Notes by Sir Thomas Barrington," *Commons Debates 1621*, ed. Wallace Notestein, Frances Helen Relf, and Hartley Simpson (New Haven, 1935), III, 111.
170. Letter to Buckingham, 20 January 1619, in *The Letters and the Life of Francis Bacon*, ed. James Spedding (1874), VII, 73.

with which he thought himself supplied. As he had told his former favorite, Robert Carr, who was languishing in the Tower in 1621, "all your being, except your breathing and soul, is from me."[171] Carr was, as James put it, his "creature." And so was Buckingham.

For all who cared to read his published words, James had written to Buckingham that *"as the person to whom wee pray ... is our heauenly Father, so am I ... not onely your politike, but also your œconomike Father...."*[172] In discussing Buckingham one early historian wrote that the King meant "to shew his own Power to raise him from nothing...."[173] In Wilson's somewhat less biased words, "the King cast his eye upon a young Gentleman, so rarely *moulded*, that he meant to make him a *Masterpiece*...."[174] And in the words of the still kindlier Wotton, James *"moulded him, (as it were) Platonically to his owne Idea, delighting first in the choyse of the Materialls; because he found him susceptible of good forme; and afterwards by degrees as great Architects use to doe in the workmanship of his Regall hand...."*[175] The very idiom of titles reinforced the royal role. It was in James's power to "create" knights and marquesses and dukes. Thus it was fitting that he be welcomed to Burley with the paradoxical assurance that there, indeed, "The Master is your creature...."

Buckingham himself, as distinguished from the writer or speaker of such lines, would readily have said the same. In one letter he addressed the King as "my good fellow, my physician, my maker, my friend, my father, my all...."[176] Gratitude is a heavy burden, but Buckingham carried it with grace. It would have been stupid of him to be ungrateful, and he was not. As he put the matter to James, "I have not so much unthankfulness to deny ... that my former excuse of the disproportion of my estate is taken away; for you have filled a consuming purse; given me fair houses, more land than I am worthy of, to maintain both me and them; fill my coffers to full with patents of honour, that my shoulders cannot bear more."[177]

171. Halliwell-Phillips, II, 130–131.
172. *A Meditation upon the Lords Prayer* (1619), A6[r] & [v].
173. Thomas Frankland, *The Annals of King James and King Charles the First* (1681), p. 30.
174. *History of Great Britain*, p. 79.
175. *A Parallell betweene Robert Late Earle of Essex, and George Late Duke of Buckingham* (1641), p. 2.
176. From Halliwell-Phillips, II, 244.
177. Quoted by Hugh Ross Williamson, *George Villiers*, p. 310.

In 1621, when he welcomed James so warmly and entertained him so well, George Villiers, Marquess of Buckingham, was every inch a King's creature.

Such facts as these are obviously relevant to the gypsy masque. Less obvious is the fact that they are essential for understanding the hieroglyphic of the gypsies' metamorphosis. Of course one may argue that to seek reasons for the metamorphosis is to take too seriously what is basically a delightful game. Jonson probably banked on the realization that many people would hold this view. On the other hand, we have now seen sufficient evidence to suggest that Jonson's apparently casual playfulness in this masque is generally calculated and meaningful. His handling of the metamorphosis and the epilogue simply provides further evidence of his dualistic approach.

Despite the many merry notes of the masque, its high spirits are significantly qualified when we begin to understand—or even suspect —that the change announced in the title is by no means so profound as the transformations in most masques. The change here is one of appearance, not essence, and ironically it is the King who, in accord with conventional decorum and historical fact, has made even this change possible. It is he who has suffered the gypsies to come into the royal presence. It is he who has provided the titles and clothes ("Birdlime of *Fools*," says Jonson) with which Jonson shows them to be adorned. A major center of power such as the court is traditionally a difficult place in which to distinguish a person from his *persona*, but in this masque Jonson, ironically and satirically, has succeeded in unmasking James's chief courtier and his companions by the witty expedient of putting a disguise on his gypsies. This is quite in keeping with Jonson's practice in his plays, which typically lead to the unmasking of rogues and fools. The fox is uncased and the poetaster's papers are burned. In *The Gypsies Metamorphos'd* it is the nature of the gypsy-courtiers that is revealed. In some other masque King James may be shown to have the power to revive a corpse or blanche an Ethiope, but here we see his creative powers working only in a diminished way. In *The Gypsies Metamorphos'd* we see that he has welcomed into the sphere of the court a devilishly charming rogue who has brought along a ragtag pack of friends and relations, and we are given to think that their change to more glorious forms, a change wrought by royal power with the rogues' eager aid, is no more profound than the turning of counterfeit gypsies into counterfeit *"Lords . . . / With . . . their attenders"* (B 903–904).[178]

178. In Jonson's *Staple of News* (1626) there is an interesting parallel for the extrinsic sort of change we have in *The Gypsies Metamorphos'd*. As Mirth says to Tattle in that play, *"That was the old way, Gossip, when* Iniquity *came in like* Hokos Pokos, *in a Iuglers ierkin, with false skirts, like the* Knaue *of* Clubs! *but now they are attir'd like men and women o' the time, the* Vices, *male and female!"* (HS VI, 323: second "Intermeane"). As noted here previously, it would be wrong to equate gypsies with vices, and yet the fact remains that the elegant speakers and dancers at the end of the Burley masque, *"attir'd like men . . . o' the time,"* have only lately come forth from what we have seen to be the Egyptian darkness of the Devil's Arse.

Chapter IV. *Conclusion*

i. *Jonson's Achievement of a Middle Realm*

> If things oppos'd must mixt appeare. . . .
> (B 936)

The final moments of *The Gypsies Metamorphos'd* are bright with crystalline flattery. After the gypsies have "*chang'd*," they dance in their finery before the King, then alternately speak and sing his praises. More particularly, eager to "hurle his name/ About the globe in thousand aëry rings" (B 967–968), they "speake a hymne" which the Jackman proceeds to "sweeten with an under song" (B 938–941). The ungainly old King is assured that he is as fair, fresh, and fragrant as a summer sky and blessed with the look of a new-blown lily (B 956–960), and then finally, drawing the spoken part of the summer night's entertainment to a close in accord with dramatic convention, the last words of all are delivered by the spokesman of highest rank. Buckingham closed the masque thus:

> Love, love his fortune then,
>   And vertues knowne,
>   Who is the top of men,
>   But make the happinesse our owne;
> Since where the Prince for goodnesse is renoun'd,
> The subject with felicity is crown'd.
> (B 1003–08)

As we come to the almost ode-like ending of the masque, however, we also come across some puzzles. Why, for example, is Buckingham's final speech assigned in the text to the "Captaine," and the one before it to the Fourth Gypsy, and the one before that to the Third Gypsy? Practical necessity might be an excuse, but it is insufficient as an answer. Though the Patrico has promised to show the gypsies as "*true men*" (B 907), and though the appearance of the performers doubtless changed greatly between their two entrances, the underlying continuity of their roles is suggested—and by some

means could have been avoided—in the written text. Witnessed or
read, moreover, the glittering finale is remarkably shorter than what
has preceded it. When the metamorphosed gypsies enter, over ninety
per cent of the lines have been spoken, and all but the last dance
danced. Just what has Jonson achieved here? Schelling decided to
call the whole thing *The [Anti] Masque of Gipsies.*[1]

The "mixt" nature of the world attained at the close of *The
Gypsies Metamorphos'd* may be understood best if we compare it
with those realms that are found in the final portions of some of
Jonson's earlier masques. In *The Masque of Beauty*, for instance, the
Chorus proclaims that "the'*Elysian* fields are here" (HS VII, 194:
l. 407). In *The Golden Age Restored* Astraea exclaims, "It is become a heau'n on earth" (HS VII, 429: l. 229). And as these masques
come to a close, they remain unstreaked by dubious shadows. Jonson, of course, was neither blind nor sycophantic. He was, as he
long ago had signed himself in *Cynthia's Revels*, a servant, not a
slave, to the court. How then could he write such things? We have
previously had occasion to consider this question. Without flattery,
Jonson could not have functioned at court at all, but by using it
thoughtfully he could depict and recommend real virtue in terms of
the court.[2] As Orgel says, "the idealization of the virtue embodied
in the king and aristocracy was in the highest sense a moral act."[3]
It was therefore morally fitting for a masque to display a Platonic
universe. This was no less true after Jonson discovered that he could
enhance his presentation of idealized virtue by providing it with a
foil. If the foil happened to have more dramatic appeal than its opposite, the virtue was no less ideal (or Platonic) for that. In fact,
The Masque of Queens, in which the queens are ideal absolutes and
the hags their antitheses, provides us with an unmistakably clear
embodiment of his belief that virtue is *"more seene, more knowne,
when Vice stands by."*[4]

In a typical masque there is not merely a gap between the masque
proper and its antimasque, but another one as well (and this is why
the flattery catches our eye) between both of these and real life.
In Meagher's words, "We, and *a fortiori* the original audiences of the
masques, see the difference between the Jacobean reality and the

1. *Elizabethan Playwrights* (New York, 1925), pp. 238–239.
2. See pp. 37–42.
3. *Ben Jonson: The Complete Masques* (New Haven, 1969), p. 2.
4. *Pleasure Reconciled to Virtue*, HS VII, 491: l. 342.

perfection of order toward which the masques point."[5] In fact, it is the closing of this gap towards which the typical masque works. Everything leads up to the revels dances, where the masquers mingle with their courtly but merely mortal audience, and thus draw into the idealized "image" of the piece those who have been observers, dissolving for a magic while the line between fiction and reality.[6] Burton was straining to close the same fundamental gap in a passage in *The Anatomy of Melancholy* (1621), in which he wrote of James himself as the *Rex Platonicus*.[7] The truth is that James in 1621 was a frowzy, ailing old man, not by any means the *Rex Platonicus*. Except for rhetorical purposes a gap had always been evident. Had this not been true, the satirical master-dramatist probably could not have brought himself to engage in what was virtually a separate career of masque-writing. As matters stood, Jonson's extravagant praise could be taken seriously, but nobody need take it—indeed, they could *not* take it—literally.

Though *The Gypsies Metamorphos'd* affords several glimpses of that rarefied "world of glass" which one finds in more conventional masques, these comments should help us to see how it also differs from some of Jonson's other masques, both in its presentation of "absolutes" and "antitheses" and in its management of the distance between "the Jacobean reality and the perfection of order." In *The Masque of Queens* we have an old-fashioned hell, complete with flames from below, contrasted to the radiant and quasi-divine realm of Queen Anne and her ladies. Here the offstage cave where the gypsies entertain the Devil is not quite hell, nor is the sphere of the King's influence quite divine, despite his potential to create. The whole situation is made quite ambiguous early in the entertainment when the King, through his association with the gypsies, is actually drawn into the antimasque world. Not a gypsy blanches. In fact, far from metamorphosing or vanishing at the sight of the King, the gypsies tell his fortune, dance another strain, then move on to their usual business of duping.[8] With the ideal thus qualified in the action, it is qualified in our mind's eye, too. Even

5. *Method and Meaning in Jonson's Masques* (Notre Dame, Ind., 1966), p. 175.
6. See Alan L. Levitan, "The Life of Our Design: The Jonsonian Masque as Baroque Form," unpub. diss., Princeton, 1965, p. 45 *et passim*.
7. Pt. I, sec. 2, memb. 3, subs. 15 (p. 182).
8. Some of the flattery they give him is touchingly close to life: "You'are an honest good man, and have care of your barnes [bairns]," and "Some book-craft you have, and are pretty well spoken" (B 267, 269).

if it does not occur to us at once that the King is something like the clowns in allowing himself to be seduced by gypsy charms while his pockets are picked (and that, like Clod, he has a particular responsibility as the custodian of the common wealth), we may see that the images of both gypsy and King are qualified by being juxtaposed. The gypsies are prettied up even at the outset, and eventually they are "changed," but the situation is such that whatever they gain by being in the King's presence, the King loses by being in theirs. Jonson manages a neat, bold thrust when he has Cockrell hazard the guess that the Patrico and his companions are some of *"the Kings Gypsies"* (B 781–782).

What becomes, then, of traditional, idealized royal glory? After the gypsies change, the Captain assures James that he is "Glory of ours, of [i.e., *and*] grace of all the earth" (B 943). But even before his change he had said as much. Still clad in tatters and bells, he had assured the King that he was "High! bountifull! just! a Jove for your parts!" (B 272). In fact, *as a gypsy* he had gone on at Windsor to express his personal gratitude for the King's favors (W 307–318)!

We have, then, a real continuity as well as a contrast between the Captain's roles before and after the "metamorphosis." The blending is made yet more explicit when the Patrico refers to the Gypsy Captain as ready to feed the clowns *at Burley* "With his bread, beere, and biefe" (B 912). Jonson could scarcely make clearer the overlapping identities of the Captain and Buckingham.[9] Of course it is all in fun, but thus, too, is continued the theme of Cock-lorrel's feast. At Windsor Jonson added yet another stroke to the Cock-lorrellian quality of these gypsies by having Cockrell assume that the current Captain *is* Cock-lorrel. Cockrell tells the Patrico he hopes that now "your Captaine keepes better chere then he made the Deuill" (W 970–971). Something has gone intriguingly awry here, for though Buckingham was not yet Constable of the Castle at Windsor (that came in 1624), he doubtless kept cheer with the King.[10]

It is all very well to protest against poking too closely into such

9. Little sense could have been made of the passage, by the way, had Charles played the Captain's role.
10. One should not make much of the matter since it postdates Jonson's work, but a cut used in about 1642 to illustrate Jonson's ballad catches precisely the ambiguity which I am trying to point out: *A Strange Banquet, or, The Divels Entertainment by Cook Laurell* depicts Cock-lorrel at table with a crowned king. (See plate No. 10, reproduced here from BM C.20f.2.292.)

mechanical details of the masque. The point is that, taken together, their meaning is hard to ignore. Let us take another example. In some other masque the King may be able to "salue the rude defects of euery creature," but during the gypsy masque and at its close the "queen" of the gypsies sits in honor with James and his court. Nothing happens to change her because she is also the Countess of Buckingham. She is merely revealed to be *also* the gypsy queen, and after the gypsies change, no indication is given that this particular lady undergoes any alteration for the better. One is inclined to wonder how many other gypsies there may be in the audience. It is worth noting that after the clowns first enter and begin to chatter about gypsies, Puppy, bumbling in later than the rest, inquires, "which be they?" (B 508). *Which?* What does the word tell us if not that Puppy has glanced at the gypsies and the spectators and not been able to tell one from the other? Puppy is a clown, of course, and "which be they?" is an obvious bid for a laugh. Still, we may go so far as to suggest that it is the nature of this laugh that is in question for anyone hoping to come to terms with the masque. For the thoughtful, at any rate, it is likely to be a laugh which is shaded by the fact that the distinction between gypsies and courtiers is not nearly so clear as that which Jonson once had made between wicked witches and virtuous queens.

The Patrico and probably the Jackman provide further illustrations of the fact that at the end of *The Gypsies Metamorphos'd* the antimasque world is partially absorbed by the masque-court world, not banished or transformed by it. Masques were supposed to end by blending masquers with spectators, thereby raising the latter at least briefly into the brighter and better world of the former. In this masque, however, the spectators and masquers have been merged almost from the outset, thanks to the fortune-telling, and towards the end, after most of the gypsies have changed clothes and washed their faces, the Patrico remains standing in the royal presence. Whatever is supposed to have effected the gypsies' change, the Patrico not only remains as he was, but he also remains in full view.[11] Nothing is said about whether the Jackman changes, but he certainly

---

11. When he adds the comment at Windsor, "And so will I/ Be my selfe by and by" (W 1094-95), he apparently refers to the fact that after the masque is over he again will become the actor he really is rather than a gypsy. An acting actor will become a non-acting actor. But the point is that even during the most exalted moments of the masque he stands as a gypsy who is unvanquished by the royal presence.

continues to sing *as* the Jackman after the gypsies have metamorphosed. Since the role of the Jackman is likely to have been played by
a professional performer, perhaps it would have been indecorous
for him to change to a "lord's" costume and blend in with the real
lords. In any case, the show which began with antimasque elements
(the entry of the gypsies) has proceeded in its mid-section to still
greater disorder (the gypsies interacting with the clowns), and
now it concludes with the expected fine costumes and rippling
paeans of praise while at least some elements of the antimasque world
still stand unchanged and unchallenged in the presence of the King.
It is not enough to say that the men who play the Patrico and Jackman are paid performers, hence need not transform. In terms of
the masque they are two of the Captain's most skillful gypsies, and
most gypsies before the law are felons and rogues. They are weeds
in the English garden.[12]

The fact is that a blending of worlds—antimasque, masque, and
"real" worlds—seems to be much more important here than any
simple contrasting of them. As a further example, it might be noted
that in the Windsor version Jonson adds a "morning-after" glimpse
of the world in which the King will arise. In the long blessing of
the King's senses by the Patrico, the very first line blesses James
against "a Gypsie in the morninge" (W 1129). Is James, then,
normally subject to seeing a gypsy in the morning? A question to
be asked. And will he see any gypsy tomorrow? Another valid question, but before its original auditors had a chance to think about it,
the Patrico proceeded cheerfully on his way, mentioning a whole
series of things *besides gypsies* which the real James disliked—a
"smock rampant" and "Heapes of phrases and no stile," tobacco
("with the type/ Of the Diuells glister pipe"), pork, and, not least,
his gout and a fall (Jonson is discreet enough not to specify *another*
fall) from his horse.[13] The masque world and the real world, though
not congruent, are nevertheless adjoining and interpenetrating
spheres which share areas here that are much larger than in most
masques.

Also coming toward the close of the gypsy masque is a sticho-
mythic chorus of gypsy-courtiers who define the ideal king in
terms of James. There is one last idealizing song ("O that we under-

12. Probably the clowns remain, too, since there is no device indicated to get
them offstage. At Windsor the Patrico asked them to "beare the bob" (W 1120)—
sing the chorus—of his final song.
13. W 1135, 1144, 1159–60, 1165–66, 1180, and 1185.

stood/ Our good...."), and finally those concluding verses by the Captain lauding James. Perhaps one has the impression for a moment that James is at last being purified to his essential kingly self, refined to an ideal kingliness just as Buckingham earlier has been sublimated to *his* essential self, an appealing gypsy. But the whole process is ambiguous. Only God is what he would be, and despite those final bright verses and songs, the ideality of the King and his court, like the shrunken Main Masque itself, remains negatively qualified. Not only is it overshadowed by the sheer bulk of antimasque material that has gone before, but the closing passages themselves have been invaded by elements of the antimasque. In the *Epilogue*, when all else is said, sung, danced, and done, we find not a reaffirmation that former gypsies have now been transmuted to courtiers, but the plain, true statement that "wee are Gipsies of no common kind Sir" (W 1272). The ending of *The Gypsies Metamorphos'd*, in other words, has what one might term a relative reality.

Though this masque is probably unique in the thoroughness with which its contrasting elements are "mixt," it is not unique as a Jonsonian effort to mix "things oppos'd." Orgel, who offers a rather extended discussion of *Pleasure Reconciled to Virtue*, points out that neither Comus nor Daedalus emerges at the end of that masque as master of all he surveys. Hence that masque provides an illustration of what Orgel calls a "middle realm," a more or less realistic mean between the extremes of order and disorder, masque and antimasque.[14] "Middle realm" is exactly the term we need for

14. *The Jonsonian Masque* (Cambridge, Mass., 1965), p. 190. "Indeed," says Orgel, "this masque asserts with equal strength both the power of the individual will to overcome disorder and the insubstantiality of the ideal vision."
   Barish is also interested in the changing relationship between Jonson's masques and antimasques. He writes that

> Jonson's masques ... move ... toward irony instead of away from it, toward a less and less convincing image of the ideal society in the ascendant. He starts with the "pure" antimasque of grotesques, the witches in *The Masque of Queens*, abstract embodiments of sinister forces. He moves then to the antimasques of *Love Restored* and *Mercury Vindicated*, where figures like Plutus and Vulcan, conceived realistically up to a point, nevertheless retain their symbolic function as emissaries of darkness. In the third stage, he abandons the symbolic scaffolding for the antimasquers entirely: the city humors of *The Masque of Augurs* or *News from the New World* represent little but their own oddity. No triumph or vindication is possible, because the antimasquers represent nothing to be triumphed over; a meaningful transition from prologue to apotheosis becomes almost out of the question.

(*Ben Jonson and the Language of Prose Comedy* [Cambridge, Mass., 1960], pp. 266–267) Provided one accept this general schema and the main thesis of the present

the close of the gypsy masque. Jonson was obliged by convention to end with some rhetorical flowers for the King, but in arranging them he created only a "middle realm," a realm poised somewhere off to the side of both an ideally perfect court and an underworld of felonious gypsies, and partaking of the nature of both of these as well as of the everyday Jacobean world. Clearly it is a major means by which Jonson expresses himself in the gypsy masque. It is a complex, make-believe realm, the creation of a scholar-poet, and yet it provides some relatively firm ground on which we may stand to view the realm which James really ruled. It is a sort of mirror, as Jonson said a masque should be, in which we may glimpse an image of James's court.

Beyond gratulatory entertainment, what is its point? The gypsies who dance before the King change in appearance so as to conform to the external requirements of life at court, but they speak the lines of a writer who held that the only power which can really make man a "beautiful object" is "*a mind, shining through any sute, which needes no false light either of riches, or honors to helpe it.*" In order to be great a man must have virtue: " 'Tis Vertue alone, is true Nobilitie."[15] As has been said here now in various ways, this is a basic theme of the gypsy masque, and Jonson summarizes it forcefully in the conclusion of his final song:

There's happinesse indeed in blood,
   And store,
  But how much more,
  When vertues flood
In the same streame doth hit!
   (B 996–1000)

---

study, Jonson's gypsies slip readily enough into the second category here. They are "conceived realistically up to a point" and yet "retain their symbolic function as emissaries of darkness." Judging from Barish's suggested chronology, however (*Mercury Vindicated* is 1616 and *News* is 1620), one might suppose he himself would place the gypsies in his third category. His only direct comment is that "in country *divertissements* like . . . *The Masque of Gypsies*, where stage machinery must have been almost nonexistent and elaborate transformation scenes out of the question, Jonson can make the masque and antimasque virtually coextensive, mingling them and overlapping them at pleasure, so as to disguise the dualism inherent in the genre" (p. 269).

15. Ded. to *Cynthia's Revels*, HS IV, 33, and "To Kenelme, John, George," HS VIII, 282; l. 21. A man as confident of his worth as Jonson may have clung to such a view partly as a means of affording himself a sort of "nobility," but that is another matter.

The specific reference is to James himself, but the "streame" that Jonson writes of is capable of much wider application. Given its setting and its language—pure and neat, such as Jonson loved best— the passage is clear enough.[16] Read aright, it is not only a caveat for the present, but a pattern for the days to come.

ii. *Responses to the Masque*

> *King.* Have you heard the argument? Is there
> no offense in 't?
>
> *Hamlet.* No, no, they do but jest....
> III.ii.242–244

On the grounds which have been surveyed here one may hold that *The Gypsies Metamorphos'd* is worthy of that serious second look which modern readers generally have denied it, as, until fairly recently, all masques save Milton's *Comus* have also been denied. Like *Comus* the gypsy masque presents a significant theme, a theme which is topically relevant and perhaps permanently so. Moreover, it does so with considerable expertise.[17] Though exegesis rather than value judgment has been the goal of this study, it is impossible to ignore altogether the qualitative aspects of Jonson's work. Especially is this true when the exegesis, which suggests that the masque has a broader relevance and deeper meaning than previously was thought,

16. Almost as if daring to emphasize the point, Jonson returned to it in the Earl Marshall's fortune at Windsor:

Yours shall be to make true gentrie knowne
From the fictitious; not to prise blood
So much by the greatenes as by the good;
To shewe and to open cleare vertue the way
Both whether she should and how far she may....

(W 446–450)

17. Jonson's satire is not such that we may assert whether he is concerned here merely with the Buckinghamian milieu or with both that milieu and also the forces and failings which might lead to Buckinghamian behavior in another time and place. His other works would lead us to think that the latter is the case. Basil Willey observes that "it is of the essence of allegory to assume that the *most real thing*, that which is to be demonstrated, illustrated, or inculcated, is something abstract [in the present case, Buckinghamianism], while the image, the personification [a troupe of gypsies], is created for the sake of the abstraction, and points only thither" (*The Seventeenth Century Background* [New York, 1953; 1st ed., 1934], p. 69). Surely Jonson's masque is first and foremost topical, but he appears to be working with a moral construct which is universal.

is so dependent on Jonson's impressive verbal skills. No bells will ring at this late date for the news that literary form and meaning are interdependent. In terms of any specific masque, however, it still may be worth observing that it is hard to disengage a mirror from the reflection it shows us. Such an observation is particularly helpful if used to clear the way for saying also that we cannot understand and appraise the reflection if we lack a basic knowledge of the "real world" it reflects. Viewed in the light of its topical meaning, however, the gypsy masque may be seen to have greater literary interest. It may be seen not only to have utilized a traditional form and to have moved skillfully beyond it, but also in a number of ways to have reversed its normal direction. It may be seen, that is, to have greater complexity and subtlety. It may be seen to have (pehaps one may borrow from Eliot) that coherence, maturity, and truth to experience which some readers, at least, expect of a major literary work.[18] Viewed thus, its various speeches, songs, and poems are no longer likely to be seen as so many more or less arbitrary items created and displayed so as to catch the fancy of a frivolous court, but as carefully designed integers thematically informed so as to constitute a patterned and meaningful whole. The bigness of the piece—it is much longer than any other Jonson masque—is an indication not that Jonson has gone to comic seed, but that he has grasped the opportunity to increase the intricacy of expression and the breadth of an exciting theme. Bigness alone could prove a puzzling irritant if we found no meaning in the masque, if we saw the text simply as the skeleton of an oversized dodo. Meaning is not all but it is very important, and a search for it in the gypsy masque gives us a chance to discover that this work may be quite as interesting and worthwhile to us as, for different reasons, it was to James.

Of course one does well to remain critical of any attempt, including the present one, to label layers in a literary work. Jonson's mind and Jonson's age worked with such layers, however, and so must we if we hope to read them aright. On its literal surface *The Gypsies Metamorphos'd* displays an attractive-but-noxious band of gypsies who charm their way into the highest social circles and, with little ado, change to fine folk, speaking fine lines and dancing with grace. Perhaps this is enough. In the course of the present study, however, we have seen a number of reasons for holding that Jonson is using

18. *The Use of Poetry and the Use of Criticism* (1950; 1st ed., 1933), p. 96.

these gypsies to display Thievish Opportunism and Fraud (or some such traits—we should not be narrowly specific) *as they are embodied* in Buckingham, his family, and his friends. Jonson has trusted our intuition here. Skelton in his political morality called *Magnificence* (*ca.* 1515–23) could afford to be precise in pinning labels on abstract political vices—Counterfeit Countenance, Crafty Conveyance, Cloaked Collusion, and Courtly Abusion—but Jonson, writing a masque, has had to content himself with giving his Buckinghamian crew the name of "gypsy," the name that the dying Sussex gave the upstart Leicester. As this last fact suggests, Jonson does not comport himself like a man whose hands are completely tied. Throughout the masque he seems to delight in his dual mode of presentation, negative in one sense (the implied criticism of gypsy ways, whether practiced by gypsies or someone else) and positive in another (the praise of virtues such as the King should have, virtues which should make him a shining example of how to deal with "gypsies"). These are all matters, however, which lose by over-explicitness and oversimplification. Jonson's skillful handling of the gypsy-courtier conceit may be viewed to best advantage—the old cliché is true—when we return to the text of the masque.[19]

To praise Jonson's handling of his major conceit is by no means to praise the political insight which underlies it. The fact is that the gypsy masque is grounded on Jonson's convictions of what a kingdom should be like, and Jonson, like James, believed in an old-fashioned paternalistic monarchy with a wise and good king at the top of a fixed social hierarchy.[20] Neither James nor Jonson saw, or at least admitted seeing, that such an idea was anachronistic in 1621.[21]

19. If one feels the need for a summarizing statement, it is striking that one can use almost verbatim an analysis which David Bevington has written of Skelton's *Magnificence*:

A king . . . must beware of temptations inherent in his own extraordinary power and wealth. If he should fail, no human agency will undertake to correct abuses. All may be righted if the king can only admit his folly and recover the use of his innate wisdom, with God's help throwing off his sycophants and listening to conservative advice.

(*Tudor Drama and Politics* [Cambridge, Mass., 1968], p. 63) It is instructive to know that Jonson, who admired Skelton and imitated him in the gypsy masque, came so close to telling James what Skelton had told Henry.

20. K. W. Evans provides a good analysis in "*Sejanus* and the Ideal Prince Tradition," *SEL*, XI (1971), 249–264.

21. Nor, of course, was either man blind. Parliament was no longer willing to take a subordinate position in the state, and, as Godfrey Davies points out, "the king was too shrewd not to see that a new power had arisen in the land, as was

In literary ways Ben Jonson laid some solid foundations for several generations of writers, but, paradoxically, a major aspect of his "classicism" was an attachment to the past which was almost romantic. As Evans puts it, Jonson was "Unsympathetic towards social and economic developments that ran counter to the old organic ideal of society, and contemptuous of parliamentary assemblies, as also of the political capacity of most men. . . ." How like *James* this is! Hence Jonson could "only oppose to his changing world the time-honored paternalism of the ideal prince tradition" (p. 264). The tradition was not enough, as James (if not Jonson) discovered to his frustration and bemusement. Meanwhile Jonson did what he could. He not only wrote in praise of it, in masques and elsewhere, but in most of his writings he took arms against its varied enemies.

As a matter of fact, Jonson's interest in affairs of state was probably always more moral than political. Hence it is no surprise to find that Evans, in discussing Jonson's Sejanus, describes the favorite of Tiberius in terms which one may apply to James's Buckingham: he was a representative of those "gentry" whose attempt "to hold power for which they were morally unfit was symptomatic of a general degradation, at the root of which lay the irresponsibility of ambitious monarchs, who preferred flattery to good counsel, and had discarded their exemplary . . . role . . ." (p. 250). It has been noted here already that Buckingham could hardly have been in Jonson's mind in 1603, but an abhorrence for the ills he came to represent had long been fixed there.[22] Though Jonson and James concurred in holding to the old paternal prince tradition, Jonson (if not James) realized that they viewed their times very differently with regard to it, and in the gypsy masque he tried to create a mirror which would convey something of his own view to James and the court. Given Jonson's view and the self-assurance which un-

---

proved by his famous remark [of 10 December 1621], on receiving a parliamentary deputation: 'Chairs for the ambassadors'" (*The Early Stuarts 1603–1660* [Oxford, 2nd ed., 1959, printing of 1967; 1st ed., 1937], p. 29).

22. See p. 29. Kernan comes at essentially the same point from another direction when he writes of Jonsonian characters who are "satiric portraits of Renaissance aspiration, of the belief that man can make anything he will of himself and of his world, that he can storm heaven and become one with the gods, or make of earth a new paradise" (*The Cankered Muse* [New Haven, 1959], p. 180). D. J. Enright's generalization fits a still larger number of Jonson's characters, for he says simply that Jonson concerned himself mainly with "the acknowledgment by the individual of his proper and ordained position in the universe" ("Crime and Punishment in Ben Jonson," *Scrutiny*, IX [Cambridge, 1940], p. 231).

derlay it, it is not surprising that he said his masques were designed
to provide "nourishing, and sound meates" for their spectators.[23]

Obviously the expressed intentions of any writer are suspect as
rationalizations, especially when they are not made about the particular piece of writing at hand. Nonetheless, Jonson's stubborn
repetition of his views gives them weight, and especially when they
really do seem pertinent to the work in question. From such be-
ginnings, at any rate, and via such evidence as we have seen here,
one comes to the delicious irony of Buckingham, the most "glorious
Starre" in James's firmament, sponsoring and sparkling his way
through a masque which is critical of himself and, more subtly,
monitory to the King. The gypsy masque may be viewed as a tri-
umphant example of Jonson's willingness to take a calculated risk.

Jonson met with resounding success. He received £100, far
more than his usual fee for a masque (Buckingham could afford to
be generous);[24] he narrowly escaped being knighted ("his majesty
would have done it, had there not been means made [himself not
unwilling] to avoid it");[25] and shortly afterwards he was granted
the reversion of a significant and appropriate post at court, the
Mastership of the Revels (though he never held the post, the fact
that he was placed in line for it indicates the esteem he had won).
Jonson must have felt elated at having pulled the whole thing off,

At the same time, however, the rewards which were contemplated
for him suggest that the King had not understood. How could James
have been so obtuse? Jonson had presented his criticism not only
in his central conceit but also in a good many details of his masque,
and he naturally would have wanted at least some of the more alert
among his auditors to sense if not articulate what he was driving at.
The King and everyone else had heard, after all, that gypsies "committ infinite thifte, insolenceis, and oppressionis upoun his Majesteis
goode subjectis in all pairtis quhair they hant and frequent...."[26]
But Jonson accompanied his criticism with sufficient praise and
good humor to protect himself in the event that anyone, the King
included, was so foolish as to cry out that his shafts had struck home.

23. *Hymenaei*, HS VII, 210: ll. 27–28.

24. Orgel estimates that £100 would have been twice what Jonson usually received (*Complete Masques*, p. 489).

25. From a letter of the Reverend Joseph Mead to Sir Martin Stuteville, 15
September 1621, cited in Thomas Birch, *The Court and Times of James the First*
(1849), II, 275.

26. See p. 47.

Praise and humor: the former we have now considered a couple
of times. It was an ideal stalking horse, not merely the traditional
idiom of masques, but a device to which James was infinitely susceptible. The humor was another multi-purpose device, and one
which Jonson relied on heavily. In some passages, we may be sure,
he aimed specifically at James's own taste. In the Windsor prologue
Jonson informed the King that the purpose of the masque was "To
haue you still merry" (W 13). Possibly Jonson knew that in the
masque which James himself wrote, there was a "zani" (a zany or
fool), as well as a naïve old country fellow who stumbles into the
presence of exotic strangers and, like Jonson's country folk, happily
contemplates the fun to come. The taste of someone other than
James must account for the fact that there are more early transcripts
of the Cock-lorrel song than of any other poem by Jonson, but we
know it must have caught James's fancy because, unlike the fas-
tidious Prince, James particularly enjoyed indecorous jests and gross
horseplay. David Lloyd in a sketch of William, Earl of Pembroke,
tells us how James, knowing that Pembroke "naturally hated a Frog,
threw one into his neck," and Pembroke, "in requital, caused a Pig
(of an equal disgust with the same Prince) to be put under his Close-
stool. . . ."[27] Sir Edward Zouch was wont to entertain the King with
bawdy jests and bawdy songs—some of which had been composed by
Sir John Finett. And apparently James took pleasure in watching
such fools as David Droman and Archie Armstrong tilting at each
other from the backs of yet other fools.[28] Wit, of course, was not

27. *The States-men and Favourites of England Since the Reformation* (1665),
pp. 688–689. Buckingham and his mother are also reported to have played a pig-
prank on James. Wilson writes that

> they caus[e]d Mistris *Aspernham*, a young Gentlewoman of the Kindred,
> to dress a *Pigg* like a *Child*, and the *Old Countess* like a *Midwife* brought it
> in to the King in a rich Mantle. *Turpin* that married one of the Kindred . . .
> was drest like a *Bishop*, . . . who (with the *Common Prayer* book) began the
> words of *Baptism*, one attending with a silver Bason of *Water* for the Service,
> the King hearing the *Ceremonies of Baptism* read, and the squeeking noise
> of that *Brute* he most abhorred, turned himself to see what *Pageant* it was,
> and finding *Turpin*'s face, which he well knew, drest like a *Bishop*; and the
> *Marquess*, whose face he most of all loved, stand as a Godfather; he cryed
> out, *away for shame*, what *Blasphemy is this*?

(*History of Great Britain* [1653], p. 218) From this and other evidence we know
that James had his limits.

28. *The Court and Character of King James*, attrib. to Sir Anthony Weldon
(1650), p. 92. Finett was Assistant to the Master of Ceremonies.

Naturally many who lived closest to the King found it convenient to share his

totally absent from the court. After all, Lancelot Andrewes and John Donne were two of James's favorite preachers. In the year of the gypsy masque Donne was named Dean of St. Paul's. James simply did not mind if, when wit appeared, it, too, was sometimes full-bodied. Moreover, as far as the present masque is concerned, it may be significant that James always tended to feel freer when away from the pressures of London. Bearing these several matters in mind, and also the fact that Jonson himself was no pressed violet, we should not be dismayed to find that Jonson's sense of the risible in the gypsy masque has through the years occasioned some critical sniffs. Standards never cease to vary.

The important fact customarily overlooked in all this is that Jonson's humor and wit are not only entertaining but useful. Perhaps one may draw a parallel between the purposes of the gypsy masque and the purposes of Archie Armstrong, James's "principall foole of *State*," as Jonson dubbed him in *Timber* (HS VIII, 573). Since we have already considered parallels between gypsies and morris fools and between gypsies and vices, and since Jonson himself used "vice" as a synonym for "fool," the relating of gypsies to the royal jester may seem the more plausible.[29] In any case, it was the function of jesters in royal households to amuse their masters by making bold and startling observations on current events, and by offering ludicrous representations of events and people. Writing about affairs in Spain in 1623, when the Spanish Match still seemed possible, James Howell reports that Archie "hath more privilege than any,

---

tastes. William Cavendish, looking back on James's reign with a certain elegiac acerbity, had a character in *The Variety* (*ca.* 1641; pub. 1649) reminisce,

> those were the dayes indeed, oh there was then such a company for dancing singing and fooling, I doe not meane the wits, for fooling is another thing cleare from it; It does so bravely in company, when there is a great many that care not for wit, and pleases better than all the wit in the world; and then there was such brave jeasts, at the death of a Stag, and Buck, to throw blood up and downe, upon folkes faces; the very Footmen and Pages understood those Jeasts then; there was a time. . . .

(pp. 48–49)

29. *The Devil Is an Ass*, I.i.84–85 (HS VI, 167). See also pp. 121–123.

One might add that Jonson knew the passage in which Dekker said gypsies were "neither absolutely mad, nor yet perfectly in their wits." Dekker had wanted to explain that the gypsies' nickname of moon-men was borrowed "from the Moone, because as the Moone is neuer in one shape two nights together, but wanders vp and downe Heauen, like an Anticke, so these changeable-stuffe-companions neuer tarry one day in a place. . ." *Villanies Discovered by Lanthorne and Candle-light* [1620], Fiᵛ).

for he often goes with his Fool's-coat where the *Infanta* is with her *Menina's* and Ladies of Honour, and keeps a-blowing and blustering among them, and flurts out what he lists."[30] Furthermore, though the idea of having a court fool may have seemed a bit old-fashioned in the 1620's, the fact remains that James did bring along Archie on his 1621 progress. However much the salty Scot may have differed from his professional forebears, he was King James's allowed fool, and a palpable reminder at Burley of an old tradition. Apt indeed, therefore, is the observation of Herford and Simpson that "The extraordinary success of the [Gypsy] Masque was clearly due in the main to the zest of the personal allusions. Jonson had, in fact, discovered a literary substitute, fresh and unexplored, for the antiquated institution of the Court fool" (II, 316). Herford and Simpson seem not to have realized the implications of their suggestion. Pursuit of the idea that the gypsies in the masque function something like court jesters might have led them to ponder that these gypsies, like allowed fools, were allowed to make fools of other people, that they shared not only the tradition of patches and bells, but the amoral and social insularity which both of these suggest, and perhaps even that the boat of Cock-lorrel (he who is here a gypsy captain) was very much a ship of fools, its first illustrator going so far as to depict the passengers wearing fools' caps tipped with bells.[31] Perhaps, too, we should recall again Jonson's reference to the gypsy penchant for "saffron'd linnen," since yellow (as Malvolio forgets) was commonly known as the color of the fool.[32]

More important still, pursuit of the affinity between traditional jesters and Jonson's gypsies opens a path to the idea that perhaps the man who gave them their lines to speak was himself, in a larger sense, functioning in a similar way. The humor and wit in the masque—and they are scattered nearly everywhere—were certainly designed to draw forth some merely casual smiles and laughs, but they represent also an effort to enlist thoughtful laughter in the

30. *Epistolae Ho-elianae*, ed. Joseph Jacobs (1890), p. 169.

31. The woodcuts for Sebastian Brant's *Narrenschiff* (Basel, 1494) were the models for the illustrations in Alexander Barclay's *Shyp of Folys* (1509), and the Henry Watson version of *The Shyppe of Fooles* (1509) was the source of the similar cuts published by Wynkyn de Worde in *Cocke Loreles Bote* (*ca.* 1510).

32. John Doran, *The History of Court Fools* (1858), p. 182, and M. Channing Linthicum, *Costume in the Drama of Shakespeare and His Contemporaries* (Oxford, 1936), p. 49. Cf. above, pp. 118–119. Probably more important, nonetheless, is the variety of colors in the gypsy costume. A multi-colored costume, Craik notes, was in the Tudor interludes commonly a sign that its wearer was to be condemned (*The Tudor Interlude* [Leicester, 1967; 1st impression, 1958], p. 66).

cause of curbing certain excesses at James's court. As Crites observes in *Cynthia's Revels*, "The scope of wise mirth vnto fruict is bent" (HS IV, 180: V.xi.160).

Orgel, in writing of Jonson's masques generally, links together these elements of praise and comedy which we have noted and produces a summary statement which exactly fits *The Gypsies Metamorphos'd*: "the form was not, for Jonson, ultimately spectacular, but didactic and moral, providing a logical concomitant to satiric comedy on the one hand and the poetry of praise on the other."[33]

Setting aside the sugar-coating of comic appeal and praise, at least three hypotheses (or some combination of them) might be advanced to explain why James spoke not of hanging Jonson but of knighting him. The first concerns the carefully proportioned mixture of clarity and obscurity in the masque. Very early on, as we have seen, the Patrico rattles off the avowal that "If here we be a little obscure, it is our pleasure, for rather then we will offer to be our owne interpreters, we are resolv'd not to bee understood" (B 84–86). From the evidence of the text it would appear that Jonson might have said much the same about the masque as a whole. He did take care to preserve the major amenities: his masque is a festive occasional piece designed to celebrate the visit of the monarch to the country home of his favorite; deep in the country the antimasque clowns are, appropriately, country folk; and the main characters, a band of gypsies, are very much associated with country villages and fleeting revels. In the gypsies, however, Jonson had an ambiguous device to which every listener and viewer was at least ostensibly free to respond according to his own experience and capability. This is where the difficulty comes. Jonson could speak directly to the King in a masque only in the sense that the King was one of his immediate auditors. He could afford to be only so clear and no clearer in recording his conviction that at James's court all was not sweet, all was not sound. To a greater degree than most, then, this masque, and particularly its central device, became illustrative of what his friend Bacon said of parabolical writing generally: "it serves for *Obscuration*; and serveth also for *Illustration*...."[34] It serves to disguise and veil meaning, and also to clarify and throw light on it. In other words Jonson may be said to have chosen here

33. Introd., *Complete Masques*, p. 3.
34. *Of the Advancement and Proficience of Learning*, trans. Gilbert Wats (Oxford, 1640), p. 107.

exactly what T. S. Eliot believes was the typical Jonsonian solution: he hid his major meaning by placing it where it would be most readily available, namely, on the surface.[35] If Jonson has failed to enlist the sympathy of modern readers, Eliot believes, it is because they are unwilling to do the intellectual work necessary to analyze what has been so obviously placed. Three hundred years before Eliot, Sidney Godolphin conveyed something of the same idea. Jonson's, he said, is "The deepest, plainest, highest, cleerest pen. . . ."[36]

Gabriele Jackson has protested against Eliot's analysis. According to her, Jonson responded intuitively (like any man) and (unlike most) was sufficient poet to record his response in such a way that "his auditors, the mass of men, respond intuitively . . . in order to receive the artist's transmission of what he has beheld." She speaks up for the "alogical faculty" (Jonson says "inmost affection") as a sort of intuitional spark which jumps the gap between artist and audience and thereby makes artistic communication possible (p. 97).

Perhaps one can have it two ways, both Eliot's and Jackson's. Jonson's gypsies lie very much on the surface of the masque, and if given the close look Eliot calls for, they may be recognized on intellectual grounds for what they are, charming representatives of disorder. (It should also be obvious that any figurative meaning they have is inextricable from, indeed impossible without, the literal level of the masque. One should be wary of saying that "the allegory says" when clearly no allegory says anything except by means of its literal surface. One tries now and then to distinguish between two or more levels in a work—our forefathers often sought three or four—but always it should be with the hope of bringing them together again and coming back up to the surface.) As Eliot says, Jonson's meaning *does* lie on the surface. On the other hand, Jonson has not merely extracted some colorful character types from the pamphlets of Dekker and Rid. He also has intuited them from what he knew of life, from what he sensed not only about a specific royal favorite but about the whole ethos of the Jacobean court. One result is that he displays his gypsies in such terms that he seems almost to be thinking through them and by means of them rather than simply using them as counters. In some ways, therefore, he moves well

35. "Ben Jonson," in *Elizabethan Essays* (1934), pp. 65–85; discussed by Gabriele Bernhard Jackson, *Vision and Judgment in Ben Jonson's Drama* (New Haven, 1968), pp. 95–96.
36. In *Jonsonus Virbius*, reprinted in HS XI, 450.

beyond the pale of simple, mechanistic allegory. This is not the place to fuss over drawing a divisory line through that shadowy area where allegory and symbolism converge, especially when Bacon's larger concept of "parabolical" writing will serve as well here as either of the narrower terms. It is necessary to say only—to repeat—that it would be wrong to assign Jonson's gypsies a meaning that is too fixed and narrow, quite as wrong as it would be to deny that they do *have* meaning. One hesitates to apply the word "alogical" to anything Ben Jonson ever made, but perhaps part of the reason for the "obscurity" of his very clear gypsy masque is that in part he is working intuitively, and so must we if we are to catch as much as possible of his meaning.[37]

There is yet another point to be made regarding Jonson's mix of clarity and obscurity in this masque, and it is no less significant for being true of Jonson's other masques. It is very simple: among the appeals of a removed mystery is the fact that it is mystifying. Though one need not deny the various pleasures belonging to the same genus as unravelling, unlocking, unsnarling, and deciphering, the fact remains that there is something profoundly appealing about a sphinx who knows and keeps secrets. Stephen Orgel comments on this subject in relation to seventeenth-century courtly masques in general:

> A viewer's understanding ... depended on his ability to *read* what he saw. If he could not interpret the symbolism, as must almost invariably have been the case, it had to be explained to him, either in the dialogue or more often in the printed text of the work, as in *The Masque of Blackness* or *Tempe Restored*. The fact that even this proceedure was exceptional only means that we must not underestimate the Renaissance's love of mysteries and enigmas. To find oneself in the presence of mystic and impenetrable truths afforded considerable pleasure.[38]

Seating oneself to dine at Jonson's "full tables," in other words, did not necessarily mean that one could or should lick the platter clean. A persevering student might attempt it over a period of time, of

37. John Gordon Nichols has a comment akin to this. Jonson, he says, was a master of poetic structures in which each part contributes "to a whole which is intelligible to the reason though not to be exhausted by it" (*The Poetry of Ben Jonson* [1969], p. 43).
38. "The Poetics of Spectacle," *New Literary History*, II (1971), 384.

course, and Jonson would have approved the attempt. The immediate audience or audiences, however, need not have lost face had they made a decent effort, then given over their attention to the dancing which followed, or perhaps to those quite different tables which their host had had laden for them in some nearby room.

A second hypothesis, for practical purposes inseparable from the first, is that the gypsy masque was happily accepted rather than well understood because its audience, as usual at a masque, derived much of their impression from nonverbal sources. We who are so dependent on the text can only conjecture about the actors' costumes, gestures, and dancing—some of it rather spirited dancing, if Jonson followed the example of Middleton in *More Dissemblers*, where the gypsies perform "*a strange wilde fashion'd dance to the Hoboys or Cornets.*"[39] Surely one may assume that some of the words and phrases which have been anatomized here were for various reasons simply lost in the air at Burley. Some passages could have been lost merely because it is often hard to catch the words in a show, especially words in a song, even a simple song, and some of Jonson's are anything but simple. Words could have been lost because of the jingle of a gypsy's bells or a sudden cough from somewhere across the crowded hall. Perhaps, too, some of those expository words at the beginning lost out to the novelty of having two horses and some pigs, plus little flocks of children and poultry onstage. Then, again, modern readers should bear in mind that it is distracting as well as pleasurable to watch a performance by someone we know. An amateur performer's personal life has a tendency to permeate and come through the fictional character he plays, and though Jonson, for his own purposes, needed to take no pains to avoid this palimpsest effect in his gypsy masque, it probably served as much for "*Obscuration*" as "*Illustration.*"

One need not suppose, either, that the King and his court sat down to the evening's entertainment unfortified by drink. The French Ambassador, Tillières, wrote that "The end of all is ever the bottle." Late in the month of the gypsy masque, he reported, "They have no thoughts here of a war either in France or in Germany, nor of any occupation whatever, other than that of eating, drinking, and making merry. The house of the Duke of Buckingham is a chief

39. In *Two New Playes* (1657), p. 57; performed *ca.* 1615. On the day after the Belvoir performance, by the way, Buckingham paid not only a "tabbarer" and some fiddlers, but also a "corniter" (Public Record Office, State Papers, July–Sept., 1621, CXXII, 32).

resort for these pursuits. . . ."⁴⁰ James had a stronger head than most for that sweet wine and Scotch ale which Oglander says he loved so well, but on an occasion so festive as the Burley visit it is unlikely that either he or the other guests would have been cold, stone sober when they seated themselves for the main entertainment.⁴¹ Nor is it probable that the performers themselves danced with dry throats. The text appears to allude to the custom of serving performers backstage. On some occasions, we know, performers did not receive all that was coming to them, but the Patrico here reminds the bumpkins that

> . . . tis not long syne
> Yee dranke of his [the Captain's] wine,
> And it made you fine,
> Both clarret and sherry. . . .
>
> (B 913–916)

Doubtless for some the lamps glowed double.

Though it is a matter affecting the perception only of James, not his court, it should be recalled also that at fifty-five the King was fully sunk into ill health and premature old age. He looks out at us from his portraits of this period as a sad-eyed, tired old man, rather unlikely, with or without imbibing, to be looking for slings or arrows in a masque at his beloved Buckingham's—at Steenie's— house.⁴² In short, even though some of the audience, notably the King, heard the masque twice more, circumstances did not encourage or even permit many of those present to consider its text closely.

40. Quoted in Frederick Von Raumer, *History of the Sixteenth and Seventeenth Centuries*, trans. from the German (1835), II, 266, 259.

41. *A Royalist's Notebook: The Commonplace Book of Sir John Oglander Kt. of Nunwell*, ed. Francis Bamford (1936), p. 196.

It also happens that the Belvoir performance the following Sunday fell on one of James's personal holidays. His narrow escape from the Gowrie Plot of 1600, apparently an attempt on his life, was a matter for commemorations, sermons, and feasting the rest of his life. Within the text of the gypsy masque, Jonson alludes to the fact that it was no occasion for dry throats in 1621:

> The fift of August
> Will not let saw-dust
> Lie in your throats,
> Or cob-webs, or oates;
> But helpe to scoure yee.
> This is no Gowrie
> Hath drawne James hether,
> But the good man of Bever,
> Our Buckinghams father[-in-law]. . . .

(Belvoir replacement for, presumably, B 908–924)

42. See plate No. 2.

It might be argued that Jonson was a practical dramatist, well aware of the need to compete with outside influences both on a stage and within an audience. His occasional complaints on the subject tell us, though, that he did not always emerge a victor in the competition. When he addressed the readers of *The Staple of News*, he complained that "the *allegory*, and purpose of the *Author* hath hitherto beene wholly mistaken..." (HS VI, 325). In some cases— in the gypsy masque, for instance—total clarity would have meant total defeat. Throughout his career, nevertheless, he continued to be interested in adumbrating the more removed mysteries which give a masque its moral backbone, and this despite his lament for "the wit/ There wasted."[43] As for the court, it was perhaps always more interested in "shows" than "words," and in recent years it had demonstrated a growing interest in the revels of the antimasque rather than the dignity of the main masque. The success of *The Gypsies Metamorphos'd* itself doubtless derived largely from the fact that, finer points aside, it was nearly all antimasque.

Still one would suppose that there must have been at least a little curiosity as to what the masque meant. Jonson's comments in the Windsor epilogue are difficult to explain unless viewed as a response to questions which someone had posed. Conceivably the questioner was James himself. As he told Buckingham, he himself had "satt vpon Parnassus forked hill."[44] And he was used to receiving credit for the transformations in the masques he attended. Whether the questions were ever verbalized or not, though, Jonson crafted such obscure answers for them that the removed mysteries remained mysterious. He had said in the masque what he meant, and if the King did not catch it, who would presume to tell him? Who would tell the old emperor he was naked if he thought himself clad in royal robes?

A third hypothesis grows out of this last point. As Owen Feltham wrote in his *Resolves* (1628), "In things that may haue a *double sense*, 'tis good to thinke, the *better* was intended..." (p. 118). Jonson had had cause to consider this matter. In *Timber* we find that he has posed it as a rhetorical question: "*Whilst* I name no persons, but deride follies; why should any man confesse, or betray himselfe?" And he discussed it thus:

43. "To Sir Robert Wroth," HS VIII, 97: ll. 11–12.
44. "Votum," *The Poems of James VI. of Scotland*, ed. James Craigie (Edinburgh, 1958), II, 177.

they that take offence where no Name, Character, or Signature doth blazon them, seeme to mee like affected as woemen; who, if they heare any thing ill spoken of the ill of their Sexe, are presently mov'd, as if the contumely respected their particular: and, on the contrary, when they heare good of good woemen, conclude, that it belongs to them all. If I see any thing that toucheth mee, shall I come forth a betraier of my selfe, presently? No; if I be wise, I'le dissemble it; if honest, I'le avoid it: lest I publish that on my owne forehead, which I saw there noted without a title. . . . The Person offended hath no reason to bee offended with the writer, but with himselfe; and so to declare that properly to belong to him, which was so spoken of all men, as it could bee no mans severall, but his that would willfully and desperately clayme it.

(HS VIII, 633–634)

The usefulness of this point, which Jonson borrowed directly from Erasmus, is that it leaves the door open to conjecture that some at the court did, indeed, understand what Jonson had achieved in the gypsy masque. Even if some had passing doubts, why would any —the King included—start like a guilty creature? Often at court it is wisest to seem not to know, and on the present occasion there were rationalizations aplenty. The masque had been concocted by one who for some five years had been officially regarded as a "welbeloved Servaunt" of the King (HS I, 231–232), and the royal favorite had not only commissioned the piece but performed in it. Besides, it was an entertaining business, with its fast-talking gypsies and bumbling bumpkins, and it certainly said some pleasant things about the King. Why spoil everything by frowning like Good Friday and mentioning an inkling of some dark message which might not have been meant? In other words, the fact that Jonson was praised and petted rather than clapped into prison at the close of the masque does not mean that no one in his audience—in a generation of emblem-viewers, and with the King himself a sometime allegorist—it does not mean that absolutely no one could witness the work, grasp some of its implications, and still hold his peace.

All things considered, *The Gypsies Metamorphos'd* may be Jonson's most interesting achievement as a writer of masques. In the process of praising the King he has managed here both to amuse and give a public warning, something like a jester who aims to make

his master laugh while serving up a trencher of truth. He has gone
so far as to bless his "sweet Masters . . . / From . . . the stroak of the
tongue" (B 248–249) while he himself is making use of various
tongues from James's own court to administer some strokes of his
own. There is no indication that Jonson succeeded in catching the
conscience of the King. Perhaps James simply accepted as a compliment the dramatized fact of George Villiers's rise to eminence.
That is, he may have accepted and enjoyed some implications of
the masque and mistaken or let others go. One may conjecture,
nonetheless, and even hope that a few of those seated in the audience
or standing on the sidelines at Burley must have winked or gawked
at certain of Jonson's thrusts. Jonson might call the court "the
Inne of *Ignorance*" (HS VIII, 633), but he knew and we know
that not everyone in it was ignorant. The satirist and allegorist
appeal to an aristocracy of brains, and there were still "some men,"
as Gabriel Harvey had observed back in Elizabeth's day, who could
"giue a shrewd gesse at a courtly allegory. . . ."[45] All we may
say for sure, though, is that the wisest fool in Christendom called
for his bowl and his gypsies two more times, and Buckingham, the
star, continued to dance.

45. From *Pierce's Supererogation* in *Elizabethan Critical Essays*, ed. G. Gregory
Smith (Oxford, 1904), II, 252.

THis glorious *Starre* attending on the *Sunne,*
Having, from this low world, iuſt wonder wonne
For brightnes;*Enuie,*that foule *Stygian* brand,
T' extinguiſh it thruſts forth her greedie *hand :*
To catch it from its mounted moving place,
And hurle it lower to obſcur'd *Diſgrace :*
But while ſhe ſnatches, to put out the flame,
Fooliſhly *fiers* her *fingers* with the ſame.
Who others glories ſtriue t' eclipſe(poore Elues)
Doe but drawe downe ſelfe-miſchiefe on themſelues..
You waiting on the *Sunne* of *Maieſtie*
May that *clamping Heliotropium* be :
Still bright in your *Eclipticke* circle runne,
Y' are out of *Enuies* reach,ſo neare the *Sunne*.
Moue fairely, freely in your wonted *Orbe,*
Aboue the danger of *Detractions* curbe,.
And her ſelfe-burſting Brood : ſit there,contemne,
Nay laugh, and ſcorne both their deſpight,and them..

1. An emblem depicting the relationship of George Villiers and
James I, from *The Mirrour of Majestie* (1618) (from the British
Museum, C.71.d.17)

POTENTISS · IACOBUS · D · G · MAGNA · BRITANNIÆ · GALLIÆ · ET · HIBERNIÆ · REX · FIDEI · DEFENSOR

Behold Greate Britaines, France and Irelands King,
About whose Browes Clusters of Crownes doe springe
Whose faith him Champion of the FAITH en-stiles
Vpon whose head fortune and Honnor smiles —
The Rod of vice and Vertues Recompence —
Longe liue Kinge JAMES in all Magnifence —

Are to be sould by
Roger Daniell
Att the Angellin
Lumbardstrete

I·Br: excudit
Anno Dom̄:
1621

2. The aging James I in a portrait dated 1621 (from the British Museum, Department of Prints and Drawings, Vol. XIV, O.D. 70)

3. George Villiers, favorite of James I, *ca.* 1625, by Daniel
Mytens (from the collection of the Duke of Buccleuch)

4. (Left) Beggars—probably gypsies—as they appeared in Barclay's *Shyp of Folys* (1509) (from the British Museum, G.11593)

5. English gypsies as depicted on the broadside ballad called *The Brave English Jipsie* (1626 or earlier) (from the British Museum, C.20f.7[544])

Burley Stables on the East side.

6. Buckingham's stables at Burley-on-the Hill as pictured in *The History and Antiquities of the County of Rutland* (1684), by James Wright (from Perkins Library, Duke University)

7. A view of the ruins of the old castle at Castleton, Derbyshire, with the entrance to the Devil's Arse, a drawing made by Elias Ashmole *ca.* 1662 (from the Bodleian Library, Oxford, MS Ashmole 854)

The Divils Arse, or Peaks Arse in Darbyshire, is a wide Subterrane=ous Cavern, running under a Hill. At its entrance it is large & capacious but further in it grows narrow & contracted. The Roof is lofty & appears like a most graceful Arch chequer'd with variety of Collour'd Stone. From y Top of it there is continually dropping a Sparry petrifying water. AA are house where many poor people live within y. Arch. B. a river running cross. C. a second river, where y. Rock opens again D. a third river, where y. rock & water closes y whole

8. The Devil's Arse as depicted on an eighteenth-century map by Charles Rice (from the British Museum, Map Room, uncatalogued)

9. An illustration for Jonson's ballad of Cock-lorrel from John Mennes's *Recreation for Ingenious Head-peeces* (1650) (from the British Museum, 11601.bb.18)

10. An illustration for a broadside version of *A Strange Banquet, or, The Divels Entertainment by Cook Laurell at the Peak in Devonshire* [!] in which the Devil appears as a crowned monarch (from the British Museum, C.20f.2 [292])

Appendix. *A Glance at* Wither's Motto *(1621)*

About the same time as Jonson's gypsy masque and James's reaffirmation of his proclamation *Against Excesse of Lavish and Licentious Speeche of Matters of State*, the poet George Wither produced *Wither's Motto*. On 27 June 1621 a warrant went out to commit Wither close prisoner in the Marshalsea, and on 7 July the Reverend Joseph Mead reported to Sir Martin Stuteville that the King was "threatening to pare" Wither's "whelp's claws."[1] Frank Sidgwick has offered the explanation that "a hidden satire was discovered by some enemy in high position. . . ."[2] On the other hand, though Wither previously had been refused a license to print the book, Sidgwick notes that it was not questioned further until the first impression was sold and a second in preparation. In short, events surrounding Wither's imprisonment and the sale of the book are not clear.

Whatever Wither's offense was thought to be so far as officialdom was concerned, *Wither's Motto* treats some of the same raw materials which Jonson found useful in *The Gypsies Metamorphos'd*. Having noted scornfully, "I neuer yet a Fauourite did see/ So happy, that I wished to be hee . . ." (B4ʳ), Wither launches into some rather extended commentary on favorites. Naturally claiming that his satire is general, not particular, he writes:

> Yet, Princes (by experience) we haue seene,
> By those they loue, haue greatly wronged beene.
> Their too much trust, doth often danger breed,
> And Serpents in their Royall bosoms feed.
> For, all the fauours, guifts, and places, which
> Should honour them; doe but these men enrich.
> With those, they further their owne priuate ends:
> Their faction strengthen, gratifie their friends:
> Gaine new Associates, daily to their parts,
> And from their Soueraigne, steale away the hearts,
> Of such as are about them; For those be
> Their Creatures; and but rarely, thankes hath He,
> Because the Grants of *Pension*, and of *Place*;
> Are taken as Their fauors, not *His* grace.

(D5ʳ)

1. Quoted in Thomas Birch, *The Court and Times of James the First* (1849), II, 266.
2. Ed., *The Poetry of George Wither* (1902), I, xxix.

Since there was only one sovereign in England, and since his close favorites were few, this passage would seem to cut close to the bone. A little farther on, Wither even makes use of the star image, Buckingham's special emblem in *The Mirrour of Majestie* (1618). Though a star is an obvious figure for a favorite and Buckingham had no monopoly on it, it is of interest to find Wither complaining that "Those rising *Starres*, would neuer deigne to shine,/ On any good endeauour, yet, of mine" (D6ʳ). Most striking of all, however, is Wither's attack on the "gaudy Vpstarts" at court, the "braue-bespangl'd Rabblement" (D8ᵛ) who have really made themselves less noble, in any significant sense, than the "most betatter'd Pesant. . . ." These "foes to Vertue"

> Haue now to couer o're their knau'ry,
> Got on the Robes, of Wealth, and Brau'ry;
> And dare behaue their Rogueships sawcily,
> In presence of our old Nobility. . . .

(E1ʳ)

This, *sans* flattery, takes us close to what Jonson says in his gypsy masque.

Bibliography

The following list is comprised of two parts. The first includes (i) a handful of manuscripts, (ii) a good many publications before 1700, (iii) some early works published in editions after 1700, and, (iv) a variety of secondary works printed since 1700. This first part is a fairly complete record of writings cited or used in the text, the only items omitted being standard sources such as the *DNB*, *OED*, and Shakespeare, and a few titles which are merely mentioned. Though a complete bibliography of the topic is beyond the aim of this study, the second part offers a supplementary sampling of titles which a reader may find helpful.

Part I. Works Cited in the Text

i. *Manuscripts*

Account of payment from Buckingham to Jonson and Lanier. Public Record Office, State Papers, July–September, 1621, CXXII, 32.

Elias Ashmole's sketch of the Devil's Arse. MS Ashmole 854, p. 41. Bodleian, Oxford.

"An Humble Oblation to the Pretiouse Memory of . . . S^r: Gervas Clifton Kn^t: & Baronet." MS Ashmole 36, 205^r–206^r. Bodleian, Oxford.

Inventory of Buckingham's art collection. MS Rawlinson A.341.(30). Bodleian, Oxford.

"The True Tragi-comedie Formerly Acted at Court & Now Revi[v]ed by ane Eie Witnes." British Museum Add. MS 25348.

Verses on Buckingham and his family. MS Ashmole 38, 229^r–229^v cited. Bodleian, Oxford.

Verses on seventeenth-century social conditions. British Museum Add. MS 5832, 206^v cited.

ii. *Works printed before 1700*

Adamson, John, ed. *Ta Ton Mouson Eisodia*. Edinburgh, 1618.

Anno Quinto Reginae Elizabethe. At the Parliament Holden at West-mynster the .xii. of January . . . Were Enacted as Foloweth. 1562.

Anno xxxix. Reginae Elizabethae. At the Parliament. . . . 1597.

Armstrong, Archibald (attrib.). *A Banquet of Jeasts*. 1630.

Awdeley, John. *The Fraternitye of Vacabondes*. 1575; 1st ed., 1565.

B., A. D., *The Court of the Most Illustrious and Most Magnificent James, the First.* . . . 1619.

Bacon, Francis. *Of the Advancement and Proficience of Learning.* Trans. Gilbert Wats. Oxford, 1640.

———. *The Essaies of Sr Francis Bacon Knight.* . . . 1624.

———. *A Letter of Advice Written by S^r. Francis Bacon to the Duke of Buckingham . . . Never before Printed.* 1661.

Barclay, Alexander. *The Shyp of Folys.* 1509.

Boissard, Jean Jacques. *Habitus Variarum Orbis Gentium.* Mechlin (?), 1581.

A Booke of Proclamations, Published Since the Beginning of His Majesties Most Happy Reigne. . . . 1609.

Borde, Andrew. *The Fyrst Boke of the Introduction of Knowledge.* 1542.

The Brave English Jipsie. A broadside, 1626 or earlier.

Bullokar, John. *An English Expositor.* 1616.

Burnell, Henry. *Landgartha.* Dublin, 1641.

Burton, Robert. *The Anatomy of Melancholy.* Oxford, 1621.

Camden, William. *Britain.* Trans. Philemon Holland. 1610.

Carmichael, James (?). *Newes from Scotland. Declaring the Damnable Life of Doctor Fian a Notable Sorcerer.* . . . 1591.

A Cat May Look upon a King. 1652.

Cavendish, William. *The Country Captaine, and the Variety, Two Comedies.* . . . 1649.

Cokayne, Aston. *A Masque Presented at Bretbie,* in *A Chain of Golden Poems.* 1658.

Cotton, Charles. *The Wonders of the Peake.* 2nd ed., 1683.

Cowell, John. *The Interpreter: Or Booke Containing the Signification of Words.* Cambridge, 1607.

Dekker, Thomas. *Villanies Discovered by Lanthorne and Candle-light.* 1620. (*STC* 6489; cf. *STC* 6480–88.)

Digges, Dudley. *A Speech Delivered in Parliament . . . Concerning the Evill Consequences, That Doe Attend This State, by Committing Places of Trust, into the Hands of Court-Favourites.* 1643.

Drayton, Michael. *The Second Part, or A Continuance of Poly-olbion.* 1622.

Eglisham, George. *The Fore-runner of Revenge.* 1642.

Feltham, Owen. *Resolves or, Excogitations. A Second Centurie.* 1628.

Finett, John. *Finetti Philoxenis.* . . . 1656.

Flecknoe, Richard. *Heroick Portraits.* 1660.

———. *Miscellania. Or, Poems of All Sorts, with Divers Other Pieces.* 1653.

Foure Statutes, Specially Selected and Commanded by His Majestie to

Be Carefully Put in Execution by All Justices and Other Officers of the Peace Throughout the Realm. 1609.

Frankland, Thomas. *The Annals of King James and King Charles the First*. 1681.

Fuller, Thomas. *The History of the Worthies of England*. 1662.

G., H. (Henry Goodyer?). *The Mirrour of Majestie*. 1618.

Gascoigne, George. *The Pleasant Fable of Ferdinando Jeronimi, and Leonora de Valasco*, in *The Whole Woorkes of George Gascoigne*. 1587.

Goodcole, Henry. *The Wonderfull Discoverie of Elizabeth Sawyer*. . . . 1621.

Hall, Edward. *The Union of the Two Noble and Illustrate Famelies of Lancastre & Yorke*. 1548.

Harman, Thomas. *A Caveat for Commen Cursetors Vulgarly Called Vagabones*. . . . 1567.

Harrison, William. *The Description of Britaine*, in *The Firste Volume of the Chronicles of England, Scotlande, and Irelande . . . by Raphaell Holinshed*. 1577.

Hobbes, Thomas. *De Mirabilibus Pecci: Being the Wonders of the Peak in Darby-shire*. Trans. "by a Person of Quality." 1678.

James I (and VI of Scotland). *Basilikon Doron*. Edinburgh, 1599.

————. *Daemonologie, in Forme of a Dialogue*. Edinburgh, 1597.

————. *A Meditation upon the Lords Prayer*. 1619.

————. *Ane Metaphoricall Invention of a Tragedie Called Phoenix*. 1584.

————. *The Workes of the Most High and Mightie Prince, James*. . . . Ed. James, Bishop of Winton, 1616.

Jonson, Ben. *A Strange Banquet, or, The Divels Entertainment by Cook Laurell at the Peak in Devonshire*[!]. A broadside, 1642(?)

Lambard, William. *Eirenarcha, or Of the Office of the Justices of Peace*. 1619.

The Lawes and Actes of Parliament, Maid Be King James the First and His Successours Kings of Scotlãd. . . . Edinburgh, 1597.

Lilly Lash't with His Own Rod. A broadside, 1660.

Lloyd, David. *The States-men and Favourites of England Since the Reformation*. 1665.

Markham, Francis. *The Booke of Honour*. 1625.

Markham, Gervase. *Markhams Farwell to Husbandry*. 1620.

Mason, George, and John Earsden. *The Ayres That Were Sung and Played, at Brougham Castle in Westmerland, in the Kings Entertainment: Given by the Right Honourable the Earl of Cumberland, and His Right Noble Sonne the Lord Clifford*. 1618.

Melton, John. *Astrologaster, or, The Figure-caster*. 1620.

Mennes, John. *Recreation for Ingenious Head-peeces.* 1650.

Middleton, Thomas. *Two New Playes. More Dissemblers Besides Women. Women Beware Women.* 1657.

More, Thomas. *A Dyalog of Syr Thomas More Knyghte.* 1514.

Naunton, Robert. *Fragmenta Regalia.* 1641.

Needham, Marchemount. "The Cities Feast to the Lord Protector. To the Tune of Cooke Lorrell," in *Rump: or an Exact Collection of the Choycest Poems and Songs Relating to the Late Times.* Vol. I. 1662.

Osborne, Francis. *Historical Memoires on the Reigns of Queen Elizabeth, and King James.* 1658.

Peyton, Edward. *The Divine Catastrophe of the Kingly Family of the House of Stuarts.* 1652.

Playford, John. *The English Dancing Master.* 1651.

Rid, Samuel. *Martin Mark-all, Beadle of Bridewell.* 1610.

Sanderson, William. *A Compleat History of the Lives and Reigns of Mary Queen of Scotland, and of Her Son and Successor, James the Sixth. . . .* 1656.

Skelton, John. *Here After Foloweth Certayne Bokes, Cōpyled by Mayster Skelton.* 1545(?)

Slatyer, William. *The History of Great Britanie . . . to This Present Raigne.* 1621.

Speed, John. *The Theatre of the Empire of Great Britaine.* 1611.

Tomkis, Thomas. *Lingua.* 1607.

Weldon, Anthony. *The Court and Character of King James.* 1650.

Wilson, Arthur. *The History of Great Britain.* 1653.

Wither, George. *Wither's Motto.* 1621.

The Wonderful Discoverie of the Witchcrafts of Margaret and Phillip Flower . . . Neere Bever Castle. . . . 1619.

Worde, Wynkyn de. *Cocke Lorelles Bote.* Ca. 1510.

Wotton, Henry. *A Parallell betweene Robert Late Earle of Essex, and George Late Duke of Buckingham.* 1641.

―――. *Reliquiae Wottonianae.* 1651.

Wright, James. *The History and Antiquities of the County of Rutland.* 1684.

iii. *Early works in editions after 1700*

Ashton, Robert, ed. *James I by His Contemporaries.* 1969.

Bacon, Francis. *The Letters and the Life of Francis Bacon.* Ed. James Spedding. Vol. VII. 1874.

Barrington, Thomas. *Notes,* in *Commons Debates 1621.* Ed. Wallace Notestein, Frances Helen Relf, and Hartley Simpson. Vol. III. New Haven, 1935.

Beaumont, Francis, and John Fletcher. *The Maid's Tragedy.* Ed. Robert

K. Turner, in *The Beaumont and Fletcher Canon*. Vol. II. Gen. ed., Fredson T. Bowers. Cambridge, 1970.

Beaumont, John. *The Poems of Sir John Beaumont, Bart.* Ed. Alexander B. Grosart. N.p., priv. circ., 1869.

The Belasyse Diary, in *Commons Debates 1621*. Ed. Wallace Notestein, Frances H. Relf, and Hartley Simpson. Vol. V. New Haven, 1935.

Browne, Edward, and Thomas Browne, *Journal of a Tour*, in *Sir Thomas Browne's Works*. Ed. Simon Wilkin. Vol. I. 1836.

Chamberlain, John. *The Letters of John Chamberlain*. Ed. Norman Egbert McClure. Vol. II. Philadelphia, 1939.

Chapman, George. *The Memorable Masque*. Ed. G. Blakemore Evans. In *The Plays of George Chapman: The Comedies*. Gen. ed., Allan Holaday, asstd. by Michael Kiernan. Urbana, Ill., 1970.

———. *The Poems of George Chapman*. Ed. Phyllis Brooks Bartlett. New York, 1941.

The Brave English Jipsie. Reptd. by William Chappell in *The Roxburghe Ballads*. Vol. III, pt. 1. Hertford, 1875.

Charles I. *The Letters Speeches and Proclamations of King Charles I*. Ed. Sir Charles Petrie. New York, 1968; 1st ed., 1935.

Chaucer, Geoffrey. *The Works of Geoffrey Chaucer*. Ed. F. N. Robinson. Boston, 1957.

Chaworth, George. *Diary*, in *The Loseley Manuscripts*. Ed. Alfred John Kempe. 1835.

Child, Francis James, ed. *The English and Scottish Popular Ballads*. Vol. IV. Boston, *ca.* 1898.

Clarendon, Edward Hyde, Earl of. *The Characters of Robert Earl of Essex, . . . and George D. of Buckingham . . . with a Comparison.* 1706.

Cook, David, ed., asstd. by F. P. Wilson. *Dramatic Records in the Declared Accounts of the Treasurer of the Chamber 1558–1642*. Malone Society Collections, VI. Oxford, 1962.

Davies, Randall. "An Inventory of the Duke of Buckingham's Pictures, etc., at York House in 1635." *Burlington Magazine*, vol. X, no. xlviii (1907), 376–382.

Dekker, Thomas. *The Dramatic Works*. . . . Ed. Fredson T. Bowers. Vols. I and III. Cambridge, 1953 and 1958.

Devereux, Walter Bourchier, ed. *Lives and Letters of the Devereux, Earls of Essex*. Vol. II. 1853.

D'Ewes, Simonds. *The Autobiography and Correspondence of Sir Simonds D'Ewes, Bart.* Ed. James Orchard Halliwell[-Phillipps]. Vol. I. 1845.

Donne, John. *John Donne: Selected Prose*. Chosen by Evelyn Simpson, ed. Helen Gardner and Timothy Healy. Oxford, 1967.

Drummond, William, of Hawthornden. *Conversations*. See Jonson, Ben, *Ben Jonson*, Herford and Simpson.

Evelyn, John. *The Diary of John Evelyn*. Ed. E. S. de Beer. Vol. III. Oxford, 1955.

Fairholt, Frederick W., ed. *Poems and Songs Relating to George Villiers, Duke of Buckingham*. 1850.

Fiennes, Celia. *The Journeys of Celia Fiennes*. Ed. Christopher Morris, 1947.

Ford, John. *The Broken Heart*. Ed. Donald K. Anderson, Jr. Lincoln, Neb., 1968.

———. *A Line of Life*, in *The Works of John Ford*. Ed. William Gifford and Alexander Dyce. Vol. III. 1869.

Gardiner, Samuel Rawson, ed. *Documents Illustrating the Impeachment of the Duke of Buckingham in 1626*. 1889.

Gervase of Tilbury. *De Antipodibus et Eorum Terra*, in *Radulphi de Coggeshall Chronicon Anglicanum*. Ed. Josephus Stevenson. 1875.

Glanvill, Joseph. *The Vanity of Dogmatizing: The Three "Versions."* Introd. Stephen Medcalf. Hove, Sussex, 1970.

Goodman, Godfrey. *The Court of King James the First*. Ed. John S. Brewer. 2 vols. 1839.

Green, Mary Anne Everett, ed. *Calendar of State Papers, Domestic . . . 1611–1618; . . . 1619–1623; and . . . 1623–1625*. Vols. IX and X, 1858. Vol. XI, 1859.

Halliwell-Phillipps, James Orchard, ed. *Letters of the Kings of England*. Vol. II. 1848.

Harington, John. *Sir John Harington's A New Discourse of a Stale Subject, Called the Metamorphosis of Ajax*. Ed. Elizabeth Story Donno. New York, 1962.

———. *Nugae Antiquae: Being a Miscellaneous Collection of Original Papers*. Sel. by Henry Harington and arr. by Thomas Park. 2 vols. 1804.

Harvey, Gabriel. *Pierce's Supererogation*, in *Elizabethan Critical Essays*. Ed. G. Gregory Smith. Vol. II. Oxford, 1904.

Hinds, Allen B., ed. *Calendar of State Papers and Manuscripts . . . Venice . . . 1617–1619*. Vol. XV. 1909. Also . . . *1619–1621*. Vol. XVI. 1910. And . . . *1621–1623*. Vol. XVII. 1911.

Howell, James. *Epistolae Ho-elianae*. Ed. Joseph Jacobs. 1890.

Innes, Cosmo Nelson, ed. *The Acts of the Parliaments of Scotland*. Vol. IV. Edinburgh, 1826.

James I (and VI of Scotland). *The Poems of James VI. of Scotland*. Ed. James Craigie. Vol. I, Edinburgh, 1955. Vol. II, 1958.

Jonson, Ben. *Ben Jonson*. Ed. C. H. Herford and Percy Simpson. 11 vols. Oxford, 1925–1952.

————. *Ben Jonson: The Complete Masques.* Ed. Stephen Orgel. New Haven, 1969.

————. *Ben Jonson's Literary Criticism.* Ed. James D. Redwine. Lincoln, Neb., 1970.

————. "Cock-Lorrel's Strange Banquet," in *The Roxburghe Ballads.* Ed. J. Woodfall Ebsworth. Vol. VII, pt. i, pp. 217–221. Hertford, 1890.

————. *The Gipsies Metamorphosed,* in *English Drama 1580–1642.* Ed. C. F. Tucker Brooke and Nathaniel Burton Paradise. Boston, 1933.

————. *The Gypsies Metamorphosed . . . Edited from Original and Unexpurgated Sources . . . A Variorum Edition.* Ed. George Watson Cole. New York, 1931.

————. *Jonson's Masque of Gipsies in the Burley, Belvoir, and Windsor Versions: An Attempt at Reconstruction by W. W. Greg.* 1952.

Jonsonus Virbius. See Herford and Simpson, under Jonson, Ben.

Journals of the House of Lords, Beginning Anno Decimo Octavo Jacobi Regis, 1620. Vol. III. 1771 (?)

Kyd, Thomas. *The Spanish Tragedy.* Ed. Philip Edwards. Cambridge, Mass., 1959.

Lilly, William. *The Lives of Those Eminent Antiquaries Elias Ashmole, Esquire, and Mr. William Lilly, Written by Themselves; Containing . . . Lilly's Life and Death of Charles the First. . . .* 1774.

Lyle, J. V., ed. *Acts of the Privy Council of England 1621–1623.* 1932.

Marlowe, Christopher. *The Plays of Christopher Marlowe.* Ed. Roma Gill. Oxford, 1971.

Marston, John. *The Malcontent.* Ed. M. L. Wine. Lincoln, Neb., 1964.

Masson, David, ed. *The Register of the Privy Council of Scotland.* Vol. XII. Edinburgh, 1895.

Middleton, Thomas. *A Game at Chesse.* Ed. R. C. Bald. Cambridge, 1929.

————, and William Rowley. *The Spanish Gipsie. . . .* Ed. Edgar C. Morris. Boston, 1908.

North, Roger. *The Musicall Gramarian.* Ed. Hilda Andrews, foreword by Sir Richard Trevy. 1925.

Notestein, Wallace, Frances Helen Relf, and Hartley Simpson, eds. *The Anonymous Journal,* in *Commons Debates 1621.* Vol. II. New Haven, 1935. See also Barrington, Thomas, and *Belasyse Diary.*

Oglander, John. *A Royalist's Notebook: The Commonplace Book of Sir John Oglander Kt. of Nunwell.* Ed. Francis Bamford. 1936.

Raumer, Frederick Von. *History of the Sixteenth and Seventeenth Centuries.* Trans. from the German. Vol. II. 1835.

Shipman, Roger, and William Taylor (?). *Grobiana's Nuptialls.* Ed. Ernst Rühl, in *Grobianus in England, Palaestra,* XXXVIII (1904), 164–191.

Shirley, James. *The Poems of James Shirley.* Ed. Ray Livingstone Armstrong. New York, 1941.

Simpson, Claude M. *The British Broadside Ballad and Its Music.* New Brunswick, N.J., 1966.

Summerson, John, ed. *The Book of Architecture of John Thorpe in Sir John Soane's Museum.* The Walpole Society, vol. XL. 1966.

Wither, George. *The Poetry of George Wither.* Ed. Frank Sidgwick. Vol. I. 1902.

Yonge, Walter. *Diary of Walter Yonge, Esq.* Ed. George Roberts. 1848.

iv. *Secondary works from 1700 to the present*

Apel, Willi. *Harvard Dictionary of Music.* 2nd ed., Cambridge, Mass., 1969.

Aydelotte, Frank. *Elizabethan Rogues and Vagabonds.* Oxford, 1913.

Barcroft, John H. "Carleton and Buckingham: The Quest for Office," in *Early Stuart Studies: Essays in Honor of David Harris Willson.* Ed. Howard S. Reinmuth, Jr. Minneapolis, 1970.

Barish, Jonas A. *Ben Jonson and the Language of Prose Comedy.* Cambridge, Mass., 1960.

Barron, Oswald. "Heraldry," in *Shakespeare's England.* Ed. Sidney Lee and C. T. Onions. Vol. II. Oxford, 1932; 1st ed., 1916.

Barrow, Albert S. ("Sabretache," pseud.). *Monarchy and the Chase.* 1948.

Baum, Helena Watts. *The Satiric & the Didactic in Ben Jonson's Comedy.* Chapel Hill, N.C., 1947.

Bennett, Josephine Waters. "Oxford and *Endimion*," *PMLA*, LVII (1942), 354–369.

Bentley, Gerald Eades, gen. introd. *A Book of Masques in Honour of Allardyce Nicoll.* Cambridge, 1967.

Betcherman, L.-R. "Balthazar Gerbier in Seventeenth-Century Italy," *History Today*, XI (1961), 325–331.

Bevington, David. *Tudor Drama and Politics: A Critical Approach to Topical Meaning.* Cambridge, Mass., 1968.

Birch, Thomas. *The Court and Times of James the First.* Vol. II. 1849.

Black, George F. *A Calendar of Cases of Witchcraft in Scotland 1510–1727.* New York, 1938.

Blair, F. G. "The Costume of Gypsies in the Masque," *Journal of the Gypsy Lore Society*, 3rd series, XXXIII (1954), 74–75.

Bloomfield, Morton W. "Allegory as Interpretation," *New Literary History*, II (1972), 301–317.

Borrow, George. *Romano Lavo-lil.* Reprint of 1st (1876) ed., 1923.

Bowen, Catherine Drinker. *The Lion and the Throne: The Life and*

Times of Sir Edward Coke (1552–1634). Boston, 1957; copyright, 1956.

Bridenbaugh, Carl. *Vexed and Troubled Englishmen 1590–1642*. New York, 1968.

Brooksbank, J. H. "Castleton: Its Traditions, Sayings, Place-Names, Etc.," *Transactions of the Hunter Archaeological Society*, III (1929), 34–52.

Burton, Elizabeth. *The Jacobeans at Home*. 1962.

Cammell, Charles Richard. *The Great Duke of Buckingham*. 1939.

Carpenter, Frederic Ives. *A Reference Guide to Edmund Spenser*. Chicago, 1923.

Carrington, W. A. "The Early Lords of Belvoir," *Journal of the British Archaeological Association*, N.S. VII (1901), 299–326.

Chancellor, E. Beresford. *The Life of Charles I. 1600–1625*. 1886.

Clébert, Jean-Paul. *The Gypsies*. Trans. Charles Duff. New York, 1963.

Colie, Rosalie L. *Paradoxia Epidemica: The Renaissance Tradition of Paradox*. Princeton, 1966.

Collins, Arthur. *Collins's Peerage of England*. Aug. by Sir Egerton Brydges. 1812.

Craik, T. W. *The Tudor Interlude: Stage, Costume, and Acting*. Leicester, 1967; 1st impression, 1958.

Crofton, Henry Thomas. *The English Gipsies under the Tudors*. Manchester, 1880.

———. "The Former Costume of the Gypsies," *Journal of the Gypsy Lore Society*, N.S. II (1908–1909), 207–231.

Cunningham, Dolora. "The Jonsonian Masque as a Literary Form," *ELH*, XXII (1955), 108–124.

Cutts, John P. "Robert Johnson and the Court Masque," *Music and Letters*, XLI (1960), 111–126.

———. "Robert Johnson: King's Musician in His Majesty's Public Entertainment," *Music and Letters*, XXXVI (1955), 110–125.

Davies, Godfrey. "The Character of James VI and I," *HLQ*, V (1941–1942), 33–63.

———. *The Early Stuarts 1603–1660*. 1st ed., Oxford, 1937; 1967 printing of 2nd ed., 1959.

———. "English Political Sermons, 1603–1640,"*HLQ*, III (1939), 1–22.

Defoe, Daniel. *A Tour Thro' the Whole Island of Great Britain Divided into Circuits or Journies*. Vol. III. 1727.

DeLuna, Barbara. *Jonson's Romish Plot: A Study of "Catiline" and Its Historical Context*. Oxford, 1967.

Dolmetsch, Mabel. *Dances of England and France from 1450 to 1600*. 1949.

Doran, John. *The History of Court Fools*. 1858.

Dunlap, Rhodes. "The Allegorical Interpretation of Renaissance Literature," *PMLA*, LXXXII (1967), 39–43.

Eliot, T. S. "Ben Jonson," in *Elizabethan Essays*. 1934.

———. *The Use of Poetry and the Use of Criticism*. 1950; 1st ed., 1933.

Eller, Irvin. *The History of Belvoir Castle*. 1841.

Emslie, McD. "Nicholas Lanier's Innovations in English Song," *Music and Letters*, XLI (1960), 13–27.

Enright, D. J. "Crime and Punishment in Ben Jonson," *Scrutiny*, IX (Cambridge, 1940), 231–248.

Erlanger, Philippe. *George Villiers Duke of Buckingham*. Trans. Lionel Smith-Gordon. 1953.

Evans, K. W. "*Sejanus* and the Ideal Prince Tradition," *SEL*, XI (1971), 249–264.

Ewen, C. L'Estrange. *Witchcraft and Demonianism*. 1933.

Finch, Pearl. *History of Burley-on-the-Hill Rutland*. 1901.

Fletcher, Angus. *The Transcendental Masque: An Essay on Milton's "Comus."* Ithaca, N.Y., 1971.

Fraser, Angus M., and François de Vaux de Foletier. "The Gypsy Healer and the King of Scots," *Journal of the Gypsy Lore Society*, 3rd ser., LI (1972), 1–8.

Furniss, W. Todd. "Ben Jonson's Masques," in *Three Studies in the Renaissance: Sidney, Jonson, Milton*. New Haven, 1958.

Gardiner, Samuel Rawson. *History of England from the Accession of James I. to the Outbreak of the Civil War*. Vol. III. New ed., New York, 1901.

Gibb, M. A. *Buckingham 1592–1628*. 1935.

Gilbert, Allan H. "The Function of the Masques in *Cynthia's Revels*," *PQ*, XXII (1943), 211–230.

Gordon, D. J. "The Imagery of Ben Jonson's *The Masque of Blacknesse* and *The Masque of Beautie*," *Journal of the Warburg and Courtauld Institutes*, VI (1943), 122–141.

———. "Poet and Architect: The Intellectual Setting of the Quarrel Between Ben Jonson and Inigo Jones," *Journal of the Warburg and Courtauld Institutes*, XII (1949), 152–178.

Gotch, J. Alfred. "Architecture," in *Shakespeare's England*. Ed. Sidney Lee and C. T. Onions. Vol. II. Oxford, 1932; 1st ed., 1916.

Gregory Smith, George. *Ben Jonson*. 1919.

Grigson, Geoffrey. *The Englishman's Flora*. 1955.

Gross, Allen. "Contemporary Politics in Massinger," *SEL*, VI (1966), 279–290.

Hardison, O. B., Jr. *The Enduring Monument: A Study of the Idea of Praise in Renaissance Literary Theory and Practice*. Chapel Hill, N.C., 1962.

Heffner, Ray L., Jr. "Unifying Symbols in the Comedy of Ben Jonson," in *English Stage Comedy*. Ed. W. K. Wimsatt, Jr. New York, 1955.

Hoyland, John. *A Historical Survey of the Customs, Habits, & Present State of the Gypsies*. 1816.

Huxley, Gervas. *Endymion Porter: The Life of a Courtier 1587–1649*. 1959.

Jackson, Gabriele Bernhard. *Vision and Judgment in Ben Jonson's Drama*. New Haven, 1968.

Kernan, Alvin. *The Cankered Muse: Satire of the English Renaissance*. New Haven, 1959.

Knights, L. C. *Drama & Society in the Age of Jonson*. 1937.

Krishnamurthi, M. G. "The Ethical Basis of Ben Jonson's Plays," *Journal of the Maharaja Sayajirao University of Baroda*, XI (1962), 139–157.

Lal, Chaman. *Gipsies: Forgotten Children of India*. Delhi, 1962.

Levitan, Alan Lloyd. "The Life of Our Design: The Jonsonian Masque as Baroque Form." Unpub. diss. Princeton, 1965.

Leyburn, Ellen Douglass. *Satiric Allegory: Mirror of Man*. New Haven, 1956.

Linthicum, M. Channing. *Costume in the Drama of Shakespeare and His Contemporaries*. Oxford, 1936.

Longueville, Thomas. *The Curious Case of Lady Purbeck*. 1909.

McPeek, James A. S. *The Black Book of Knaves and Unthrifts in Shakespeare and Other Renaissance Authors*. Storrs, Conn., 1969.

MacQueen, John. *Allegory*. 1970.

MacRitchie, David. "The Crime of Harbouring Gypsies," *Journal of the Gypsy Lore Society*, N.S. VII (1913–14), 243–247.

————. *Scottish Gypsies under the Stewarts*. Edinburgh, 1894.

Mares, Francis Hugh. "The Origin of the Figure Called 'the Vice' in Tudor Drama," *HLQ*, XXII (1958–59), 11–29.

Mayes, Charles R. "The Sale of Peerages in Early Stuart England," *Journal of Modern History*, XXIX (1957), 21–37.

Meagher, John C. *Method and Meaning in Jonson's Masques*. Notre Dame, Ind., 1966.

Mee, Arthur. *Derbyshire*. Rev. and ed. F. R. Banks. 1969.

Meier, T. "The Naming of Characters in Jonson's Comedies," *English Studies in Africa*, VII (1964), 88–95.

Miller, Henry K. "The Paradoxical Encomium with Special Reference to Its Vogue in England, 1600–1800," *MP*, LIII (1956), 145–178.

Murrin, Michael. *The Veil of Allegory*. Chicago, 1969.

Nason, Arthur Huntington. *Heralds and Heraldry in Ben Jonson's Plays, Masques and Entertainments*. New York, 1968; 1st printed, 1907.

Nichols, John. *The Progresses, Processions, and Magnificent Festivities of King James the First. . . .* Vol. IV. 1828.

Nichols, John Gordon. *The Poetry of Ben Jonson*. 1969.

Nuttall, Anthony David. *Two Concepts of Allegory.* 1967.

Orgel, Stephen. *The Jonsonian Masque.* Cambridge, Mass., 1965.

──────. "The Poetics of Spectacle," *New Literary History*, II (1971), 367–389.

──────. "To Make Boards to Speak: Inigo Jones's Stage and the Jonsonian Masque," in *Renaissance Drama*, N.S. I (1968), 121–152.

Page, William, ed. *The Victoria History of the County of Rutland*, in *The Victoria History of the Counties of England.* Vol. I, 1908. Vol. II, 1935.

Parfitt, G. A. E. "Ethical Thought and Ben Jonson's Poetry," *SEL*, IX (1969), 123–134.

Partridge, Edward B. *The Broken Compass: A Study of the Major Comedies of Ben Jonson.* 1958.

──────. "The Symbolism of Clothes in Jonson's Last Plays," *JEGP*, LVI (1957), 396–409.

Partridge, Eric. *A Dictionary of the Underworld.* 3rd ed., 1968.

──────. *A Dictionary of Slang and Unconventional English.* 6th ed., New York, 1967.

Prestwich, Menna. *Cranfield: Politics and Profits under the Early Stuarts.* Oxford, 1966.

Pulver, Jeffrey. *A Dictionary of Old English Music & Musical Instruments.* 1923.

Rathmell, J. C. A. "Jonson, Lord Lisle, and Penshurst," *English Literary Renaissance*, I (1971), 250–260.

Rice, Charles. *A New & Correct Map of Great Britain and Ireland.* Ca. 1727–53.

Ross Williamson, Hugh. *George Villiers First Duke of Buckingham.* 1940.

Sackton, Alexander H. "The Paradoxical Encomium in Elizabethan Drama," *University of Texas Studies in English*, XXVIII (1949), 83–104.

Schelling, Felix E. *Elizabethan Playwrights.* New York, 1925.

Sharp, Cecil J., and Herbert C. MacIlwaine. *The Morris Book.* Part I. 2nd ed., 1912.

Sheavyn, Phoebe. *The Literary Profession in the Elizabethan Age.* Rev. by J. W. Saunders. New York, 1967.

Simson, Walter. *A History of the Gipsies.* Ed. James Simson. New York, 1866.

Soulis, George C. "The Gypsies in the Byzantine Empire and the Balkans in the Late Middle Ages," *Dumbarton Oaks Papers*, XV (1961), 143–165.

Spivack, Bernard. *Shakespeare and the Allegory of Evil: The History of a Metaphor in Relation to His Major Villains.* New York, 1958.

Stone, Lawrence. *The Crisis of the Aristocracy 1558–1641*. Oxford, 1965.

Swinburne, Algernon Charles. *A Study of Ben Jonson*. 1889.

Talbert, Ernest W. "The Interpretation of Jonson's Courtly Spectacles," *PMLA*, LXI (1946), 454–473.

Tawney, R. H. *Business and Politics under James I*. Cambridge, 1958.

Thoms, William J., ed. *Anecdotes and Traditions, Illustrative of Early English History and Literature*. 1839.

Thomson, Katharine. *The Life and Times of George Villiers, Duke of Buckingham*. 3 vols. 1860.

Townshend, Dorothea. *Life and Letters of Mr. Endymion Porter*. 1897.

Trevor-Roper, H. R. *Religion the Reformation and Social Change*. 1967.

Tuve, Rosemond. *Allegorical Imagery: Some Mediaeval Books and Their Posterity*. Princeton, 1966.

Vaux de Foletier, François de. "Iconographie des 'Egyptiens': Précisions sur le Costume Ancien des Tsiganes," *Gazette des Beaux-Arts*, ser. 6, vol. LXVIII (1966), 165–172.

Waith, E. M. "The Comic Mirror and the World of Glass," *Research Opportunities in Renaissance Drama*, IX (1966), 16–23.

Weinberger, G. J. "Jonson's Mock-Encomiastic 'Celebration of Charis,' " *Genre*, IV (1971), 305–328.

Willeford, William. *The Fool and His Scepter: A Study in Clowns and Jesters and Their Audience*. Evanston, Ill., 1969.

Willey, Basil. *The Seventeenth Century Background*. New York, 1953; 1st ed., 1934.

Willson, D. Harris. *King James VI and I*. 1956.

Winstedt, Eric Otto. "Early British Gypsies," *Journal of the Gypsy Lore Society*, N.S. VII (1913–14), 5–37.

Woodfill, Walter L. *Musicians in English Society from Elizabeth to Charles I*. New York, 1969; 1st printing, 1953.

Zaller, Robert. *The Parliament of 1621: A Study in Constitutional Conflict*. Berkeley, Calif., 1971.

Part II. Some Supplementary Works

(Though not cited in the text, these sources cast additional light from various significant angles.)

Akrigg, G. P. V. *Jacobean Pageant*. Cambridge, Mass. 1962.

Allen, Don Cameron. "Ben Jonson and the Hieroglyphics," *PQ*, XVIII (1939), 290–300.

———. *Mysteriously Meant: The Rediscovery of Pagan Symbolism and*

Allegorical Interpretation in the Renaissance. Baltimore, 1970.

Baskervill, Charles Read. *English Elements in Jonson's Early Comedy.* Austin, Texas, 1911.

Bentley, Gerald Eades. *The Jacobean and Caroline Stage.* 7 vols. Oxford, 1941–68.

Bergeron, David M. *English Civic Pageantry 1558–1642.* Columbia, S. C., 1971.

Berlin, Normand. *The Base String: The Underworld in Elizabethan Drama.* Rutherford, N.J., 1968.

Brett, S. Reed. *The Stuart Century 1603–1714.* 1961.

Dent, Edward J. *Foundations of English Opera: A Study of Musical Drama in England During the Seventeenth Century.* New York, 1968 reprint; 1st ed., 1928.

DeSante, Paul J. "An Analysis of the Antimasques in the Court Masques of Ben Jonson." Unpub. diss., St. John's University, N.Y., 1963.

Dessen, Alan C. *Jonson's Moral Comedy.* Evanston, Ill., 1971.

Dunlap, Rhodes. "King James's Own Masque," *Philological Quarterly,* XLI (1962), 249–256.

Enck, John J. *Jonson and the Comic Truth.* Madison, Wis., 1957.

Ewbank, Inga-Stina. " 'The Eloquence of Masques': A Retrospective View of Masque Criticism," *Renaissance Drama,* N.S. I (1968), 307–327.

Gilbert, Allan H. *The Symbolic Persons in the Masques of Ben Jonson.* Durham, N.C., 1948.

Gum, Coburn. *The Aristophanic Comedies of Ben Jonson: A Comparative Study of Jonson and Aristophanes.* The Hague, 1969.

Hayes, Charles. "Symbol and Allegory: A Problem in Literary Theory," *The Germanic Review,* XLIV (1969), 273–288.

Hill, Christopher. *The Century of Revolution, 1603–1714.* New York, 1961.

Janicka, Irena. "The Popular Background of Ben Jonson's Masques," *Shakespeare Jahrbuch,* CV (1969), 183–208.

Jonson, Ben. *The Complete Poetry of Ben Jonson.* Ed. William B. Hunter, Jr. New York, 1963.

Judges, A. V. *The Elizabethan Underworld.* New York, 1930.

Kenyon, J. P. *The Stuarts: A Study in English Kingship.* 1958.

McClennen, Joshua. *On the Meaning and Function of Allegory in the English Renaissance.* University of Michigan *Contributions in Modern Philology,* No. 6. Ann Arbor, 1947.

MacLean, Hugh. "Ben Jonson's Poems: Notes on the Ordered Society," in *Essays in English Literature from the Renaissance to the Victorian Age Presented to A. S. P. Woodhouse 1964.* Ed. Millar MacLure and F. W. Watt. Toronto, 1964.

Nicoll, Allardyce. *Stuart Masques and the Renaissance Stage.* 1937.

Parrott, T. M. "Comedy in the Court Masque: A Study of Ben Jonson's Contribution," *PQ*, XX (1941), 428–441.

Ribton-Turner, C. J. *A History of Vagrants and Vagrancy and Beggars and Begging.* 1887.

Rid, Samuel. *The Art of Jugling or Legerdemaine.* 1612.

Sabol, Andrew J. *Songs and Dances for the Stuart Masque.* Providence, R. I., 1959.

Sackton, Alexander H. *Rhetoric as a Dramatic Language in Ben Jonson.* New York, 1948.

Thompson, T. W. "Consorting with and Counterfeiting Egyptians," *Journal of the Gypsy Lore Society*, 3rd ser., II (1923), 81–93.

Thomson, Patricia. "The Literature of Patronage, 1580–1630," *Essays in Criticism*, II (1952), 267–284.

Vesey-Fitzgerald, Brian. *Gypsies of Britain: An Introduction to Their History.* 1944.

Wedgwood, C. V. *Poetry and Politics under the Stuarts.* Cambridge, 1960.

Welsford, Enid. *The Court Masque.* Cambridge, 1927.

Wren, Robert M. "Ben Jonson as Producer," *Educational Theatre Journal*, XXII (1970), 284–290.

Index